How to Start a Business in Michigan

Edward A. Haman

Attorney at Law

Fifth Edition

SPHINX® PUBLISHING
AN IMPRINT OF SOURCEBOOKS, INC.®
NAPERVILLE, ILLINOIS
www.SphinxLegal.com

Fifth Edition: 2008

Published by: **Sphinx® Publishing, A Division of Sourcebooks, Inc.®**

Naperville Office
P.O. Box 4410
Naperville, Illinois 60567-4410
630-961-3900
Fax: 630-961-2168
www.sourcebooks.com
www.SphinxLegal.com

This publication is designed to provide accurate and authoritative information in regard to the subject matter covered. It is sold with the understanding that the publisher is not engaged in rendering legal, accounting, or other professional service. If legal advice or other expert assistance is required, the services of a competent professional person should be sought.

From a Declaration of Principles Jointly Adopted by a Committee of the
American Bar Association and a Committee of Publishers and Associations

This product is not a substitute for legal advice.

Disclaimer required by Texas statutes.

Library of Congress Cataloging-in-Publication Data

Haman, Edward A.
    Start a business in Michigan / by Edward A. Haman. -- 5th ed.
        p. cm.
    Rev. ed. of: How to start a business in Michigan. 4th ed. 2004 (2005 printing)
    Includes index.
    ISBN 978-1-57248-682-9 (pbk. : alk. paper) 1. New business enterprises--Law and legislation--Michigan--Popular works. I. Haman, Edward A. How to start a business in Michigan. II. Title.

KFM4407.Z9H36 2008
346.774'065--dc22
                                                    2007050946

Printed and bound in the United States of America.
SB — 10 9 8 7 6 5 4 3 2 1

Contents

Using Self-Help Law Books

Before using a self-help law book, you should realize the advantages and disadvantages of doing your own legal work and understand the challenges and diligence that this requires.

The Growing Trend

Rest assured that you will not be the first or only person handling your own legal matter. For example, in some states, more than 75% of the people in divorces and other cases represent themselves. Because of the high cost of legal services, this is a major trend and many courts are struggling to make it easier for people to represent themselves. However, some courts are not happy with people who do not use attorneys and refuse to help them in any way. For some, the attitude is, "Go to the law library and figure it out for yourself."

We write and publish self-help law books to give people an alternative to the often complicated and confusing legal books found in most law libraries. We have made the explanations of the law as simple and easy to understand as possible. Of course, unlike an attorney advising an individual client, we cannot cover every conceivable possibility.

Cost/Value Analysis

Whenever you shop for a product or service, you are faced with various levels of quality and price. In deciding what product or service to buy, you make a cost/value analysis on the basis of your willingness to pay and the quality you desire.

When buying a car, you decide whether you want transportation, comfort, status, or sex appeal. Accordingly, you decide among such choices as a Neon, a Lincoln, a Rolls Royce, or a Porsche. Before making a decision, you usually weigh the merits of each option against the cost.

When you get a headache, you can take a pain reliever (such as aspirin) or visit a medical specialist for a neurological examination. Given this choice, most people, of course, take a pain reliever since it costs only pennies, whereas a medical examination costs hundreds of dollars and takes a lot of time. This is usually a logical choice because it is rare to need anything more than a pain reliever for a headache. But in some cases, a headache may indicate a brain tumor and failing to see a specialist right away can result in complications. Should everyone with a headache go to a specialist? Of course not, but people treating their own illnesses must realize that they are betting on the basis of their cost/value analysis of the situation. They are taking the most logical option.

The same cost/value analysis must be made when deciding to do one's own legal work. Many legal situations are very straightforward, requiring a simple form and no complicated analysis. Anyone with a little intelligence and a book of instructions can handle the matter without outside help.

But there is always the chance that complications are involved that only an attorney would notice. To simplify the law into a book like this, several legal cases often must be condensed into a single sentence or paragraph. Otherwise, the book would be several hundred pages long and too complicated for most people. However, this simplification necessarily leaves out many details and nuances that would apply to special or unusual situations. Also, there are many ways to interpret most legal questions. Your case may come before a judge who disagrees with the analysis of our authors.

Therefore, in deciding to use a self-help law book and to do your own legal work, you must realize that you are making a cost/value analysis. You have decided that the money you will save in doing it yourself outweighs the chance that your case will not turn out to your satisfaction. Most people handling their own simple legal matters never have a problem, but occasionally people find that it ended up costing them more to have an attorney straighten out the situation than it would have if they had hired an attorney in the beginning. Keep this in mind while handling your case, and be sure to consult an attorney if you feel you might need further guidance.

Local Rules   The next thing to remember is that a book that covers the law for the entire nation, or even for an entire state, cannot possibly include every procedural difference of every jurisdiction. Whenever possible, we provide the exact form needed; however, in some areas, each county, or even each judge, may require unique forms and procedures. In our state books, our forms usually cover the majority of counties in the state, or provide examples of the type of form that will be required. In our national books, our forms are sometimes even more general in nature but are designed to give a good idea of the type of form that will be needed in most locations. Nonetheless, keep in mind that your state, county, or judge may have a requirement, or use a form, that is not included in this book.

You should not necessarily expect to be able to get all of the information and resources you need solely from within the pages of this book. This book will serve as your guide, giving you specific information whenever possible and helping you to find out what else you will need to know. This is just like if you decided to build your own backyard deck. You might purchase a book on how to build decks. However, such a book would not include the building codes and permit requirements of every city, town, county, and township in the nation, nor would it include the lumber, nails, saws, hammers, and other materials and tools you would need to actually build the deck. You would use the book as your guide, and then do some work and research involving such matters as whether you need a permit of some kind, what type and grade of wood are available in your area, whether to use hand tools or power tools, and how to use those tools.

Before using the forms in a book like this, you should check with your court clerk to see if there are any local rules of which you should be aware, or local forms you will need to use. Often, such forms will require the same information as the forms in the book but are merely laid out differently or use slightly different language. They will sometimes require additional information.

Changes in the Law   Besides being subject to local rules and practices, the law is subject to change at any time. The courts and the legislatures of all fifty states are constantly revising the laws. It is possible that while you are reading this book, some aspect of the law is being changed.

In most cases, the change will be of minimal significance. A form will be redesigned, additional information will be required, or a waiting period will be extended. As a result, you might need to revise a form, file an extra form, or wait out a longer time period; these types of changes will not usually affect the outcome of your case. On the other hand, sometimes a major part of the law is changed, the entire law in a particular area is rewritten, or a case that was the basis of a central legal point is overruled. In such instances, your entire ability to pursue your case may be impaired.

Again, you should weigh the value of your case against the cost of an attorney and make a decision as to what you believe is in your best interest.

Introduction

Each year thousands of new corporations and limited liability companies are registered in Michigan and thousands more partnerships and sole proprietorships open for business. Nationwide, the 1990s were called the *Decade of the Entrepreneur*. Especially with the popularity of home-based and Internet businesses, the trend is continuing in the twenty-first century.

The best way to take advantage of this trend is to run your own business. With the *Computer Age* in full swing, it is easier than ever to conduct business out of your home or a small office, or to expand a larger business—even taking it nationwide through the Internet. However, if you do not follow the laws of local, state, and federal governments, your progress can be slowed or stopped by fines, civil judgments, or even criminal penalties.

This book is intended to give you the framework for legally opening a business in Michigan. It also includes information on where to find special rules for various types of businesses. If you have legal questions or problems that are not covered by this book, you should seek out an attorney who can be available for your ongoing needs.

Chapters 1 and 2 will help you decide if you really want to start your own business and what type of business entity would be best for you. Chapter 3 will discuss naming your business. Chapter 4 will explore financing options. Chapter 5 covers the location of your business. Chapter 6 considers possible licensing requirements, while Chapter 7 gives an overview of the law of contracts. Chapter 8 explains various types of insurance to consider. Chapter 9 covers legal issues relating to doing business on the Internet.

Chapters 10 through 12 discuss legal requirements relating to health and safety, employment relations, and advertising. Chapter 13 relates to payment and collection matters, while Chapter 14 explains various laws regarding business relations. Chapter 15 covers various miscellaneous legal issues. Chapter 16 explores bookkeeping and accounting matters. Chapters 17 through 19 cover federal, state, and out-of-state taxes.

You will also find a glossary and several appendices. Appendix A contains a business start-up checklist. Appendix B includes sample, filled-in forms, and blank forms are found in Appendix C.

In order to cover all of the aspects of any business you are thinking of starting, you should read through this entire book, rather than skipping to the parts that look most important. There are many laws that may not sound like they apply to you but that do have provisions that will affect your business.

In recent years the government bureaucracies have been amending and lengthening their forms regularly. The forms included in this book were the most recent versions available at the time of publication. It is possible that some may be revised by the time you read this book, but in most cases they will be similar and require the same information.

References to Michigan laws are to the *Michigan Compiled Laws Annotated* (abbreviated by lawyers and judges as M.C.L.A., but in this book as Mich. Comp. Laws Ann.). The symbol "§" means section; however, "section" is abbreviated as "Sec." in this book.

NOTE: *Outside of this book you may come across references to Michigan laws designated* Michigan Statutes Annotated *(abbreviated M.S.A. or MSA). This was an alternative set of books containing Michigan laws; however, it is no longer updated and has been phased out. The M.S.A. used a different numbering system. If you come across a reference to only an M.S.A. statute number, there are cross-reference tables in the Michigan Compiled Laws Annotated that may enable you to find the current statute in the M.C.L.A. books; however, these tables will not be up to date.*

Deciding to Start a Business

If you are reading this book, you have probably made a serious decision to take the plunge and start your own business. Hundreds of thousands of people make the same decision each year and many of them become very successful. Some merely eke out a living, while others become billionaires. But a lot of them also fail. Knowledge can only help your chances of success. Some of what follows may seem obvious, but to someone wrapped up in a new business idea, some of this information is occasionally overlooked.

KNOW YOUR STRENGTHS

The last thing a budding entrepreneur wants to hear is that he or she is not cut out for running his or her own business. Those *do you have what it takes* quizzes are ignored with the fear that the answer might be one the entrepreneur does not want to hear. But even if you lack some skills, you can be successful if you know where to get them.

You should consider all of the skills and knowledge that running a successful business needs and decide whether you have what it takes. If you do not, it does not necessarily mean you are doomed to be an employee all your life. Perhaps you just need a partner who has the skills you lack. Perhaps you can hire someone with the skills you need. Or, you can structure your business to avoid areas where you are weak. If those stratagies do not work, maybe you can learn the skills.

For example, if you are not good at dealing with employees (either you are too passive and get taken advantage of or are too tough and scare them off), you can:

✪ handle product development yourself and have a partner or hired manager deal with employees;

✪ take seminars in employee management; or,

✪ structure your business so you do not need employees, use independent contractors, or become an independent contractor.

Here are some of the factors to consider when planning your business.

✪ If it takes months or years before your business turns a profit, do you have the resources and emotional ability to hold out? Businesses have gone under or have been sold just before they were about to take off. Some people just give up too easily if their business does not take off rapidly. Staying power is an important ingredient to success.

✪ Are you willing to put in a lot of overtime to make your business a success? Owners of businesses do not set their own hours; the business sets them for the owner. Many business owners work long hours, seven days a week. But they enjoy running their business more than family picnics or fishing.

✪ Are you willing to do the dirtiest or most unpleasant work of the business? Emergencies come up and employees are not always dependable. You might need to mop up a flooded room, spend a weekend stuffing 10,000 envelopes, or work Christmas if someone calls in sick.

✪ Do you know enough about the product or service? Are you aware of the trends in the industry and what changes new technology might bring? Think of the people who started typesetting or printing businesses just before type was replaced by laser printers.

✪ Do you know enough about accounting and inventory? Do you have a good head for business? Some people naturally know how to save money and do things profitably. Others are in the habit of buying the best and the most expensive of everything, which can be fatal to a struggling new business.

✪ Are you good at managing employees?

✪ Do you know how to sell your product or service? You can have the best product on the market, but people will not beat a path to your door if you do not know how to sell it. If you are a wholesaler, shelf space in major stores can be hard to get, especially for a new company without a record, a large line of products, or a large advertising budget.

✪ Do you know enough about getting publicity? The media receive thousands of press releases and announcements each day and most are thrown away. Do not count on free publicity to put your name in front of the public.

KNOW YOUR BUSINESS

You do not only need to know the concept of a business, you need the experience of working in the type of business you intend to operate. Maybe you always dreamed of running a bed and breakfast or having your own pizza place. Now you want to use your savings to fulfill that dream. Have you ever worked in such a business? If not, you may have no idea of the day-to-day headaches and problems of the business. For example, do you really know how much to allow for theft, spoilage, and returns from unhappy customers? Or, what can you expect in the way of employee turnover?

You might feel silly taking an entry level job at a pizza place when you would rather start your own, but it might be the most valuable preparation you could have. A few weeks of seeing how a business operates could mean the difference between success and failure.

Working in a business as an employee is one of the best ways to be a success at running such a business. New people with new ideas who work in old stodgy industries have been known to revolutionize them with obvious improvements that no one before dared to try.

DO THE MATH

Conventional wisdom says you need a business plan before committing yourself to a new venture, but some businesses are started successfully without the owner even knowing what a business plan is. He or she has a great concept, puts it on the market, and it takes off. But you at least need to do some basic calculations to see if the business can make a profit. Below are some examples.

- ✪ If you want to start a retail shop, figure out how many people are close enough to become customers and how many other stores will be competing for those customers. Visit some of those others and see how busy they are. Without giving away your plans to compete, ask staff members some general questions like *how's business?* and maybe they will share their frustrations or successes.

- ✪ Whether you sell a good or a service, do the math to find out how much profit is in it.

Example:

If you plan to start a house painting company, find out what you will have to pay to hire painters; the cost of paint, brushes, rollers, thinner, rags, drop cloths, and other supplies; the cost for all of the insurance, bonding, and licensing you will need; and, the cost of advertising. Figure out how many jobs you can do per month and what other painters are charging.

Depending upon such things as the industry and the area of the country you are in, there may be a large margin of profit or there may be almost no profit.

- ✪ Find out if there is a demand for your product or service. Suppose you have designed a beautiful new kind of candle and your friends all say you should open a shop because "everyone will want them." Before making a hundred of them and renting a store, bring a few to craft shows or flea markets and see what happens.

✪ Figure out what the income and expenses would be for a typical month of your new business. List monthly expenses such as rent, salaries, utilities, insurance, taxes, supplies, advertising, services, and other overhead. Then figure out how much profit you will average from each sale. Next, figure out how many sales you will need to cover your overhead and divide by the number of business days in the month. Can you reasonably expect that many sales? How will you get those sales?

Most types of businesses have trade associations, which often have figures on how profitable its members are. Some even have start-up kits for people wanting to start businesses. One good source of information on such organizations is the *Encyclopedia of Associations* published by Thomson Gale, available in many library reference sections. Producers of products to the trade often give assistance to small companies getting started to win their loyalty. Contact the largest suppliers of products your business will be using and see if they can be of help.

SOURCES FOR FURTHER GUIDANCE

The following offices offer free or low-cost guidance for new businesses.

Small Business Administration

The *Small Business Administration* (SBA) is a federal government agency set up to provide assistance to small businesses. The SBA offers educational programs for small businesses through *Small Business Development Centers* at many Michigan colleges and universities. In addition to the SBA website **www.sba.gov**, the SBA has a website to help small businesses at **www.business.gov**. To find the SBA office nearest to you, check in your local phone directory under the U.S. Government listings. The SBA is a good place to check for licensing requirements, financing information, and general assistance with what you need to start and to run a successful business. If you cannot find a local listing, try the following.

Small Business & Technology Development Center

A good starting point is the Small Business & Technology Development Center. The statewide main office is located at:

MI-SBTDC State Headquarters
Grand Valley State University
Seidman College of Business
510 West Fulton Street
Grand Rapids, MI 49504

616-331-7480
email: sbtdchq@gvsu.edu
www.gvsu.edu/misbtdc

In addition to this main office, there are twelve regional offices, and over thirty satellite offices. The regional offices are listed as follows, along with the counties they serve. Contact the regional office for your county to find out if there is a satellite office closer to you.

Region 1: All fifteen Upper Peninsula counties: Alger, Baraga, Chippewa, Delta, Dickinson, Gogebic, Houghton, Iron, Keweenaw, Luce, Mackinac, Marquette, Menominee, Ontonagon, and Schoolcraft.

Region 1-M1-SBTDC
2950 College Avenue
Escanaba, MI 49829
906-789-0558
jschultz@jobforce.org
www.gvsu.edu/misbtdc/region1

Region 2: Antrim, Benzie, Charlevoix, Emmet, Grand Traverse, Kalkaska, Leelenau, Manistee, Missaukee, and Wexford.

Chris Wendel, Regional Director
1209 South Garfield Avenue, Suite C
P.O. Box 506
Traverse City, MI 49685
231-922-3780
cwendel@nwm.cog.mi.us
www.gvsu.edu/misbtdc/region2

Region 3: Alcona, Alpena, Cheboygan, Crawford, Iosco, Montmorency, Ogemaw, Oscoda, Otsego, Presque Isle, and Roscommon.

MI-SBTDC
Alpena Community College
665 Johnson Street
Newport Center, Room 108
Alpena, MI 49707
989-358-7375

mehargk@alpenacc.edu
www.gvsu.edu/misbtdc/region3

Region 4: Clare, Gladwin, Gratiot, Isabella, Lake, Mason, Mecosta, Montcalm, Newaygo, Oceana, and Osceola.

MI-SBTDC, Region 4
Mid Michigan Community College
M-TEC Building
1375 South Clare Avenue
Harrison, MI 48625
989-386-6630
misbtdc4@midmich.edu
www.gvsu.edu/misbtdc/region4

Region 5: Arenac, Bay, Huron, Midland, Saginaw, Sanilac, and Tuscola.

MI-SBTDC, Region 5
Delta College
1961 Delta Road, H Wing
University Center, MI 48710
989-686-9597
sbtdc@delta.edu
www.gvsu.edu/misbtdc/region5

Region 6: Genessee and Lapeer.

Marsha Lyttle, Regional Director
Kettering Universtiy
Campus Center Building
5th Floor, Room 5-100
1700 West Third Avenue
Flint, MI 48504
810-762-9660
mlyttle@kettering.edu
www.gvsu.edu/misbtdc/region6

There is also a satellite office:

Patricia Lucas, Satellite Director
Lapeer Development Corporation
449 McCormick Drive
Lapeer, MI 48446
810-667-0080
patricia@lapeerdevelopment.com

Region 7: Kent, Muskegon, and Ottawa.

MI-SBTDC
Grand Valley State University
401 West Fulton Street
DeVos Center, 318C
Grand Rapids, MI 49504
616-331-7370
sbtdcinfo@gvsu.edu
www.gvsu.edu/misbtdc/region7

Region 8: Clinton, Eaton, Ingham, Ionia, Livingston, and Shiawassee.

MI-SBTDC
6400-Lansing Community College
309 North Washington Square, Suite 115
P.O. Box 40010
Lansing, MI 48933
517-483-1921
sbtdc@lcc.edu
www.gvsu.edu/misbtdc/region8

Region 9: Monroe, Oakland, and Wayne.

MI-SBTDC Regional Host Office
Eastern Michigan University
306 Gary M. Owen Building
300 West Michigan Avenue
Ypsilanti, MI 48197
734-487-0355
emu.sbdc@emich.edu
www.gvsu.edu/misbtdc/region9

Region 10: Macomb and St. Clair

Michigan Small Business & Technology Development Center
1 South Main Street, 7th Floor
Mount Clemens, MI 48043
586-469-5118
SBTDC@macombcountymi.gov
www.gvsu.edu/misbtdc/region10

Region 11: Allegan, Barry, Berrien, Branch, Calhoun, Cass, Kalamazoo, St. Joseph, and Van Buren.

MI-SBTDC
Haworth College of Business
3110 Schneider Hall
Western Michigan University
Kalamazoo, MI 49008
269-387-6004
sbtdc-kzoo@wmich.edu
www.gvsu.edu/misbtdc/region11

Region 12: Hillsdale, Jackson, Lenawee, and Washtenaw.

MI-SBTDC
Washtenaw Community College
301 West Michigan Avenue, Suite 101
Ypsilanti, MI 48197
734-547-9170
sbtdc@wccnet.org
www.gvsu.edu/misbtdc/region12

SCORE The Service Corps of Retired Executives (SCORE) is an organization of retired businesspeople who volunteer their time to help people starting new businesses. SCORE is sponsored by the Small Business Administration. They also sponsor loan information clinics for a small fee (usually about $5.00).

To contact your nearest SCORE organization, check in your local phone directory under the U.S. Government listings (SCORE will be listed under the heading for the Small Business Administration). If you cannot find it in the phone directory, call one of the phone numbers previously listed for the SBA and ask for the phone number of the SCORE office nearest you. You can also check the SCORE website:

www.score.org

chapter 2

Choosing the Form
of Your Business

One of the first decisions you will need to make in relation to setting up a business is how you will structure your business. Will you be in business alone, in a relatively loose association with one or more other persons, or will you use one of the more formal statutory organizations such as a corporation or limited liability company? This chapter explores the various forms of organizing a business to help you determine which is best for you.

BASIC FORMS OF DOING BUSINESS

Traditionally, the four primary forms for a business were proprietorship, partnership, limited partnership, and corporation. Since 1993, another option has been a *limited liability company*. The characteristics, advantages, and disadvantages of each are as follows.

Proprietorship   *Characteristics.* One person does business in his or her own name, or under an assumed name. There are no specific state laws covering the setting up of a proprietorship.

Advantages. Proprietorships are simple. There is no organizational expense and no partners to potentially come into conflict with in making business decisions.

Disadvantages. There is personal liability for all debts and obligations, and no continuation after death. All profits are directly taxable and business affairs easily mix with personal affairs.

Partnership

Characteristics. Two or more people carry on a business together and share the profits and losses. Laws covering partnerships are found in the *Michigan Uniform Partnership Act.* (Mich. Comp. Laws Ann., beginning with Sec. 449.1.)

Advantages. Partners can combine expertise and assets. Liability may be spread among more persons. Business can be continued after the death of a partner if bought out by a surviving partner and there is relatively little regulation.

Disadvantages. Each partner is personally liable for acts of him- or herself and other partners within the scope of the business. All profits are taxable, even if left in the business. Control is shared by all parties and the death of a partner may result in liquidation. Also, it is often hard to get rid of a bad partner.

Corporation

Characteristics. A corporation is a *person* created by the law that carries on business through its officers for its shareholders. (In Michigan one person may form a corporation and be the sole shareholder and officer.) Laws covering corporations are contained in the *Michigan Business Corporation Act.* (Mich. Comp. Laws Ann., beginning with Sec. 450.1101.)

An *S corporation* is a corporation that has filed **IRS FORM 2553** (form 3, p.199), choosing to have all profits taxed to the shareholders, rather than to the corporation. An S corporation files a tax return but pays no federal or state tax. The profit shown on the S corporation tax return is reported on the owners' tax returns.

A *C corporation* is any corporation that has not elected to be taxed as an S corporation. A C corporation pays income tax on its profits. The effect of this is that when dividends are paid to shareholders they are taxed twice, first as income to the corporation and second as they are paid to the shareholders.

A *professional service corporation* is a corporation formed by a licensed professional such as a doctor or accountant. Michigan has special rules for professional service corporations that differ slightly from those of other corporations. These are included in the Michigan *Professional Service Corporation Act.* (Mich. Comp. Laws Ann., beginning with Sec. 450.221.) There are also special tax rules for professional service corporations.

A *nonprofit corporation* is usually used for such organizations as churches and condominium associations. However, with careful planning, some types of businesses can be set up as nonprofit corporations and save in taxes. While a nonprofit corporation cannot pay dividends, it can pay its officers and employees fair salaries. Some of the major American nonprofit organizations pay their officers well over $100,000 a year. Michigan's special rules for nonprofit corporations are covered in the *Michigan Nonprofit Corporation Act.* (Mich. Comp. Laws Ann., beginning with Sec. 450.2101.)

Advantages. If properly organized, shareholders have no liability for corporate debts and lawsuits and officers usually have no personal liability for their corporate acts. The existence of a corporation may be perpetual and there are tax advantages allowed only to corporations. There is prestige in owning a corporation. Capital may be raised by issuing stock and it is easy to transfer ownership upon death. A small corporation can be set up as an S corporation to avoid corporate taxes but still retain corporate advantages. Some types of businesses can be set up as nonprofit corporations, which provide significant tax savings.

Disadvantages. There are start-up costs for forming a corporation, as well as certain formalities such as annual meetings, separate bank accounts, and tax forms. Unless a corporation registers as an S corporation, it must pay income tax separate from the tax paid by the owners.

Limited Partnership

Characteristics. A limited partnership has characteristics similar to both a corporation and a partnership. There are two types of partners in a limited partnership: *general partners* who have the control and liability; and, *limited partners* who put up money, but have no control over the business and whose liability is limited to what they paid for their share of the partnership (like corporate stock). See the *Michigan Revised Uniform Limited Partnership Act.* (Mich. Comp. Laws Ann., beginning with Sec. 449.1101.)

Advantages. Capital can be contributed by limited partners who have no control of the business or liability for its debts.

Disadvantages. General partners are personally liable for partnership debts and for the acts of each other. There are high start-up costs and an extensive partnership agreement is required.

Characteristics. In 1993, Michigan enacted the *Michigan Limited Liability Company Act.* (Mich. Comp. Laws Ann., Secs. 450.4101 to 450.5200.) An LLC has characteristics of both a corporation and a partnership. None of the partners (called *members*) have personal liability and all can have some control.

Limited Liability Company

Advantages. The limited liability company offers the tax benefits of a partnership (if structured properly) with the protection from liability of a corporation. It offers more tax benefits than an S corporation because it may pass through more depreciation and deductions, it may have different classes of ownership, it may have an unlimited number of members, and it may have aliens as members. It is similar to a Latin-American *Limitada* or a German *GmbH & Co. K.G.* A name can also be reserved with the Department of Commerce.

Disadvantages. There are start-up costs and because from a legal standpoint it is still a fairly new invention, there may not be a definite answer to some legal questions that may arise. However, the courts will probably rely on corporation and limited partnership law. As the Internal Revenue Service (IRS) has not ruled that all Michigan LLCs automatically receive partnership tax treatment, an attorney or tax accountant should be consulted to be sure documents are phrased in such a manner to assure the desired tax treatment.

NOTE: *Michigan no longer has limited liability partnerships. It just recognizes limited liability companies.*

Choosing the Form for Your Business

The selection of a form of doing business is best made with the advice of an accountant and an attorney. If you were selling harmless objects by mail, a proprietorship would be the easiest way to get started. But if you own a taxi service, it would be important to incorporate or form a limited liability company. That way, you avoid losing your personal assets if one of your drivers were to injure someone in an accident if the damages exceeded your insurance.

If you can expect a high cash buildup the first year, then a corporation may be the best way to keep taxes low. If you expect the usual start-up losses, then a proprietorship, a partnership, or an S corporation would probably be best.

START-UP PROCEDURES

This section explains how to go about setting up each type of business organization.

Proprietorship   There are no formal procedures to set up a sole proprietorship. This is the most simple and basic form of business operation. All bank accounts and any necessary licenses are in the name of the owner. If you wish to use a name other than your own, you will need to register that business name. (See Chapter 3 for more information about using an assumed name.)

Partnership   To form a partnership, a written agreement should be prepared to spell out the rights and obligations of the partners. You must also file a *co-partnership certificate* with the county clerk, although an assumed name certificate will meet this requirement. (Mich. Comp. Laws Ann., Sec. 449.101.) (See Chapter 3 for information about using an assumed name.)

Corporation   To form a corporation, *articles of incorporation* must be filed with the Department of Labor and Economic Growth in Lansing, along with a $10 filing fee. An organizational meeting is then held at which officers are elected, stock is issued, and other formalities are complied with to avoid the corporate entity being later declared invalid. Licenses and accounts are titled in the name of the corporation. (See Chapter 3 for information about selecting a corporate name and about using an assumed name.)

Limited Partnership   To start a limited partnership, a written *certificate of limited partnership* must be filed with the Department of Labor and Economic Growth in Lansing, and a lengthy disclosure document must be given to all prospective limited partners. Because of the complexity of securities laws and the criminal penalties for violation, it is advantageous to have an attorney organize a limited partnership.

Limited Liability Company   Two or more persons may form a limited liability company by filing *articles of organization* with the Department of Labor and Economic Growth in Lansing, and paying a $50 filing fee. Licenses and accounts are in the name of the company. It is similar to filing for a corporation.

SECURITIES LAWS

Both the state and federal governments have long and complicated laws dealing with the sales of *securities* (interests in businesses sold to investors, such as shares of stock, corporate bonds, or certain limited partnership interests). There are also hundreds of court cases attempting to explain what these laws mean. A thorough explanation of this area of law is beyond the scope of this book.

Basically, securities exist whenever a person provides money with the expectation that he or she will get a profit through the efforts of another person. This can apply to any situation where someone buys stock in or makes a loan to your business. What the laws require is disclosure of the risks involved and, in some cases, registration of the securities with the government. There are some exemptions such as for small amounts of money and for a limited numbers of investors.

Penalties for violation of securities laws are severe, including triple damages and prison terms. Consult a specialist in securities laws before issuing any security. You can often get an introductory consultation at a reasonable rate to have your options explained.

A copy of Michigan's securities law (known as the *Blue Sky Law*) may be obtained from:

Department of Labor and Economic Growth
Office of Financial and Insurance Services
Ottawa Building, 3rd Floor
611 West Ottawa
Lansing, MI 48909
877-999-6442
517-373-0220
ofis-sec-info@michigan.gov
www.michigan.gov/ofis

A brochure regarding Michigan's securities law can be downloaded at:

www.michigan.gov/documents/cis_ofis_guide_25011_7.pdf

Federal securities laws are enforced by the Securities and Exchange Commission.

FOREIGN NATIONALS

Persons who are not citizens nor legal permanent residents of the United States are free to start any type of business organization in Michigan. The type that would be most advantageous would be the LLC because it allows foreign owners (unlike an S corporation) and it avoids corporate taxation (unlike a C corporation).

Immigration Status

Two legal issues that foreign persons should be concerned with when starting a business in Michigan are their immigration status and the proper reporting of the business's foreign owners.

The ownership of a U.S. business does not automatically confer rights to enter or remain in the United States. Different types of visas are available to investors and business owners and each of these has strict requirements.

A visa to enter the United States may be permanent or temporary. *Permanent visas* for business owners usually require investments of $500,000 to $1,000,000 that result in the creation of new jobs. However, there are ways to obtain visas for smaller investments if they are structured right. For more information on this area, you should consult an immigration specialist or a book on immigration.

Temporary visas may be used by business owners to enter the United States; however, these are hard to get because in most cases the foreign person must prove that there are no U.S. residents qualified to take the job.

Reporting

U.S. businesses that own real property and are controlled by foreigners are required to file certain federal reports under the *International Investment Survey Act*, the *Agricultural Foreign Investment Disclosure Act*, and the *Foreign Investment in Real Property Tax Act* (FIRPTA). If these laws apply to your business, consult an attorney who specializes in foreign ownership of U.S. businesses.

Naming Your Business

One early consideration is naming your business. In addition to being important from a marketing standpoint, you also need to be aware of certain legal issues relating to business names.

PRELIMINARY CONSIDERATIONS

Before deciding upon a name for your business, be sure that it is not already being used by someone else. Many business owners have spent thousands of dollars on publicity and printing and then had to throw it all away because another company owned the name. A company that owns a name can take you to court and force you to stop using that name.

If you will be running a small local shop with no plans for expansion, you should at least check out whether the name has been trademarked. If another business is using the same name anywhere in the country and has registered it as a federal trademark, that business can sue you. If you plan to expand or to deal nationally, then you should do a thorough search of the name.

The first places to look are the local phone books and official records of your county. Next, you should check with the Department of Labor and

Economic Growth in Lansing to see if another company is using the name you have chosen or a name that would be confusingly similar. The department can be reached at 517-241-6470 or **www.michigan.gov/corporations**.

To do a national search, check trade directories and phone books of major cities. These can be found at many libraries and are usually reference books that cannot be checked out. The *Trade Names Directory* is a two volume set of names compiled from many sources and is published by Gale Research Co.

If you have a computer with Internet access, you can use it to search all of the Yellow Pages listings in the United States at a number of sites (at no charge). Some of the sites that offer free Yellow Pages searches are:

www.yellowpages.com
www.yellow.com
www.yp.com

A thorough search would include a check of all trademarks registered in the U.S. Patent and Trademark Office (USPTO) in Washington. Start by going to the USPTO website at **www.uspto.gov**. Some public libraries can do a preliminary search with their computers. There may be a fee for such a search. There are also companies that do such searches for a fee, usually under $100. One such company is:

Government Liaison Services, Inc.
200 North Glebe Road, Suite 321
Arlington, VA 22203
703-524-8200
800-642-6564
GLS@trademarkinfo.com
www.trademarkinfo.com

They also offer searches of 100 trade directories and 4,800 phone books.

No matter how thorough your search, there is no guarantee that there is not a local user somewhere with rights to the mark.

Example:
You register a name for a new chain of restaurants and later find out that someone in Winnemucca, Nevada, has been using the name longer than you. That person will still have the right to use the name, but just in his

local area. If you do not want his restaurant to be confused with your chain, you can try to buy him out.

Similarly, if you are operating a small business under a unique name and a law firm in New York writes and offers to buy the right to your business name, you can assume that some large corporation wants to start a major expansion under that name.

The best way to make sure a name you are using is not already owned by someone else is to make up a name. Names such as Xerox, Kodak, and Exxon were made up and did not have any meaning prior to their use. But remember that there are millions of businesses and even something you make up may already be in use. Do a search anyway.

ASSUMED NAMES

In Michigan, as in most states, unless you do business in your own name you must register the name you are using. (Mich. Comp. Laws Ann., beginning with Sec. 445.1.) Such a business name is called an *assumed name* in Michigan. Some other states call this a *fictitious name*.

The assumed name must be registered with the county clerk in each county where you own, conduct, or transact business. There is a filing fee of $6.00, although this may be higher in counties with a population of more than 2,000,000.

The law also says you should register in every county where you *intend* to conduct business. However, unless you know with a fair degree of certainty that you will soon be doing business in a particular county, there seems little point in registering until you are about to conduct business there. There is a special exception to the requirement of registering in a county if all you do is sell goods there through a traveling salesperson, by sample, or through the mail.

An assumed name registration is good for five years. It can be renewed for additional five-year periods for a $4.00 renewal fee. The county clerk is required to mail you a renewal form prior to the expiration.

It is a misdemeanor to fail to register an assumed name, with a possible penalty of a $25 to $100 fine and thirty days in jail. Each day of failing to register is considered a separate offense. Also, you may not sue anyone in your business name unless you are registered.

Example:

John Doe operates a masonry business. He may operate his business as John Doe, Mason without registering it. But he would need to register if he used other names, such as:

Doe Masonry	Doe Masonry Company
Doe Company	Michigan Masonry

Corporations and Assumed Names

Do not confuse an assumed name with the name of a corporation. Corporations are registered with the Michigan Department of Labor and Economic Growth, not the county clerk. You cannot use the words "corporation," "incorporated," "corp.," or "inc.," unless you have legally formed a corporation. If a corporation is doing business only under its official corporate name (i.e., the name that appears on its articles of incorporation filed with the Department of Labor and Economic Growth), it is not required to register that name as an assumed name with the county clerk. However, if the corporation is doing business under a name that is different from its registered corporate name, it would have to register that assumed name with the county clerk.

Example:

Doe Masonry, Inc., would not need to register an assumed name if it conducted business under that name, because that is its registered corporate name. However, if Doe Masonry, Inc., decided to conduct business in Wayne County under the name Wayne County Masonry, it would need to register Wayne County Masonry as an assumed name with the county clerk in Wayne County.

When you use an assumed name you are *doing business as* (d/b/a) the assumed name you are using. To use the previous examples, John Doe, as a sole proprietor, would be *John Doe d/b/a Doe Masonry*. As a corporation, Doe Masonry, Inc., would be *Doe Masonry, Inc., d/b/a Wayne County Masonry*.

The registration of an assumed name only gives some protection to the name in the county of registration. The clerk may reject a name that is *likely to mislead the public, or any assumed name already filed in the county or so nearly similar thereto as to lead to confusion or deception.*

Some types of businesses or professions have special requirements for the use of an assumed name. See Chapter 6 for a list of some of the state-regulated professions, with references to the laws that apply to them.

CORPORATE NAMES

As previously stated, a corporation does not have to register its name as an assumed name because it already has a legal name. The name of a corporation must contain one of the following words or abbreviations (Mich. Comp. Laws Ann., Sec. 450.1211.):

Corporation	Incorporated
Corp.	Inc.
Company	Limited
Co.	Ltd.

There are also other restrictions on corporate names. (Mich. Comp. Laws Ann., Sec. 450.1212.) It is not advisable to use only the word *Company* or *Co.*, because unincorporated businesses also use these words and a person dealing with you might not realize you are incorporated. If this happens, you might end up with personal liability for corporate debts. You can use a combination of two of the words, such as *ABC Co., Inc.*

If the name of the corporation does not contain one of the previously listed words or abbreviations, it will be rejected by the Department of Labor and Economic Growth. It will also be rejected if:

✪ the name is already taken;

✪ it is similar to the name of another corporation or partnership;

✪ it *indicates or implies that the corporation is formed for a purpose other than [one] or more of the purposes permitted by its articles of incorporation*; or,

✪ it violates any other statutes restricting the use of a corporate name.

To check on a name, you may contact the Department of Labor and Economic Growth at **www.michigan.gov/cis** or by phone at 517-241-6470.

If a name you want is taken by another company, you may be able to change it slightly and have it accepted.

Example:

You intend to operate a furniture upholstery business in Saginaw County, and want to register your corporation as Tri-City Upholstery, Inc. Your request for this name is rejected because there is already a Tri-City Upholstery, Inc., registered, but you find out it operates in Oakland County. You may be allowed to use Tri-City Upholstery of Saginaw County, Inc. However, even if this is approved by the Department of Labor and Economic Growth, you might get sued by the other company if your business is close to theirs or there is a likelihood of confusion.

> **Warning:** Do not have anything printed until your corporate papers are returned to you. Sometimes a name is approved over the phone and rejected when sent in.

Once you have chosen a corporate name and know it is available, you should immediately register your corporation. A name can be *reserved* for ninety days for $20, but it is easier just to register the corporation than to waste time on the name reservation.

If a corporation wants to do business under a name other than its corporate name, it can register an assumed name such as *Doe Corporation d/b/a Doe Industries*. But if the assumed name leads people to believe that the business is not a corporation, the right to limited liability may be lost. If such a name is used, it should always be accompanied by the corporate name. You do not want people to be in doubt that they are dealing with a corporation.

The Word Limited

Although legally permitted for a corporation, the word *Limited*, or the abbreviation *Ltd.*, at the end of a name should only be used for a limited partnership.

PROFESSIONAL SERVICE CORPORATIONS

Professional service corporations are corporations formed by professionals such as attorneys, doctors, dentists, and architects. Under Michigan law, a professional corporation cannot use the usual corporate designations (e.g., Inc., Corp., or Co.), but *must* use the words *Professional Corporation* or the abbreviation *P.C.*

LIMITED LIABILITY COMPANIES

The term *limited liability company* should only be used with such an entity. If you form a limited liability company, your company name *must* include:

✪ Limited Liability Company;

✪ L.L.C.; or,

✪ L.C.

If you form a professional limited liability company, the name *must* include:

✪ Professional Limited Liability Company;

✪ P.L.L.C.; or,

✪ P.L.C.

Trademarks, Service Marks, and Trade Names

As your business builds goodwill, its name will become more valuable and you will want to protect it from others who may wish to copy it. You can protect your company name by registering it as a *trade name* with the Michigan Department of Labor and Economic Growth. Another way to protect your company name in Michigan is to incorporate, since a particular corporate name can only be registered once in Michigan.

To protect a name used to describe your goods or services you can register it as a *trademark* (for goods) or a *service mark* (for services), with either the Michigan

Department of Labor and Economic Growth or with the United States Patent and Trademark Office.

You cannot obtain federal registration for the name of your business, but you can trademark a name you use on your goods and services. In most cases you will use your company name on your goods as your trademark, so it, in effect, protects your company name.

State registration would be useful if you expect to use the name or mark only within the state of Michigan. Federal registration would protect your mark anywhere in the country. The registration of a mark gives you exclusive use of the mark for the types of goods for which you register it. The only exception is persons who have already been using the mark. You cannot stop people who have been using the mark prior to your registration.

Federal Registration

There are two types of applications for federal trademark and trade name registration. One depends upon whether you have already made actual use of the mark and the other on whether you merely have an intention to use the mark in the future.

For a trademark that has been in *actual use*, you must file an application form along with specimens showing actual use and a drawing of the mark that complies with all of the rules of the United States Patent and Trademark Office. For an *intent to use* application you must file two separate forms, one when you make the initial application and the other after you have made actual use of the mark as well as the specimens and drawing. Before a mark can be entitled to federal registration, the use of the mark must be in *interstate commerce* or in commerce with another country. The fee for registration is $335, but if you file an *intent to use* application there is a second fee of $100 for the filing after actual use.

State Registration

The procedure for state registration of a trade name, trademark, or service mark is simple and the cost is $50. First, you should contact the Michigan Department of Labor and Economic Growth at the address, phone number, or website at the end of this section and ask them to search your desired name and tell you if it is available.

Before a trademark or service mark can be registered, it must be used in Michigan. For goods, this means it must be used on the goods themselves or on containers, tags, or labels. For services, it must be used or displayed in the sale or advertising of the services. The use must be in connection with sales in the state of Michigan.

The $50 fee will register the mark in only one *class of goods*. If the mark is used on more than one class of goods, a separate registration must be filed.

The registration is good for ten years. It must be renewed six months prior to expiration and the Department of Labor and Economic Growth is required to send you a renewal notice before the required renewal date. The renewal fee is $25 for each class of goods.

A sample, filled-in **APPLICATION FOR REGISTRATION OF TRADEMARK/ SERVICE MARK** form may be found in Appendix B as form 5. A blank form is included in Appendix C. (see form 7, p.219.)

Forms and more information may also be obtained from:

Department of Labor and Economic Growth
Division of Commercial Services and Corporations
P.O. Box 30054
Lansing, MI 48909
517-241-6470
www.michigan.gov/dleg

DOMAIN NAMES

With the Internet being so new and changing so rapidly, all of the rules for Internet names have not yet been worked out. Originally, the first person to reserve a name owned it and enterprising souls bought up the names of most of the Fortune 500 corporations and held them for ransom. Then a few of the corporations went to court and the rule was developed that if a company had a trademark for a name that company could stop someone else from using it as a domain name.

You cannot yet get a trademark merely for using a domain name. Trademarks are granted for the use of a name in commerce. Once you have a valid trademark, you will be safe in using it for your domain name.

In the next few years there will probably be several changes to the domain name system to make it more flexible and useful throughout the world. One proposed change is the addition of more *top level domains* (TLDs), which are the last parts of the names, like *com* and *gov.*

The following TLDs are either available now or will be soon:

aero	coop	llc	school
agent	family	llp	scifi
arts	free	love	shop
auction	game	ltd	soc
biz	golf	med	sport
bz	inc	mp3	tech
cc	info	museum	travel
chat	kids	names	tv
church	kids.us	nu	us
club	law	pro	video
			xxx

If you wish to protect your domain name the best thing to do at this point is to get a trademark for it. To do this you would have to use it on your goods or services. (See Chapter 9 for more information on domain names and the Internet.)

Financing Your Business

The way to finance your business is determined by how fast you want your business to grow and how much risk of failure you are able to handle. Letting the business grow with its own income is the slowest but safest way to grow. Taking out a personal loan against your house to expand quickly is the fastest but riskiest way to grow.

GROWING WITH PROFITS

Many successful businesses have started out with little money and used the profits to grow bigger and bigger. If you have another source of income to live on (such as from a job or a spouse), you can plow all the income of your fledgling business into growth.

Some businesses start as hobbies or part-time ventures on the weekends and evenings, while the entrepreneur holds down a full-time job. Many types of businesses can start this way. Even some multimillion-dollar corporations such as Apple Computer started out this way.

This way you have no risk. If you find you are not good at running that type of business or the time or location was not right for your idea, all you are out is the time you spent and your start-up capital.

However, most businesses can only grow so big from their own income. As a business grows, in many cases, it gets to a point where the orders are so big that money must be borrowed to produce the product to fill the order. With this situation there is the risk that if your customer cannot pay or goes bankrupt, your business will also go under. At such a point, a business owner should investigate the credit worthiness of the customer and weigh the risks. Some businesses have grown rapidly, some have gone under, and others have decided not to take the risk and stayed small. You can worry about that down the road.

USING YOUR SAVINGS

If you have savings you can tap to get your business started, that is the best source. You will not have to pay high interest rates on a loan and you will not have to worry about paying someone back (such as a relative).

Using Your Home Equity

If you have owned your home for several years, it is possible that the equity has grown substantially and you can get a second mortgage to finance your business. Some lenders will even make second mortgages that exceed the equity if you have been in the home for many years and have a good record of paying your bills. Just remember, if your business does not succeed, you can lose your home.

Retirement Accounts

Be careful about borrowing from your retirement savings. There are tax penalties for borrowing from or against certain types of retirement accounts. Again, if your business does not succeed, you will have lost your retirement nest egg.

Having Too Much Money

It probably does not seem possible to have too much money with which to start a business, but many businesses have failed for that reason. With plenty of start-up capital available, a business owner does not need to watch expenses and can become wasteful. Employees get used to lavish spending. Once the money runs out and the business must run on its own earnings, it fails.

Starting with the bare minimum forces a business to watch its expenses and be frugal. It necessitates finding the least expensive solutions to problems that crop up and creative ways to be productive.

BORROWING MONEY

It is extremely tempting to look to others to get the money to start a business. The risk of failure is less worrisome and the pressure is lower than if you were using your own money. However, there is a problem with borrowing. If it is others' money, you do not have quite the same incentive to succeed as if everything you own is on the line.

Family Depending on how much money your family can spare, it may be the most comfortable or most uncomfortable source of funds for you. If you have been assured a large inheritance and your parents have more funds than they need to live on, you may be able to borrow against your inheritance without worry. It will be your money anyway and you need it much more now than you will ten, twenty, or more years from now. If you lose it all it is your own loss anyway.

If, however, you are borrowing your widowed mother's source of income or asking her to cash in a CD she lives on to finance your business, you should have second thoughts about it. Stop and consider all the real reasons your business might not take off and what your mother would do without the income.

Friends Borrowing from friends is like borrowing from family members. If you know they have the funds available and could survive a loss, you may want to risk it. However, if they would be loaning you their only resources, do not chance it.

Financial problems can be the worst thing for a relationship, whether it is a casual friendship or a long-term romantic involvement. Before you borrow from a friend, try to imagine what would happen if you could not pay it back and how you would feel if it caused the end of your relationship.

The ideal situation is if your friend were a co-venturer in your business and the burden would not be totally on you to see how the funds were spent. Still, realize that such a venture will put extra strain on the relationship.

Banks In a way, a bank can be a more comfortable party to borrow from than friends or family because you do not have a personal relationship with it. If you fail, a bank will write your loan off rather than disown you. But a bank can also be the least comfortable party to borrow from because it will demand realistic projections and be on top of you to perform. If you do not meet the bank's expectations, it may call your loan just when you need it most.

The best thing about a bank loan is that it will require you to do your homework. You will have to have plans that make sense to a banker. If he or she approves your loan, you know that your plans are at least reasonable.

Bank loans are not cheap or easy. You will be paying interest and you will have to put up collateral. If your business does not have equipment or receivables, the bank may require you to put up your house and other personal property to guarantee the loan.

Banks are a little easier to deal with when you get a Small Business Administration (SBA) loan. That is because the SBA guarantees that it will pay the bank if you default on the loan. SBA loans are obtained through local bank branches. They have the paperwork to get your loan approved.

Credit Cards   Borrowing against personal credit cards can be the most expensive source of capital. The rates can go higher than 20%. But many cards offer lower rates and some people are able to get numerous cards. Some successful businesses have used personal credit cards to get off the ground or to weather through a cash crunch. However, if the business does not begin to generate the cash to make the payments, you could soon end up in bankruptcy. A good strategy is only to use credit cards for a long-term asset, like a computer or for something that will quickly generate cash, like buying inventory to fill an order. Do not use credit cards to pay salaries or expenses that are not generating revenue.

GETTING A RICH PARTNER

One of the best business combinations is a young entrepreneur with ideas and ambition and a retired investor with business experience and money. Together they can supply everything the business needs.

How do you find such a partner? Be creative. You should have investigated the business you are starting and know others who have been in such businesses. Have any of them had partners retire over the last few years? Are any of them planning to phase out of the business?

SELLING SHARES OF YOUR BUSINESS

Silent investors are the best source of capital for your business. You retain full control of the business and if it happens to fail you have no obligation to them. Unfortunately, few silent investors are interested in a new business. It is only after you have proven your concept to be successful and built up a rather large enterprise that you will be able to attract such investors.

The most common way to obtain money from investors is to issue stock to them. For this, the best type of business entity is the corporation. It gives you almost unlimited flexibility in the number and kinds of shares of stock you can issue.

USING THE INTERNET TO FIND CAPITAL

Before attempting to market your company's shares on the Internet, be sure to get an opinion from a securities lawyer or do some serious research into securities laws. The Internet does have some sources of capital listed. The following sites may be helpful.

Business Finance

www.businessfinance.com

SBA

www.sba.gov

Inc. Magazine

www.inc.com

NVST

www.nvst.com

The Capital Network

www.thecapitalnetwork.com

Locating Your Business

The right location for your business will be determined by what type of business it is and how fast you expect to grow. For some types of businesses the location will not be important to your success or failure; in others it will be crucial.

WORKING OUT OF YOUR HOME

Many small businesses get started out of the home. Some eventually move out of the home, but many people prefer working at home and keep their businesses there. Chapter 6 discusses the legalities of home businesses. This section discusses the practicalities.

Starting a business out of your home can save you the rent, electricity, insurance, and other costs of setting up at another location. For some people this is ideal and they can combine their home and work duties easily and efficiently. But for other people it is a disaster. A spouse, children, neighbors, television, or household chores can be so distracting that no other work gets done.

Many people use their residential telephone line to conduct business or add a second residential line, since residential rates are usually lower than business lines. However, if you wish to be listed in the Yellow Pages, you will need to have a business line in your home. If you are running two or more types of businesses, you can probably add their names as additional listings on the original number and avoid paying for another business line.

You also need to consider whether operating out of your home will be compatible with the type of business you will operate. For example, if you run a consulting business in which you are usually driving to a client's workplace to do most of your work or conducting most of your business by telephone, you can probably operate comfortably out of your home. But if your business requires stocking inventory, having several employees, or having many customers come to your office, your home may not be a convenient place from which to conduct business.

CHOOSING A RETAIL SITE

For most types of retail stores, the location is of prime importance. Such things to consider are how close it is to your potential customers, how visible it is to the public, and how easily accessible it is to both autos and pedestrians. The attractiveness and safety of the building and the general area should also be considered.

Location is less important for a business that is the only one of its kind in the area (for example, the only moped parts dealer or Armenian restaurant in a metropolitan area), since people would have to come to wherever you are if they want your products or services. However, even with such businesses, keep in mind that there is competition. People who want moped parts can order them by mail and restaurant customers can choose another type of cuisine.

Look up all the businesses like the one you plan on starting in the phone book and mark them on a map. For some businesses, like dry cleaners, you would want to be far from the others so that you are the most convenient location for people in your area. But for other businesses, like antique stores, you would want to be near the others. Antique stores usually do not carry the same things, so they do not directly compete and people like to go to an *antique district* and visit all the shops.

CHOOSING OFFICE, MANUFACTURING, OR WAREHOUSE SPACE

If your business will be the type in which customers will not come to you, then locating it near customers is not as much of a concern. You can probably save money by locating away from the high traffic central business districts. However, you should consider the convenience for employees and not locate in an area that would be unattractive to them or too far from where they would likely live (such as locating far out in the country instead of near town).

LEASING A SITE

A lease of space can be one of the biggest expenses of a small business, so you should do a lot of homework before signing one. There are a lot of terms in a commercial lease that can make or break your business. These are the most critical.

Zoning   Before signing a lease you should be sure that everything that your business will need to do is allowed by the zoning of the property.

Restrictions   In some shopping centers existing tenants have guarantees that other tenants do not compete with them. For example, if you plan to open a restaurant and bakery you may be forbidden to sell carry-out baked goods if the supermarket has a bakery and a noncompete clause.

Signs   Business signs are regulated by zoning laws, sign laws, and property restrictions. If you rent a hidden location with no possibility for adequate signage, your business will have a lot smaller chance of success than otherwise.

ADA Compliance   The *Americans with Disabilities Act* (ADA) requires that reasonable accommodations be made to make businesses accessible to the handicapped. When a business is remodeled, many more changes are required than if no remodeling is done. When renting space you should be sure that it complies with the law or that the landlord will be responsible for compliance. Otherwise, you need to be fully aware of the costs you could bear.

Expansion   As your business grows you may need to expand your space. The time to find out about your options is before you sign the lease. Perhaps you can take over adjoining units when those leases expire.

Renewal For some businesses, the location is a key to success. If you spend five years building up a clientele, you do not want someone to take over when your lease is up. Therefore, you should have a renewal clause on your lease. Usually this allows an increase in rent based on inflation.

Guarantee Most landlords of commercial space will not rent to a small corporation without a personal guarantee from the leasee. This is a very risky thing for a new business owner to do. The lifetime rent on a long-term commercial lease can be hundreds of thousands of dollars. If your business fails, the last thing you want to do is be personally responsible for five years of rent.

Where space is scarce or a location is hot, a landlord can get the guarantees he or she demands and there is nothing you can do about it (except perhaps set up an asset protection plan ahead of time). But where several units are vacant or the commercial rental market is soft, often you can negotiate out of the personal guarantee or at least limit it. For example, if the lease is five years, maybe you can get away with a guarantee of just the first year. Give it a try.

Duty to Open Some shopping centers have rules requiring all shops to be open certain hours. If you cannot afford to staff it the whole time required, if your business is seasonal, or if you have religious or other reasons that make this a problem, you should negotiate it out of the lease or find another location.

Sublease At some point you may decide to sell your business as a going concern, and in many cases the location is the most valuable aspect of the business. For this reason, be sure that you have the right to either assign your lease or to sublease the property. If this is impossible, one way around a prohibition is to incorporate your business before signing the lease and then when you sell the business, sell the stock. But some lease clauses prohibit transfer of *any interest* in the business, so read the lease carefully.

BUYING A SITE

If you are experienced with owning rental property you will probably be more inclined to buy a site for your business. If you have no experience with real estate you should probably rent and not take on the extra cost and responsibility of buying. One reason to buy your site is that you can build up equity.

Expansion   You should consider the growth potential of your business. If it grows quickly, will you be able to expand at the site you are considering buying or will you have to move? If the site is a good investment, whether or not you have your business, then by all means buy it. But if its main use is for your business, think twice.

Zoning   Some of the concerns when buying a site are the same as when renting. You will want to make sure that the zoning permits the type of business you wish to start or that you can get a variance without a large expense or delay. Be aware that just because a business is now using the site does not mean that you can expand or remodel the business at that site. Some zoning laws allow businesses to be grandfathered in but not to expand. Check with the zoning department and find out exactly what is allowed.

Signs   Signs are another concern. Some cities have regulated signs and do not allow new ones or require them to be smaller. Some businesses have used these laws to get publicity; for example, a car dealer was told to take down a large number of American flags on his lot. He filed a federal lawsuit and rallied the community behind him and his business.

ADA Compliance   Compliance with the ADA is another concern when buying a commercial building. Find out from the building department if the building is in compliance or what needs to be done to put it in compliance. If you remodel, the requirements may be more strict.

NOTE: *When dealing with public officials, keep in mind that they do not always know what the law is or do not accurately explain it. They often try to intimidate people into doing things that are not required by law. Read the requirements yourself and question the officials if they seem to be interpreting it wrong. Seek legal advice if they refuse to budge from a clearly erroneous position.*

Also consider that keeping them happy may be worth the price. If you are already doing something they have overlooked, do not make a big deal over a little thing they want changed or they may subject you to a full inspection or audit.

Ownership of the Business Site   One risk in buying a business site is that if the business gets into financial trouble the creditors may go after the building as well. For this reason, most people who buy a site for their business keep the ownership out of the business. For example, the business will be a corporation and the real estate will be owned personally by the owner, by a different corporation, or by a trust unrelated to the business.

CHECKING GOVERNMENTAL REGULATIONS

When looking for a site for your business, you should investigate the different governmental regulations in your area. For example, a location just outside the city or county limits might have a lower licensing fee, a lower sales tax rate, and less strict sign requirements.

chapter 6

Licensing Your Business

Depending upon the type of business you intend to conduct and where you intend to open your business, there may be various licensing requirements.

BUSINESS LICENSES AND ZONING

Before opening your business you may need to obtain a business license from your local city, county, or township. Each city, county, or township decides which types of businesses require a license. Businesses that do work in several areas, such as builders, may need to obtain a license from each city, county, or township in which they do work. This does not have to be done until you actually begin a job in a particular area.

All cities or counties have *zoning laws*, which divide property into various types of allowed uses. Some property may only be used for residential purposes. Other property may be used for retail business, but not for heavy industry. In rural areas, much of the property is limited to agricultural use. Be sure to find out if the zoning laws will allow your type of business before buying or leasing property. The licensing authority may check the zoning before issuing your license.

If you will be preparing or serving food, you will need to check with the local health department to be sure that the premises are in compliance with their requirements.

Home Businesses

Problems occasionally arise when people attempt to start a business in their home. Small, new businesses often cannot afford to pay rent for commercial space, and cities often try to forbid businesses from operating in residential areas. Getting a business license or registering an assumed name often gives notice to the local government that a business is being conducted in a residential area.

Some people avoid the problem by starting their businesses without business licenses, figuring that the penalties are less expensive than the cost of office space. Others get the license and ignore the zoning rules. If you have commercial trucks and equipment all over your property, or even daily pick-ups and deliveries by UPS, there will probably be complaints from neighbors and the city will probably take legal action. But if your business consists merely of making phone calls out of your home and keeping supplies there, the problem may never come up.

If a problem does arise regarding a home business that does not disturb the neighbors, a good argument can be made that the zoning law that prohibits the business is unconstitutional. For hundreds of years people performed income-producing activities in their homes. But court battles with a city are expensive and probably not worth the effort for a small business. The best course of action is to keep a low profile. Using a post office box can sometimes help divert attention away from the residence.

STATE-REGULATED PROFESSIONS AND BUSINESSES

Many professions and types of businesses require special licenses. Even if your business or profession does not require licensing, some of your business activities may be subject to licensing, certification, or permitting. The best place to check the most current state licensing requirements is on either the Small Business and Technology Development Center's licensing website, **www.michigan.org/medc/services/license**, or the state government's licensing website, **www.michigan.gov/statelicensesearch**. From either of these sites you can do a key word search, or click on "View ALL Required Licenses."

You can also contact your local Small Business and Technology Development Center (see Chapter 1 for a list of these locations), or contact:

Department of Labor and Economic Growth
Licensing Division
P.O. Box 30018
Lansing, MI 48909
517-241-9288
bcslic@michigan.gov

The Licensing Division's website will also enable you to get information on specific licensing boards.

Many, but not all, occupations and businesses subject to regulation are included in *Michigan Compiled Laws Annotated*, Chapter 339. The best ways to find out about laws affecting your business are to contact the appropriate state agency or licensing authority that regulates your type of business, contact any professional association for your type of business, and conduct your own research in the index to the *Michigan Compiled Laws Annotated*.

Partial List of Regulated Professions and Businesses in Michigan

The following is a list of some of the statutes relating to various professions, businesses, and business matters. It is by no means a comprehensive list. Even if you do not think you are subject to regulation, read through the list below and check with the Licensing Division anyway. Some licensing requirements may surprise you. Governments seem to endlessly pass laws adding to the professions and businesses regulated, so do not rely exclusively on the list below. Citations are given to the *Michigan Compiled Laws Annotated*.

PROFESSION/ACTIVITY	STATUTE SECTION
Accountants	339.720
Adoption agencies (child-placing agencies)	710.22
Adult foster care facilities	400.701
Agricultural products	(See index to MCLA)
Aircraft & airports	259.1
Alarm system contractors	338.1051
Alcoholic beverages	436.1101
Ambulance services	333.20920
Amusement rides	408.660
Animal shelters	287.331
Architects	339.2001

Asbestos contractors	338.3101
Athletic services providers	333.26301
Attorneys	600.901
Auctioneers	446.51
Barbers	339.1101 & 338.2217
Beverage containers	445.571
Bingo	432.101
Boarding & lodging houses	427.1
Boat liveries	324.44515
Boat races	324.80164
Boiler safety	408.751
Boxing	339.801
Carnivals	408.660
Casinos	432.203
Cemeteries	456.1
Chiropractors	333.16401
Coal mines	324.63514
Collection agencies	339.901
Commercial feed	287.521
Community planners	339.2301
Condominiums	559.101
Construction code	125.1501
Construction contractors	(See specific type of contractor)
Cosmetology	339.1201
Counseling services	333.16341 & 333.18101
Credit cards	750.157m
Credit insurance	550.601
Dentists, dental assistants & hygienists	333.16601
Detectives	338.821
Driver training schools	256.601
Druggists (pharmacists)	333.17741
Dry cleaners & launderers	333.13301
Electrical contractors & electricians	338.881
Electrologists	339.1208
Electronic fund transfers	488.1
Elevators, dumb waiters, & escalators	408.801
Employment agencies	339.1001
Engineers	339.2001
Estheticians	339.1210
Explosives	29.41 & 750.200

Family day-care homes	125.216g
Fertilizer manufacture or distribution	324.8504
Fireworks	750.243a
Fitness centers	333.26301
Food	289.1101
Foresters	339.2101
Franchises	445.1501
Frozen desserts	288.321
Funeral directors & embalmers	339.1801
Grain dealers	285.67a
Guns	28.421 & 750.22
Gymnasiums	333.26301
Hawkers & peddlers	445.371
Hazardous materials	29.471
Hazardous substances labeling	286.451
Hazardous waste management	324.11101
Health spas	333.26301
Hearing aid dealers	339.1301
Home improvement financing	445.1101
Horse & mule dealers & brokers	287.112 & 287.121
Horse racing	431.301 & 750.330
Hotels	427.1
Insurance	500.100
Insurance adjusters, agents, & counselers	500.240 & 500.1201
Junk dealers	445.401
Junk yards	445.451
Laboratories	333.20501
Land sales	565.801
Landscape architects	339.2201
Liquidation sales	442.211
Manicurists	339.1209
Meats	287.571 & 289.1101
Mechanical contractors	338.971
Messenger companies	484.1 & 750.539
Mobile homes & mobile home parks	125.991
Mortgage brokers, lenders, & servicers	445.1651
Mortgage lending	445.1601
Motor carriers	475.1 & 476.1
Motor vehicle manufacturers, distributors, & dealers	445.1561
Motor vehicle sales financing	492.101

Motor vehicles	257.1
Natural hair cultivation	339.1210a
Notaries public	55.107
Nurseries	286.209
Nurses	333.17201
Nursing homes	339.1901
Ocularists	339.2701
Optometry	333.17401
Osteopathy	333.17501
Outdoor advertising	252.301
Pawnbrokers	445.471 & 446.201
Pest control	286.201
Pet shops	287.331
Pharmacists	333.17741
Physical therapy	333.17801
Physicians	333.17001
Physicians assistants	333.17011
Plumbers	338.901
Podiatry	333.18001
Polygraph examiners	338.1701
Poultry	445.301
Precious metal & gem dealers	445.481
Private schools	388.551
Private trade schools	395.101
Psychiatric facilities & programs	330.1134
Psychologists	333.18201
Real estate appraisers	339.2601
Real estate brokerage	339.2501
Rental-purchase agreements	445.951
Residential builders and maintenance & alteration contractors	339.2403
Restaurants	289.1101 & 691.1521
Retail installment sales	445.851
Secondhand & junk dealers	445.401
Securities transactions	451.501
Security agencies & guards	338.1051
Septic tanks	333.12751
Ski areas	408.329
Snowmobile dealers	324.82101
Storage, cleaning, or repair services (for clothing, curtains, draperies, carpets, or household furnishings)	445.1751

Summer resorts & parks	455.101
Surveyors	339.2001
Taverns & saloons	436.1525
Telegraph & telephone companies	484.1 & 750.539
Timber	324.50101; 324.52501; 426.151; 426.174; & 752.701
Transient merchants	445.371
Used-car lots	445.501
Veterinary medicine	333.18811
Warehouses & warehousement	444.1
Watches, secondhand dealers	445.551

FEDERAL LICENSES

So far there are few businesses that require federal licensing or registration. If you are in any of the types of businesses in the following list, you should check with the federal agency listed below it.

Radio or television stations or manufacturers of equipment emitting radio waves:

Federal Communications Commission
445 12th Street, SW
Washington, DC 20554
www.fcc.gov

Manufacturers of alcohol, tobacco, firearms, or explosives:

Bureau of Alcohol, Tobacco, Firearms and Explosives
99 New York Avenue, NE
Washington, DC 20226
www.atf.gov

Securities brokers and providers of investment advice:

Securities and Exchange Commission
100 F Street, NE
Washington, DC 20549
www.sec.gov

Manufacturers of drugs and processors of meat:

Food and Drug Administration
5600 Fishers Lane
Rockville, MD 20857
www.fda.gov

Interstate carriers:

Surface Transportation Board
395 E Street, SW
Washington, DC 20423
www.stb.dot.gov

Exporting:

Bureau of Industry and Security
U.S. Department of Commerce
14th Street & Constitution Avenue, NW
Washington, DC 20230
www.bis.doc.gov

Important Addresses

The following list will provide you with a quick reference to the main offices of various agencies. If you call any of the numbers listed below, you may be transferred to a specific subdivision or be given a separate number to call. Portions of this book may have information on where to contact subdivisions of these agencies for specific types of information.

Office of the Attorney General
P.O. Box 30212
Lansing, MI 48909
877-765-8388
www.michigan.gov/ag

Michigan Department of Treasury
Lansing, MI 48922
517-373-3200
Forms: 800-367-6263
www.michigan.gov/treasury

Michigan Department of Environmental Quality
P.O. Box 30473
Lansing, MI 48909
517-373-7917
www.michigan.gov/deq

Michigan Department of Community Health
Capitol View Building
201 Townsend Street
Lansing, MI 48913
517-373-3740
www.michigan.gov/mdch

Department of Labor and Economic Growth
P.O. Box 30004
Lansing, MI 48909
517-373-1820
www.michigan.gov/dleg

Department of Labor and Economic Growth
Licensing Division
P.O. Box 30018
Lansing, MI 48909
517-241-9288
www.michigan.gov/dleg

NOTE: *The Department of Labor and Economic Growth has many divisions, including unemployment compensation and workers' compensation, under it. On its website, in the left-hand column, click on "Agencies & Commissions" for a complete listing.*

Michigan Department of Civil Rights
Capitol Tower Building, Suite 800
Lansing, MI 48933
517-335-3165
www.michigan.gov/mdcr

Small Business and Technology Development Center
Grand Valley State University
Seidman College of Business
510 West Fulton Street
Grand Rapids, MI 49504
616-331-7480
www.gvsu.edu/misbtdc

Equal Employment Opportunity Commission
1801 L Street, NW
Washington, DC 20507
800-669-4000
www.eeoc.gov

East Central Region
Federal Trade Commission
1111 Superior Avenue, Suite 200
Cleveland, OH 44114
www.ftc.gov

U.S. Internal Revenue Service
477 Michigan Avenue
Detroit, MI 48226
313-628-3722
www.irs.gov

U.S. Department of Labor
Occupational Safety and Health Administration
315 West Allegan, Room 207
Lansing, MI 48933
517-487-4996
www.osha.gov

U.S. Department of Labor
200 Constitution Avenue, NW
Washington, DC 20210
www.dol.gov

U.S. Citizenship and Immigration Services
333 Mount Elliot
Detroit, MI 48207
800-375-5283
www.uscis.gov

U.S. Department of Labor
Office of Labor-Management Standards
211 West Fort Street, Suite 1313
Detroit, MI 48226
313-226-6200
www.dol.gov/esa

Contract Law

As a business owner you will need to know the basics of forming a simple contract for your transactions with both customers and vendors. This chapter gives you a quick overview of the principles that apply to your transactions and pitfalls to avoid. If you face more complicated contract questions, consult a law library or an attorney familiar with small business law.

TRADITIONAL CONTRACT LAW

One of the first things taught in law school is that a contract is not legal unless three elements are present: an *offer*, an *acceptance*, and a *consideration*. Very basically, these terms may be defined as follows.

✪ An *offer* is a proposal to make a contract, made by one party to a second party.

Example:
I promise to pay you $20 if you will promise to shovel the snow off my driveway before noon today.

✪ An *acceptance* is the second party's agreement to form a contract as proposed by the party who made the offer. The second party must accept the proposal exactly as made, without adding or changing anything; otherwise, it is not an acceptance.

Example:
You may accept the offer stated in the previous example by saying something as simple as I accept.

✪ A *consideration* is what induces a party to enter into a contract, which is usually exchanging something of value or exchanging promises.

Example:
The consideration in these examples would be my promise to pay you $20 and your promise to shovel the snow by noon.

A basic course on contracts will spend the entire semester dissecting exactly what may be a valid offer, acceptance, and consideration. For your purposes, the important things to remember are as follows.

✪ If you make an offer to someone, it may result in a binding contract, even if you change your mind or find out it was a bad deal for you.

✪ Unless an offer is *accepted* (that is, with both parties agreeing to the same contract terms), there is no contract.

✪ A contract does not always have to be in writing. Some laws require certain contracts to be in writing, but as a general rule an oral contract is legal.

✪ Without *consideration* (the exchange of something of value or mutual promises) there is not a valid contract.

As mentioned, an entire semester of a course in contracts is spent analyzing each of the three elements of a contract. The most important rules for the business owner are as follows.

✪ An advertisement is not an offer.

Example:
Suppose you intended to put an ad in the newspaper offering new IBM computers for $1,995, but there is a typo in the ad and it says $19.95. Can people come in and say, I accept, here's my $19.95, creating a legal contract? Fortunately, no.

Courts have ruled that the ad is not an offer that a person can accept. It is an invitation to come in and make offers, which the business can accept or reject.

✪ When a person makes an offer, several things may happen. It may be accepted, creating a legal contract. It may be rejected. It may expire before it has been accepted. Or, it may be withdrawn before acceptance. A contract may expire either by a date made in the offer (*This offer remains open until noon on January 29, 2009*) or after a reasonable amount of time.

What is *reasonable* is a legal question that a court must decide. If someone makes you an offer to sell goods, clearly you cannot come back five years later and accept. Can you accept a week later or a month later and create a legal contract? That depends on the type of goods and the circumstances.

✪ A person accepting an offer cannot add any terms to it.

Example:
If you offer to sell a car for $1,000 and the other party says he or she accepts as long as you put new tires on it, there is no contract.

An acceptance with changed terms is considered a rejection and a counteroffer.

✪ When someone rejects your offer and makes a counteroffer, a contract can be created if you accept the counteroffer.

These rules can affect your business on a daily basis. Suppose you offer to sell something to one customer over the phone and five minutes later another customer walks in and offers you more for it. To protect yourself you should call the first customer and withdraw your offer before accepting the offer of the second customer. If the first customer accepts before you have withdrawn your offer, you may be sued if you have sold the item to the second customer.

There are a few exceptions to the basic rules of contracts of which you should be aware.

✪ Consent to a contract must be voluntary. If it is made under a threat, the contract is not valid.

✪ Contracts to do illegal acts or acts *against public policy* are not enforceable.

✪ If either party to an offer dies, the offer expires and cannot be accepted by the heirs.

✪ Contracts made under misrepresentation are not enforceable.

Example:
If someone tells you a car has 35,000 miles on it and you later discover it has 135,000 miles, you may be able to rescind (cancel) the contract due to fraud and misrepresentation.

✪ If there was a mutual mistake, a contract may be rescinded.

Example:
If both you and the seller thought the car had 35,000 miles on it and you both relied on that assumption, the contract could be rescinded. However, if the seller knew the car has 135,000 miles on it, but you assumed it only had 35,000 but did not ask, you probably could not rescind the contract.

STATUTORY CONTRACT LAW

The previous section discussed the basics of contract law. These are not stated in the statutes, but are the principles decided by judges over several hundred years. But in recent times the legislatures have made numerous exceptions to these principles. In most cases, these laws have been passed when the legislature felt that traditional law was not fair.

Statutes of Fraud

Statute of fraud laws state what types of contracts *must* be in writing to be valid. In Michigan, some of the contracts that must be in writing are as follows:

✪ sales or assignments of any interest in real estate, including leases for more than one year (Mich. Comp. Laws Ann., Sec. 566.106);

✪ agreements to modify or discharge a contract obligation without consideration (Mich. Comp. Laws Ann., Secs. 440.2209 & 566.1);

✪ representations concerning the character, business, or credit of another (Mich. Comp. Laws Ann., Sec. 566.135);

✪ guarantees of debts of another person (Mich. Comp. Laws Ann., Sec. 566.132);

✪ antenuptial contracts (Mich. Comp. Laws Ann., Sec. 566.132);

✪ promises of a personal representative to answer damages personally (Mich. Comp. Laws Ann., Sec. 566.132);

✪ promises to pay a commission on the sale of an interest in real estate (Mich. Comp. Laws Ann., Sec. 566.132);

✪ warranties of cure relating to medical care (Mich. Comp. Laws Ann., Sec. 566.132);

✪ sales of goods of over $1,000 (Mich. Comp. Laws Ann., Sec. 440.2201);

✪ sales of personal property of over $5,000 (Mich. Comp. Laws Ann., Sec. 440.1206); and,

✪ agreements that take over one year to complete (Mich. Comp. Laws Ann., Sec. 566.132).

Uniform Commercial

If you choose to conduct business electronically, Michigan law provides that electronic records and signatures satisfy any legal requirements for a written statement and a signature. See the *Uniform Electronic Transactions Act*. (Mich. Comp. Laws Ann., Secs. 450.833 through 450.849.)

Other Laws

The *Uniform Commercial Code* is an important law that relates to sales of most goods. It is particularly applicable to dealings between merchants, such as between manufacturers and wholesalers, and between wholesalers and retailers. (This law is covered more in Chapter 14.)

There are numerous other laws governing contracts in many area of business, especially where financing contracts are involved (i.e., where money is being loaned). Some of these laws are covered in later chapters of this book, but it would be impossible to include every law relating to every kind of business.

There is also a law regarding unsolicited merchandise, which provides that any merchandise sent to a consumer without a request or order by the consumer is deemed to be a gift. In other words, if you send merchandise to a consumer without an order by the consumer, the consumer may keep the merchandise and not pay for it.

Insurance

There are few laws *requiring* you to have insurance, but if you do not have insurance you may face lawsuit liability that may ruin your business (and your personal finances if you did not incorporate or form another type of business entity to protect you from personal liability). You should be aware of the types of insurance available and weigh the risks of a loss against the cost of a policy.

Be aware that there can be a wide range of prices and coverages in insurance policies. Get at least three quotes from different insurance agents and ask each one to explain the benefits of his or her company's policy.

WORKERS' COMPENSATION

You are required by Michigan law to carry workers' compensation insurance if:

- ✪ you regularly employ three or more part-time employees at one time; or,

- ✪ you employ one or more employee(s) for at least thirty-five hours per week, for at least thirteen weeks during the preceding fifty-two weeks.

In Michigan, this type of insurance is governed by the *Workers' Disability Compensation Act of 1969*. (Mich. Comp. Laws. Ann., beginning with Sec. 418.101.) The term *employee* is specifically defined. (Mich. Comp. Laws. Ann., Sec. 418.161.) You should read this law carefully if you think you need to comply with it. Part-time employees, students, aliens, or illegal workers count as employees. However, under certain conditions, volunteers, real estate agents, and independent contractors are not considered employees. There are also different requirements for agricultural employees.

Even if you are not required to have workers' compensation insurance, you may still wish to carry it because it can protect you from litigation. This insurance can be obtained from most insurance companies and in many cases is not expensive. If you have such coverage, you are protected against suits by employees or their heirs in case of accident and against potentially ruinous claims.

For high-risk occupations, such as roofing, workers' compensation insurance can be expensive, sometimes thirty to fifty cents for each dollar of payroll. For this reason, construction companies try all types of ways to become exempt, such as hiring independent contractors or only having a few employees who are also officers of the business. However, the requirements for exemptions are strict. If you so intend to obtain an exemption, check with an attorney specializing in workers' compensation law to be sure you do it right.

Failure to provide workers' compensation insurance when required is considered serious, as you are then personally responsible for paying any claims. Failure to pay a claim is a misdemeanor, which can result in a fine of $1,000 per day, up to six months in jail, personal liability for officers and directors of the corporation, plus any damages suffered by the employee. (Mich. Comp. Laws. Ann., Sec. 418.641.)

There are other requirements of the workers' compensation law, such as maintaining records of injuries causing death or disability and reporting to the Workers' Compensation Agency (a division of the Department of Labor and Economic Growth). For more information, contact the Workers' Compensation Agency at:

Department of Labor and Economic Growth
Workers' Compensation Agency
P.O. Box 30016
Lansing, MI 48909
888-396-5041
wcinfo@michigan.gov
www.michigan.gov/wca

LIABILITY INSURANCE

In most cases you are not required to carry liability insurance. However, be sure to check the requirements for your particular profession or business, because some may require liability insurance.

Liability insurance can be divided into two main areas:

1. coverage for injuries on your premises or by your employees; and,

2. coverage for injuries caused by your products.

Coverage for the first type of injury is usually very reasonably priced. Injuries in your place of business or to your employees (such as in an auto accident) are covered by standard premises or auto policies. But coverage for injuries by products may be harder to find and more expensive. If insurance is unavailable or unaffordable, you can go without and use a corporation and other asset protection devices to protect yourself from liability.

The best way to find out if insurance is available for your type of business is to check with other businesses of the same type as yours. If there is a trade organization for your type of industry, their newsletter or magazine may contain ads for insurers.

Umbrella Policy   As a business owner you will be a more visible target for lawsuits, even if there is little or no merit to them. Some people who know they cannot win in court will file suit anyway, counting on the fact that it will be cheaper for you to pay them something than to pay your lawyer to defend you. Lawyers know that such *nuisance suits* are often settled for thousands of dollars. Because of your greater exposure, you should consider getting a personal *umbrella* insurance policy. This is a policy that covers you for large claims, typically up to one million dollars or more, which are not covered by other insurance. Umbrella policies are very reasonably priced.

HAZARD INSURANCE

One of the worst things that can happen to your business is a fire, flood, or other disaster. With lost customer lists, inventory, and equipment, many businesses have been forced to close after such a disaster.

The premium for such insurance is usually reasonable and could protect you from losing your business. You can even get *business interruption* insurance, which pays for fixed business expenses, such as utilities, rent, taxes, etc., during the period of time you are unable to operate your business due to damages from fire, flood, storms, etc.

HOME BUSINESSES AND INSURANCE

There is a special insurance problem for home businesses. Most homeowner and tenant insurance policies do not cover business activities. In fact, under some policies you may be denied coverage if you use your home for a business.

If you merely use your home to make business phone calls and send letters, you will probably not have a problem and not need extra coverage. But if you own equipment or have dedicated a portion of your home exclusively to the business, you could have a problem. Check with your insurance agent for the options that are available to you.

If your business is a sole proprietorship and you have, say, a computer that you use both personally and for your business, it would probably be covered under your homeowners' policy. But if you incorporated your business and bought the computer in the name of the corporation, coverage might be denied. If a computer is your main business asset, you could get a special insurance policy in the company name covering just the computer. One company that offers such a policy is Safeware, which may be reached at 800-800-1492.

OTHER TYPES OF INSURANCE

The following are some other types of insurance that are available and that you may want to consider and discuss with your insurance agent. However, for many small businesses some may be cost-prohibitive.

Employee Theft If you fear employees may be able to steal from your business, you may want to have them *bonded*. This means that you pay an insurance company a premium to guarantee employees' honesty and if they cheat you the insurance company pays you damages. This can cover all existing and new employees.

Key Man *Key man* insurance provides for the situation in which an owner or employee is so important to your business that the business will be unable to operate for a period of time if that key owner or employee becomes incapacitated or dies.

Officer and Director Officer and director insurance covers an officer or director for any actions that result in personal liability. While this type of insurance does not protect your business, it can be useful to:

  ✪ protect you as an officer or director; or,

  ✪ provide an incentive to someone you would like to hire as an officer or have serve as a director.

Automobile Automobile coverage can be obtained for business use of your personal vehicle, for business-owned vehicles, and for business-leased vehicles.

Health While new businesses can rarely afford health insurance for their employees, the sooner they can obtain it, the better chance they will have to find and to keep good employees. Those starting a business usually need insurance for themselves (unless they have a working spouse who can cover the family), and they can sometimes get a better rate if they get a small business package. Health insurance can be fully paid by the employee (with the employee benefit being lower premiums than if the employee obtained insurance independently), partially paid by the employee and partially by the employer, or fully paid by the employer.

Most employers that pay some or all of the employee's premiums do not pay for their spouses and children. Still, the employee gets the advantage of paying lower rates for his or her family. Some large companies, especially those subject to labor unions, as well as many government agencies, pay the full premiums for both the employee and his or her dependents.

Life and Disability

Life insurance for employees is another fringe benefit, but it is not usually perceived by employees as being nearly as important as health insurance. Disability insurance is typically even less regarded, although disability is more likely than death among people in the age range of most employees. The cost of such insurance coverages is much less than health insurance, so it can serve as an additional incentive for employees to stay with you.

Your Business and the Internet

The Internet has opened up a world of opportunities for businesses. A few years ago, getting national visibility cost a fortune. Today a business can set up a web page for a few hundred dollars and, with some clever publicity and a little luck, millions of people around the world will see it.

But this new world has new legal issues and new liabilities. Not all of them have been addressed by laws or by the courts. Before you begin doing business on the Internet, you should know the existing rules and the areas where legal issues exist.

DOMAIN NAMES

A *domain name* is the address of your website. For example, **www.apple.com** is the domain name of Apple Computer, Inc. The last part of the domain name, the ".com" (or "dot com"), is the *top level domain*, or TLD. Dot com is the most popular, but others are currently available in the United States, including ".net" and ".org." (Originally .net was only available to network service providers and .org only to nonprofit organizations, but regulations have eliminated those requirements.) (See page 28 for a complete list of existing or soon-to-exist TLDs.)

It may seem like most words have been taken as a dot-com name, but if you combine two or three short words or abbreviations, a nearly unlimited number of possibilities are available. For example, if you have a business dealing with automobiles, most likely someone has already registered automobile.com and auto.com. But you can come up with all kinds of variations, using adjectives or your name, depending on your type of business. Some examples include:

autos4u.com	joesauto.com	autobob.com
myauto.com	yourauto.com	onlyautos.com
greatauto.com	autosfirst.com	usautos.com
greatautos.com	firstautoworld.com	4autos.com

When the Internet first began, some individuals realized that major corporations would soon want to register their names. Since the registration was easy and cheap, people registered names they thought would ultimately be used by someone else.

At first, some companies paid high fees to buy their names from the registrants. But one company, Intermatic, filed a lawsuit instead of paying. The owner of the mark it wanted had registered numerous trademarks, such as britishairways.com and ussteel.com. The court ruled that since Intermatic owned a trademark on the name, the registration of its name by someone else violated that trademark and that Intermatic was entitled to it.

Since then people have registered names that are not trademarks, such as CalRipkin.com, and have attempted to charge the individuals with those names to buy their domain. In 1998, Congress stepped in and passed the *Anti-Cybersquatting Consumer Protection Act*. This law makes it illegal to register a domain with no legitimate need to use it.

This law helped a lot of companies protect their names, but then some companies started abusing it and tried to stop legitimate users of similar names. This is especially likely against small companies. One organization that has been set up to help small companies protect their domains is the *Domain Name Rights Coalition*. Its website is:

www.netpolicy.com/dnrc

For extensive information on domains, refer to the *Domain Manual* at:

www.domainmanual.com

Registering a domain name for your own business is a simple process. There are many companies that offer registration services. For a list of those companies, visit the site of the *Internet Corporation for Assigned Names and Numbers* (ICANN) at **www.icann.org**. You can link directly to any member's site and compare the costs and registration procedures required for the different top-level domains.

WEB PAGES

There are many new companies eager to help you set up a website. Some offer turnkey sites for a low flat rate. Custom sites can cost tens of thousands of dollars. If you have plenty of capital, you may want to have your site handled by one of these professionals. However, setting up a website is a fairly simple process and once you learn the basics you can handle most of it in-house.

If you are new to the web, you may want to look at the following sites that will familiarize you with the Internet jargon and give you a basic introduction to the web:

www.learnthenet.com
www.webopedia.com

Site Set-Up   There are seven steps to setting up a website—purpose, design, content, structure, programming, testing, and publicity. Whether you do it yourself, hire a professional site designer, or use a college student, the steps toward creating an effective site are the same.

Before beginning your own site, you look at other sites, including those of major corporations and of small businesses. Look at the sites of all the companies that compete with you. Look at hundreds of sites and click through them to see how they work (or do not work).

Purpose. To know what to include on your site you must decide what its purpose will be. Do you want to take orders for your products or services, attract new employees, give away samples, or show off your company headquarters? You might want to do several of these things.

Design. After looking at other sites you can see that there are numerous ways to design a site. It can be crowded or open and airy; it can have several windows (frames) open at once or just one, and it can allow long scrolling or just click-throughs.

You will have to decide whether the site will have text only; text plus photographs and graphics; or text plus photos, graphics, and other design elements such as animation or Java script. Additionally, you will begin to make decisions about colors, fonts, and the basic graphic appearance of the site.

Content. You must create the content for your site. For this, you can use your existing promotional materials, you can write new material just for the website, or you can use a combination of the two. Whatever you choose, remember that the written material should be concise, free of errors, and easy for your target audience to read. Any graphics, including photographs, and written materials not created by you require permission. Obtain such permission from the lawful copyright holder in order to use any copyrighted material. Once you know your site's purpose, look, and content, you can begin to piece the site together.

Structure. You must decide how the content (text plus photographs, graphics, animation, etc.) will be structured, what content will be on which page, and how a user will link from one part of the site to another. For example, your first page may have the business name and then choices to click on, such as *about us*, *opportunities*, *product catalog*, etc. Have those choices connect to another page containing the detailed information so that users will see the catalog when they click on *product catalog*. Or your site could have a choice to click on a link to another website related to yours.

Programming and setup. When you know nothing about setting up a website, it can seem like a daunting task that will require an expert. However, *programming* here means merely putting a site together. There are inexpensive computer programs available that make it very simple.

Commercial programs such as Microsoft FrontPage, Dreamweaver, Pagemaker, Photoshop, MS Publisher, and PageMill allow you to set up web pages as easily as laying out a print publication. These programs will convert the text and graphics you create into HTML, the programming language of the web. Before you choose web design software and design your site, determine which web hosting service you will use. Make sure that the design software you use is compatible with the host server's system. The web host will be the provider that will give you space on its server and that may provide other services to you, such as secure order processing and analysis of your site to see who is visiting and linking to it.

If you have used a page layout program, you can usually get a simple web page up and running within a day or two. If you do not have much experience with a computer, you might consider hiring a college student to set up a web page for you.

Testing. Some of the website setup programs allow you to thoroughly check your new site to see if all the pictures are included and all the links are proper. There are also websites you can go to that will check out your site. Some even allow you to improve your site, such as by reducing the size of your graphics so they download faster. Use a major search engine (listed below) to look for companies that can test your site before you launch it on the web.

Publicity. Once you set up your website, you will want to get people to look at it. *Publicity* means getting your site noticed as much as possible by drawing people to it.

The first thing to do to get noticed is to be sure your site is registered with as many *search engines* as possible. These are pages that people use to find things on the Internet, such as Yahoo and Excite. They do not automatically know about you just because you created a website. You must tell them about your site, and they must examine and catalog it.

For a fee, there are services that will register your site with numerous search engines. If you are starting out on a shoestring, you can easily do it yourself. While there are hundreds of search engines, most people use a dozen or so of the bigger ones. If your site is in a niche area, such as geneology services, then you would want to be listed on any specific geneology search engines. Most businesses should be mainly concerned with getting on the biggest ones. By far the biggest and most successful search engine today is Google (**www.google.com**). Some of the other big ones are:

www.altavista.com	www.infoseek.com
www.dejanews.com	www.lycos.com
www.excite.com	www.netcrawler.com
www.fastsearch.com	www.northernlight.com
www.goto.com	www.webcrawler.com
www.hotbot.com	www.yahoo.com

Most of these sites have a place to click to *add your site* to their system.

There are sites that rate the search engines, help you list on the search engines, or check to see if you are listed. One site is:

www.searchiq.com

A *meta tag* is an invisible subject word added to your site that can be found by a search engine. For example, if you are a pest control company, you may want to list all of the scientific names of the pests you control and all of the treatments you have available, but you may not need them to be part of the visual design of your site. List these words as meta tags when you set up your page so people searching for those words will find your site.

Some companies thought that a clever way to get viewers would be to use commonly searched names, or names of major competitors, as meta tags to attract people looking for those big companies. For example, a small delivery service that has nothing to do with UPS or FedEx might use those company names as meta tags so people looking for them would find the smaller company. While it may sound like a good idea, it has been declared illegal trademark infringement. Today many companies have computer programs scanning the Internet for improper use of their trademarks.

Once you have made sure that your site is passively listed in all the search engines, you may want to actively promote your site. However, self-promotion is seen as a bad thing on the Internet, especially if its purpose is to make money.

Newsgroups are places on the Internet where people interested in a specific topic can exchange information. For example, expectant mothers have a group where they can trade advice and experiences. If you have a product that would be great for expectant mothers, that would be a good place for it to be discussed. However, if you log into the group and merely announce your product, suggesting people order it from your website, you will probably be *flamed* (sent a lot of hate mail).

If you join the group, however, and become a regular, and in answer to someone's problem, mention that you "saw this product that might help," your information will be better received. It may seem unethical to plug your product without disclosing your interest, but this is a procedure used by many large companies. They hire people to plug their product (or *rock star*) all over the

Internet. So, perhaps it has become an acceptable marketing method and consumers know to take plugs with a grain of salt. Let your conscience be your guide.

Keep in mind that Internet publicity works both ways. If you have a great product and people love it, you will get a lot of business. If you sell a shoddy product, give poor service, and do not keep your customers happy, bad publicity on the Internet can kill your business. Besides being an equalizer between large and small companies, the Internet can be a filtering mechanism between good and bad products.

Advertising   There is no worse breach of Internet etiquette (*netiquette*) than to send advertising by email to strangers. It is called *spamming* and doing it can have serious consequences.

The *Controlling the Assault of Non-Solicited Pornography And Marketing Act of 2003* (CANSPAM) has put numerous controls on how you can use email to solicit business for your company. Some of the prohibited activities under the act are:

- ✪   false or misleading information in an email;

- ✪   deceptive subject heading;

- ✪   failure to include a functioning return address;

- ✪   mailing to someone who has asked not to receive solicitations;

- ✪   failure to include a valid postal address;

- ✪   omitting an opt-out procedure;

- ✪   failure to clearly mark the email as advertising; and,

- ✪   including sexual material without adequate warnings.

Some of the provisions contain criminal penalties as well as civil fines.

For more information on the CANSPAM Act see:

www.ftc.gov/bcp/conline/pubs/buspubs/canspam.shtm

For text of the act plus other spam laws around the world, see:

www.spamlaws.com

Many states, including California, Colorado, Connecticut, Delaware, Idaho, Illinois, Iowa, Louisiana, Missouri, Nevada, North Carolina, Oklahoma, Pennsylvania, Rhode Island, Tennessee, Virginia, Washington, and West Virginia, have also enacted antispamming legislation. This legislation sets specific requirements for unsolicited bulk email and makes certain practices illegal. Check with an attorney to see if your business practices fall within the legal limits of these laws. Additionally, many *Internet Service Providers* (ISPs) have restrictions on unsolicited bulk email (spam). Check with your ISP to make sure you do not violate its policies.

Banner ads are the small rectangular ads on many web pages that usually blink or move. Although most computer users seem to have become immune to them, there is still a big market in the sale and exchange of them.

If your site gets enough viewers, people may pay you to place their ads there. Another possibility is to trade ads with another site. In fact, there are companies that broker ad trades among websites. Such trades used to be taxable transactions, but since January 5, 2000, such trades are no longer taxable under IRS Notice 2000-6.

LEGAL ISSUES

Before you set up a web page, you should consider the legal issues described as follows.

Jurisdiction *Jurisdiction* is the power of a court in a particular location to decide a particular case. Usually you have to have been physically present in a jurisdiction or have done business there before you can be sued there. Since the Internet extends your business's ability to reach people in faraway places, there may be instances when you could be subject to legal jurisdiction far from your own state (or country). There are a number of cases that have been decided in this country regarding the Internet and jurisdiction, but very few cases have been decided on this issue outside of the United States.

In most instances, U.S. courts use the pre-Internet test—whether you have been present in another jurisdiction or have had enough contact with someone in the other jurisdiction. The fact that the Internet itself is not a *place* will not shield you from being sued in another state when you have shipped your company's product there, have entered into a contract with a resident of that state, or have defamed a foreign resident with content on your website. The more interactive your site is with consumers, the more you target an audience for your goods in a particular location, and the farther you reach to send your goods out into the world, the more it becomes possible for someone to sue you outside of your own jurisdiction—possibly even in another country.

The law is not even remotely final on these issues. The American Bar Association, among other groups, is studying this topic in detail. At present, no final, global solution or agreement about jurisdictional issues exists.

One way to protect yourself from the possibility of being sued in a faraway jurisdiction would be to have a statement on your website stating that those using the site or doing business with you agree that jurisdiction for any actions regarding the site or your company will be in your home county.

For extra protection you can have a preliminary page that must be clicked before entering your website. However, this may be overkill for a small business with little risk of lawsuits. If you are in any business for which you could have serious liability, review some competitors' sites and see how they handle the liability issue. They often have a place to click for a *legal notice* or *disclaimer* on their first page.

You may want to consult with an attorney to discuss the specific disclaimer you will use on your website, where it should appear, and whether you will have users of your site actively *agree* to this disclaimer or just *passively* read it. However, these disclaimers are not enforceable everywhere in the world. Until there is global agreement on jurisdictional issues, this may remain an area of uncertainty for some time to come.

Libel   *Libel* is any publication that injures the reputation of another. This can occur in print, writing, pictures, or signs. All that is required for *publication* is that you transmit the material to at least one other person. When putting together your website you must keep in mind that it is visible to millions of people all over the planet and that if you libel a person or company you may have to pay damages. Many countries do not have the freedom of speech that we do and a statement that is not libel in the United States may be libelous elsewhere.

Copyright Infringement

It is so easy to copy and *borrow* information on the Internet that it is easy to infringe copyrights without even knowing it. A *copyright* exists for a work as soon as the creator creates it. There is no need to register the copyright or to put a copyright notice on it. So, practically everything on the Internet belongs to someone. Some people freely give their works away. For example, many people have created web artwork (*gifs* and *animated gifs*) that they freely allow people to copy. There are numerous sites that provide hundreds or thousands of free gifs that you can add to your web pages. Some require you to acknowledge the source, some do not. Always be sure that the works are free for the taking before using them.

Linking and Framing

One way to violate copyright laws is to improperly link other sites to yours either directly or with framing. *Linking* is when you provide a place on your site to click that takes someone to another site. *Framing* occurs when you set up your site so that when you link to another site, your site is still viewable as a frame around the linked site.

While many sites are glad to be linked to others, some, especially providers of valuable information, object. Courts have ruled that linking and framing can be a copyright violation. One rule that has developed is that it is usually okay to link to the first page of a site, but not to link to some valuable information deeper within the site. The rationale for this is that the owner of the site wants visitors to go through the various levels of their site (viewing all the ads) before getting the information. By linking to the information you are giving away their product without the ads.

The problem with linking to the first page of a site is that it may be a tedious or difficult task to find the needed page from there. Many sites are poorly designed and make it nearly impossible to find anything.

The best solution, if you wish to link to another page, is to ask permission. Email the webmaster or other person in charge of the site, if one is given, and explain what you want to do. If he or she grants permission, be sure to print out a copy of his or her email for your records.

Privacy

Since the Internet is such an easy way to share information, there are many concerns that it will cause a loss of individual privacy. The two main concerns arise when you post information that others consider private and when you gather information from customers and use it in a way that violates their privacy.

While public actions of politicians and celebrities are fair game, details about their private lives are sometimes protected by law. Details about persons who are not public figures are often protected. The laws in each state are different and what might be allowed in one state could be illegal in another. If your site will provide any personal information about individuals, discuss the possibility of liability with an attorney.

Several well-known companies have been in the news lately for violations of their customers' privacy. They either shared what the customer was buying or downloading or looked for additional information on the customer's computer. To let customers know that you do not violate certain standards of privacy, you can subscribe to one of the privacy codes that have been promulgated for the Internet. These allow you to put a symbol on your site guaranteeing to your customers that you follow the code.

The websites of two of the organizations that offer this service and their fees at the time of this publication are:

www.privacybot.com	$100
www.bbbonline.org	$200 to $7,000

Protecting Yourself The easiest way to protect yourself personally from the various possible types of liability is to set up a corporation or limited liability company to own the website. This is not foolproof protection since, in some cases, you could be sued personally as well, but it is one level of protection.

COPPA If your website is aimed at children under the age of 13 or if it attracts children of that age, then you must follow the federal *Children Online Privacy Protection Act of 1998* (COPPA). This law requires such websites to:

- ✪ give notice on the site of what information is being collected;

- ✪ obtain verifiable parental consent to collect the information;

- ✪ allow the parent to review the information collected;

- ✪ allow the parent to delete the child's information or to refuse to allow the use of the information;

✪ limit the information collected to only that necessary to participate on the site; and,

✪ protect the security and confidentiality of the information.

FINANCIAL TRANSACTIONS

In the future, there will be easy ways to exchange money on the Internet. Some companies have already been started that promote their own kinds of electronic money. Whether any of these become universal is yet to be seen.

The existing services for sending money over the Internet, such as PayPal, usually offer more risk and higher fees than traditional credit card processing. Under their service agreements you usually must agree that they can freeze your account at any time and can take money out of your bank account at any time. Some offer no appeal process! Before signing up for any of these services you should read their service agreement carefully and check the Internet for other peoples' experiences with them. For example, for PayPal you can check **www.nopaypal.com**.

For now, the easiest way to exchange money on the Internet is through traditional credit cards. Because of concerns that email can be abducted in transit and read by others, most companies use a *secure site* in which customers are guaranteed that their card data is encrypted before being sent.

When setting up your website, you should ask the provider if you can be set up with a secure site for transmitting credit card data. If the provider cannot offer it, you will need to contract with another software provider. Use a major search engine listed on page 67 to look for companies that provide credit card services to businesses on the web.

As a practical matter, there is very little to worry about when sending credit card data by email. If you do not have a secure site, another option is to allow purchasers to fax or phone in their credit card data. However, keep in mind that this extra step will lose some business unless your products are unique and your buyers are very motivated.

The least effective option is to provide an order form on the site, which can be printed out and mailed in with a check. Again, your customers must be really motivated or they will lose interest after finding out this extra work is involved.

FTC RULES

Because the Internet is an instrument of interstate commerce, it is a legitimate subject for federal regulation. The Federal Trade Commission (FTC) first said that all of its consumer protection rules applied to the Internet, but lately it has been adding specific rules and issuing publications. The following publications are available from the FTC website at **www.ftc.gov/bcp/menus/business/ ecommerce.shtm** or by mail from Consumer Response Center, Federal Trade Commission, 600 Pennsylvania, NW, Room H-130, Washington, D.C. 20580.

✪ *Advertising and Marketing on the Internet: The Rules of the Road*

✪ *Big Print. Little Print. What's the Deal? How to Disclose the Details*

✪ *The CAN-SPAM Act: Requirements for Commercial Emailers*

✪ *The Children's Online Privacy Protection Rule: Not Just for Kids' Sites*

✪ *Disclosing Energy Efficiency Information: A Guide for Online Sellers of Appliances*

✪ *Dot Com Disclosures: Information About Online Advertising*

✪ *Electronic Commerce: Selling Internationally. A Guide for Business*

✪ *"Remove Me" Responses and Responsibilities: Email Marketers Must Honor "Unsubscribe" Claims*

✪ *Selling on the Internet: Prompt Delivery Rules*

✪ *Securing Your Server: Shut the Door on Spam*

✪ *Security Check: Reducing Risks to Your Computer Systems*

✪ *What's Dot and What's Not: Domain Name Registration Scams*

✪ *You, Your Privacy Policy and COPPA—How to Comply with the Children's Online Privacy Protection Act*

FRAUD

Because the Internet is somewhat anonymous, it is a tempting place for those with fraudulent schemes to look for victims. As a business consumer, exercise caution when dealing with unknown or anonymous parties on the Internet.

The U.S. Department of Justice, the FBI, and the National White Collar Crime Center launched the *Internet Crime Complaint Center* (IC3). If you suspect that you are the victim of fraud online, whether as a consumer or a business, you can report incidents to the IC3 on its website, **www.ic3.gov**. The IC3 is currently staffed by FBI agents and representatives of the National White Collar Crime Center and will work with state and local law enforcement officials to prevent, investigate, and prosecute high-tech and economic crime online.

Health and Safety Laws

If you plan to have at least one employee or if your business will involve certain products or services, you will need to be concerned with health and safety laws.

FEDERAL LAWS

Federal health and safety laws include the rules of the Occupational Safety and Health Administration, various laws concerning hazardous materials, and consumer safety regulations.

OSHA The Occupational Safety and Health Administration (OSHA) is a good example of government regulation so severe it strangles businesses out of existence. The point of the law is to place the duty on the employer to see that the workplace is free from recognized hazards that are likely to cause death or serious bodily injury, but OSHA tends to go overboard.

Fortunately for small businesses, the regulations are not as cumbersome as for larger enterprises. If you have ten or fewer employees or if you are in certain types of businesses, you do not have to keep a record of illnesses, injuries, and exposure to hazardous substances of employees. If you have eleven or more employees, you do have to keep this record, which is called *Log 200*. All employers are required to display a poster that you can get from OSHA.

Within forty-eight hours of the on-the-job death of an employee, or injury of five or more employees on the job, the area director of OSHA must be contacted.

For more information, you should write or call the OSHA office:

OSHA Regional Office
Lansing Area Office
315 West Allegan, Room 207
Lansing, MI 48933
517-487-4996

Or visit their general website, **www.osha.gov**, and obtain copies of their publication *OSHA Small Business Handbook* (OSHA 2209). They also have posters required to be posted in the workplace. Find them at **www.osha.gov** and click on "Publications/Posters."

Hazard Communication Standard

The hazard communication standard requires that employees be made aware of the hazards in the workplace. (Title 29, Code of Federal Regulations (C.F.R.), Section (Sec.) 1910.1200.) It is especially applicable to those working with chemicals, but this can include even offices that use copy machines. Businesses using hazardous chemicals must have a comprehensive program for informing employees of the hazards and for protecting them from contamination.

For more information, you can contact OSHA at the previously mentioned address, phone number, or website. They can supply a copy of the regulation and a booklet called *Chemical Hazard Communication* (OSHA 3084) that explains the law.

Pesticides

A revision of the worker protection standard for agricultural pesticides was phased in during 1994. It concerns businesses that deal with agricultural pesticides and requires safety training, decontamination sites, and, of course, posters. The Environmental Protection Agency (EPA) will provide information on compliance with this law. The EPA can be reached at 800-490-9198 or at **www.epa.gov**.

Pure Food and Drug Act

The Pure Food and Drug Act of 1906 prohibits the misbranding or adulteration of food and drugs. It also created the Food and Drug Administration (FDA), which has promulgated tons of regulations and must give permission before a new drug can be introduced into the market. If you will be dealing with any food or drugs, you must keep abreast of its policies. The website is **www.fda.gov**, and the small business site is **www.fda.gov/ora/fed_state/small_business/sb_guide/default.htm**. The FDA's local small business representative is:

FDA, Central Region
Marie Falcone, Small Business Representative
U.S. Customhouse
200 Chestnut Street, Room 900
Philadelphia, PA 19106
215-717-3703
oracersbr@fda.hhs.gov

Hazardous Materials Transportation

There are regulations that control the shipping and packing of hazardous materials. For more information, contact:

U.S. Department of Transportation
Pipeline and Hazardous Materials Safety Administration
East Building, 2nd Floor
1200 New Jersey Avenue, SE
Washington, DC 20590
202-366-4433
http://hazmat.dot.gov

CPSC

The Consumer Product Safety Commission (CPSC) has a set of rules that cover the safety of products. The commission feels that, because its rules cover products, rather than people or companies, they apply to everyone producing such products. However, federal laws do not apply to small businesses that do not affect interstate commerce. Whether a small business would fall under a CPSC rule would depend on the size and nature of your business.

The CPSC rules are contained in the Code of Federal Regulations, Title 16, in the following parts. These can be found at most law libraries, some public libraries, and on the Internet at **www.access.gpo.gov/nara/cfr/cfr-table-search.html**. The CPSC's site is **http://cpsc.gov/index.html**.

PRODUCT	PART
Antennas (CB and TV)	1402
Architectural Glazing Material	1201
Articles Hazardous to Children Under 3	1501
Baby Cribs—Full Size	1508
Baby Cribs—Non-Full Size	1509
Bicycle Helmets	1203
Bicycles	1512
Carpets and Rugs	1630 and 1631
Cellulose Insulation	1209 and 1404
Cigarette Lighters	1210
Citizens Band Base Station Antennas	1204
Coal and Wood Burning Appliances	1406
Consumer Products Containing Chlorofluorocarbons	1401
Electrically Operated Toys	1505
Emberizing Materials Containing Asbestos (banned)	1305
Extremely Flammable Contact Adhesives (banned)	1302
Fireworks	1507
Garage Door Openers	1211
Hazardous Lawn Darts (banned)	1306
Hazardous Substances	1500
Human Subjects	1028
Lawn Mowers—Walk-Behind	1205
Lead-containing Paint (banned)	1303
Matchbooks	1202
Mattresses	1632
Pacifiers	1511
Patching Compounds Containing Asbestos (banned)	1304
Poisons	1700
Rattles	1510
Self-Pressurized Consumer Products	1401
Sleepwear—Children's	1615 and 1616
Swimming Pool Slides	1207
Toys—Electrical	1505
Unstable Refuse Bins (banned)	1301

Additional Regulations

Every day there are proposals for new laws and regulations. It would be impossible to include every conceivable one in this book. To be up to date on the laws that affect your type of business, join a trade association for your industry and subscribe to newsletters that cover your industry. Attending industry conventions is a good way to learn more and to discover new ways to increase your profits.

MICHIGAN LAWS

In addition to federal laws affecting your business, Michigan has its own set of health and safety laws. You need to be aware of these laws and how they affect your business. Some of the more common ones are as follows.

Michigan Occupational Safety and Health Act

The Michigan *Occupational Safety and Health Act* is Michigan's OSHA. (Mich. Comp. Laws Ann., Sec. 408.1001) It applies to any business with one or more employees. Except for laws about labeling hazardous chemicals in the workplace, the act itself does not contain specific health and safety rules, but adopts the OSHA standards and allows additional rules to be made by the Michigan Department of Labor and Economic Growth and the Michigan Department of Community Health.

The act also creates several commissions to make rules or *standards*. These are the General Industry Safety Standards Commission, the Construction Safety Standards Commission, and the Occupational Health Standards Commission.

The act gives the Michigan Department of Labor and Economic Growth and the Michigan Department of Community Health the right to conduct unannounced inspections and obtain warrants for inspections. A representative of the employer and a representative of the employees may accompany an inspector during his or her inspection of the premises.

A violation of any of the standards subjects the employer to a fine of up to $7,000 per violation. Failure to correct the violation within the time frame allowed subjects the employer to an additional fine of up to $7,000 per day, up to a total of $70,000. If death results from a willful or repeated violation, it is a felony with a fine up to $10,000 and up to one year in jail. A second conviction carries a penalty of a fine up to $20,000 and up to three years in jail.

For more information or to obtain the standards that apply to your business, contact the following state agencies:

Michigan Department of Labor and Economic Growth
P.O. Box 30004
Lansing, MI 48909
517-373-1820
www.michigan.gov/dleg

MIOSHA
P.O. Box 30643
Lansing, MI 48909
517-322-1814
miasha_info@michigan.gov

Michigan Department of Community Health
Capitol View Building
201 Townsend Street
Lansing, MI 48913
517-373-3740
www.michigan.gov/mdch

Environmental Laws

The Michigan Department of Natural Resources was granted broad powers to promulgate regulations to protect the natural resources and the environment of the state under Michigan's *Natural Resources and Environmental Protection Act*. (Mich. Comp. Laws Ann, beginning with Section 324.101.) This act replaced numerous previous acts in an attempt to consolidate responsibility in one state agency.

For most business owners, these regulations will never have an impact on their business. However, it is good to be aware that such regulations exist. Even the owner of a toy store may find that he or she has a leaking underground storage tank beneath the building. If you wish to learn more about these regulations, contact the Michigan Department of Natural Resources.

Smoking

The Michigan *Clean Indoor Air Act* contains the following rules regarding smoking in *public places* and at *public meetings*. (Mich. Comp. Laws Ann., Sec. 333.12601.)

Public places are defined as the following areas:

✪ *an enclosed, indoor area owned or operated by a state or local governmental agency and used by the general public or serving as a place of work for public employees or a meeting place for a public body, including an office, educational facility, home for the aged, nursing home, county medical care facility, hospice, hospital long-term care unit, auditorium, arena, meeting room, or public conveyance; and,*

✪ *an enclosed, indoor area which is not owned or operated by a state or local governmental agency, is used by the general public, and is one of the following: an educational facility, home for the aged, nursing home, county medical care facility, hospice, or hospital long-term care unit, auditorium, arena, theater, museum, concert hall, or any other facility during the period of its use for a performance or exhibit of the arts.*

A public place does not include a private, enclosed room or office occupied exclusively by a smoker, even if it may be visited by a nonsmoker. A public meeting is a meeting of public bodies and includes all meetings of any state or local governing body (e.g., boards, commissions, etc.). No person may smoke in a public place or at a public meeting except in a designated smoking area, except that this prohibition does not apply to:

✪ a room, hall, or building used exclusively for a private function where seating is controlled by the function sponsor and not by the state or local government agency or the person who owns or operates the room, hall, or building;

✪ food service establishments or alcohol-licensed premises; or,

✪ a private educational facility after regularly scheduled school hours.

If a smoking area is designated, the following rules apply:

✪ existing physical barriers and ventilation systems must be used to minimize the toxic effect of smoke in smoking and adjacent non-smoking areas;

✪ a written policy must be created for the separation of smokers and nonsmokers, which must provide at a minimum that nonsmokers be located closest to the source of fresh air, that special consideration be given to persons with hypersensitivity to tobacco smoke, and that a procedure be established to receive, investigate, and take action on complaints; and,

✪ anyone who operates a single room is considered to be in compliance if one-half of the room is reserved and posted as a nonsmoking area.

Smoking is not permitted at all in the common or treatment areas of a private practice office of a person who is licensed in a health occupation; nor in, or anywhere on, real estate controlled by a child-care institution.

Smoking is also not permitted in a health facility unless prohibition of smoking would be detrimental to the patient's treatment (in which case the patient must be placed in a separate room from nonsmokers) or unless the health facility permits smoking (in which case smoking may only be allowed in designated areas that are enclosed, ventilated, or constructed to ensure a smoke-free environment in patient care areas and common areas).

Owners and operators of public places must post signs stating that smoking is prohibited, except in designated smoking areas. They must also arrange seating to provide a smoke-free area.

It is the duty of the owners and operators of public places to implement and enforce the policy for the separation of smokers and nonsmokers. Violations of this act subject the owner or operator to penalties of a fine of up to $100 for the first violation and up to $500 for a second or subsequent violation.

chapter 11

Employment and Labor Laws

If you intend to hire anyone to do work for you, you will need to become familiar with numerous state and federal legal issues.

HIRING AND FIRING LAWS

For small businesses there are not many rules regarding whom you may hire or fire. Fortunately, the ancient law that an employee can be fired at any time (or may quit at any time) still prevails for small businesses. But in certain situations, and as you grow, you will come under a number of laws that affect your hiring and firing practices.

One of the most important things to consider when hiring someone is that if you fire them, they may be entitled to unemployment compensation. If so, your unemployment compensation taxes will go up and it can cost you a lot of money. Therefore, ideally you should only hire people you are confident you will keep and you should avoid situations in which your former employees can collect compensation.

This can be done by hiring only part-time or temporary employees. The drawback to this is that you may not be able to attract the best employees. When hiring dishwashers or busboys, this may not be an issue, but when hiring someone to develop a software product, you do not want him or her to leave halfway through the development.

A better solution is to screen applicants and only hire those whom you feel confident will work out. Of course, this is easier said than done. Some people interview well, but then turn out to be incompetent or bad employees.

The intelligence of an employee is often more important than his or her experience. An employee with years of typing experience may be fast, but unable to figure out how to use your new computer, whereas an intelligent employee can learn the equipment quickly and eventually gain speed. Common sense is important in all situations.

The bottom line is that you cannot know if an employee will be able to fill your needs from a résumé and an interview. Once you have found someone whom you think will work out, offer them a job with a ninety-day probationary period. If you are not completely satisfied with them after the ninety days, you can always offer to extend the probationary period for an additional thirty, sixty, or ninety days rather than end the relationship immediately. All of these decisions should be in writing.

Checking References

Checking references is important, but beware that a former boss may be a current boyfriend or girlfriend, or even a relative. It has always been considered acceptable to exaggerate on résumés, but in today's tight job market, some applicants are completely fabricating sections of their education and experience.

Polygraph Tests

Under the federal *Employee Polygraph Protection Act*, you cannot require an employee or prospective employee to take a polygraph test unless you are in the armored car, guard, or pharmaceutical business.

Drug Tests

Under the *Americans with Disabilities Act* (ADA), drug testing can only be required of applicants who have been offered jobs conditioned upon passing a drug test.

New Hire Reporting

The *Personal Responsibility and Work Opportunity Reconciliation Act of 1996* (PRWORA) requires employers to report new hires to the state in order for child support enforcement agencies to track down deadbeat parents. However, the law leaves the reporting requirements up to each state.

Firing In most cases, unless you have a contract with an employee for a set time period or are subject to an agreement with a labor union, you can fire an employee at any time. This seems fair since the employee can quit at any time. The exceptions to this are if you fire someone based on some illegal discrimination, for filing some sort of health or safety complaint, for engaging in union activities, or for refusing your sexual advances. All of these matters are discussed in other parts of this book.

EMPLOYMENT AGREEMENTS

To avoid misunderstandings with employees you may want to use an employment agreement or an employee handbook. These can spell out in detail the policies of the company and the rights of the employee. They can protect your trade secrets and should spell out clearly that employment can be terminated at any time by either party.

In any agreement, policy statement, or handbook, you need to be careful to include a provision that the employment is *at will* and that the employee may be discharged at any time, with or without any reason being given. If you do not include such a provision, a court could determine that your agreement, employee handbook, or policy statement created a binding contract that limits your ability to fire the employee. Even oral statements can create such a contract if they are determined by a court to create in the employee a *legitimate expectation* of continued employment based upon the employer's conduct and practices.

While it may be difficult or awkward to ask an existing employee to sign an agreement, an applicant hoping to be hired will usually sign whatever is necessary to obtain the job. However, because of the unequal bargaining position, do not use an agreement that would make you look bad if the matter ever went to court.

If having an employee sign an agreement is awkward, you can obtain the same rights by putting the company policies in an employee handbook. Each existing and new employee should be given a copy along with a letter stating that the rules apply to all employees and that by accepting employment at your company they agree to abide by the rules. Having an employee sign a receipt for the letter and handbook is proof that they received it.

INDEPENDENT CONTRACTORS

One way to avoid problems with employees and taxes at the same time is to have all of your work done through independent contractors. This can relieve you of most of the burdens of employment laws and the obligation to pay Social Security and Medicare taxes for the workers.

An independent contractor is, in effect, a separate business that you pay to do a job. You pay them just as you pay any company that you have do work for you. At the end of the year, instead of issuing a W-2 form, you issue a 1099, if the amount is over $600.

This may seem too good to be true—and in some situations it is. The IRS does not like independent contractor arrangements because it is too easy for the independent contractors to cheat on their taxes. To limit the use of independent contractors, the IRS has strict regulations on who may and may not be classified an independent contractor. The IRS also audits companies that do not appear to pay enough in wages for the type of business they are in.

Especially risky are jobs that are not traditionally done by independent contractors. For example, you could not get away with hiring a secretary as an independent contractor. One of the most important factors considered in determining if a worker can be an independent contractor is the amount of control the company has over his or her work.

Example 1:

If you need someone to paint your building and you agree to pay him or her a certain price to do it according to his or her own methods and schedule, you can pay him or her as an independent contractor. But if you tell the person when to work, how to do the job, and provide the tools and materials, he or she will be classified as an employee.

Example 2:

If you just need some typing done and you take it to a typing service and pick it up when it is ready, you will be safe in treating them as independent contractors. But if you need someone to come into your office to type, on your machine, at your schedule, you will probably be required to treat that person as an employee for tax purposes.

The IRS has a form you can use in determining if a person is an employee or an independent contractor. It is the **DETERMINATION OF WORKER STATUS (IRS FORM SS-8)**. (see form 8, p.223.)

Independent Contractors versus Employees

In deciding whether to make use of independent contractors instead of employees, you should weigh the following advantages and disadvantages.

Advantages.

✪ Lower taxes. You do not have to pay Social Security, Medicare, unemployment, or other employee taxes.

✪ Less paperwork. You do not have to handle federal withholding deposits or the monthly employer returns to the state or federal government.

✪ Less insurance. You do not have to pay workers' compensation insurance and since the workers are not your employees you do not have to insure against their possible liabilities.

✪ More flexibility. You can use independent contractors when you need them and not have to pay them when business is slow.

Disadvantages.

✪ The IRS and state tax offices are strict about when workers can qualify as independent contractors and they will audit companies whose use of them does not appear to be legitimate.

✪ If your use of independent contractors is found to be improper you may have to pay back taxes and penalties and have problems with your pension plan.

✪ While employees usually cannot sue you for their injuries (if you have covered them with workers' compensation), independent contractors can sue you if their injuries were your fault.

✪ If you are paying someone to produce a creative work (writing, photography, artwork, etc.), you receive less rights to the work of an independent contractor.

✪ You have less control over the work of an independent contractor and less flexibility in terminating him or her if you are not satisfied that the job is being done the way you require.

✪ You have less loyalty from an independent contractor who works sporadically for you and possibly others than from your own full-time employees.

For some businesses the advantages outweigh the disadvantages, but for others they do not. Consider your business plans and the consequences from each type of arrangement. Keep in mind that it will be easier to start with independent contractors and switch to employees than to hire employees and have to fire them to hire independent contractors.

DISCRIMINATION LAWS

One of the more common types of employee complaints and lawsuits involves alleged violation of state or federal discrimination laws.

There are numerous federal laws forbidding discrimination based upon race, sex, pregnancy, color, religion, national origin, age, or disability. The laws apply to both hiring and firing, and to employment practices such as salaries, promotions, and benefits. Most of these laws only apply to an employer who has fifteen or more employees for twenty weeks of a calendar year or an employer who has federal contracts or subcontracts. Therefore, you most likely will not be required to comply with the law immediately upon opening your business.

Federal Law   One exception is the *Equal Pay Act* that applies to employers with two or more employees and requires that women be paid the same as men in the same type of job.

Employers with fifteen or more employees are required to display a poster regarding discrimination, available from both of the following:

U.S. Equal Employment Opportunity Commission
1801 L Street, NW
Washington, DC 20507
202-663-4900
800-669-4000

Michigan Department of Civil Rights
Capitol Tower Building, Suite 800
Lansing, MI 48933
517-335-3165
MDCR-INFO@michigan.gov
www.michigan.gov/mdcr

Employers with 100 or more employees are required to file an annual report with the Equal Employment Opportunity Commission (EEOC). Federal forms may be obtained from the EEOC at 800-669-3362 or through its websites:

www.eeoc.gov

Interview questions. When hiring employees, some questions are illegal or inadvisable to ask. The following areas of questioning should not be included on your employment application or in your interviews, unless the information is somehow directly tied to the duties of the job.

- ✪ Do not ask about an applicant's citizenship or place of birth. But after hiring an employee you must ask about his or her right to work in this country.

- ✪ Do not ask a female applicant her maiden name. You can ask if she has been known by any other name in order to do a background check.

- ✪ Do not ask if applicants have children, plan to have them, or have child care. You can ask if an applicant will be able to work the required hours.

- ✪ Do not ask if the applicant has religious objections for working Saturday or Sunday. You can mention if the job requires such hours and ask whether the applicant can meet this job requirement.

- ✪ Do not ask an applicant's age. You can ask if an applicant is 18 or over, or 21 or over for a liquor-related job.

- ✪ Do not ask an applicant's weight.

- ✪ Do not ask if an applicant has AIDS or is HIV positive.

- ✪ Do not ask about the applicant's previous health problems.

✪   Do not ask if the applicant has filed a workers' compensation claim.

✪   Do not ask if the applicant is married or whether his or her spouse would object to the job, hours, or duties.

✪   Do not ask if the applicant owns a home, furniture, or car, as it is considered racially discriminatory.

✪   Do not ask if the applicant has ever been arrested. You can ask if the applicant was ever *convicted* of a crime.

ADA. Under the *Americans with Disabilities Act* (ADA), employers who do not make *reasonable accommodations for disabled employees* will face fines of up to $100,000, as well as other civil penalties and civil damage awards. The ADA currently applies to employers with fifteen or more employees. Employers who need more than fifteen employees might want to consider contracting with independent contractors to avoid problems with this law, particularly if the number of employees is only slightly larger than fifteen.

To find out how the ADA affects your business, you might want to order the government's *ADA Technical Assistance Manual* from the following:

DBTAC: Great Lakes ADA Center
University of Illinois at Chicago
Institute on Disability & Human Development (MC728)
1640 West Roosevelt Road, Room 405
Chicago, IL 60608
312-413-1407
www.adagreatlakes.org

There are three types of tax credits to help small businesses with the burden of these laws.

✪   Businesses can deduct up to $15,000 a year for making their premises accessible to the disabled and can depreciate the rest. (Internal Revenue Code (IRC), Section 190.)

✪   Small businesses (under $1,000,000 in revenue and under thirty employees) can get a tax credit each year for 50% of the cost of making their premises accessible to the disabled, but this only applies to the amount between $250 and $10,500.

✪ Small businesses can get a credit of up to 40% of the first $6,000 of wages paid to certain new employees who qualify through the **Pre-Screening Notice and Certification Request for the Work Opportunity Credit (IRS form 8850)**. The form and instructions are in Appendix C. (see form 9, p.229.)

Records. To protect against potential claims of discrimination, all employers should keep detailed records showing reasons for hiring or not hiring applicants and for firing employees.

The *Elliot-Larsen Civil Rights Act* is Michigan's law prohibiting discrimination in employment (as well as in other areas) on the basis of religion, race, color, national origin, age, sex, height, weight, familial status, or marital status. This law also covers sexual harassment. (Mich. Comp. Laws Ann., Sec. 37.2101.)

Michigan Law *Discriminatory Job Advertisements and Applications.* Michigan law prohibits an employer from publishing any notice or advertisement that *indicates a preference, limitation, specification, or discrimination, based on religion, race, color, national origin, age, sex, height, weight, or marital status.* It also prohibits any use of a written or oral inquiry or form of application that elicits information about a prospective employee's status with respect to any of these matters. An exemption may be granted if you can convince the Civil Rights Commission that such discrimination is a *bona fide occupational qualification reasonably necessary to the normal operation of the business or enterprise.* (Mich. Comp. Laws Ann., Sec. 37.2206.)

Equal Pay. Michigan has a counterpart to the federal law providing for equal pay for the same job to both sexes. This state statute is meant to fill the gap of workers not covered by federal law and, therefore, does not apply to workers who are under the *Fair Labor Standards Act.* (Mich. Comp. Laws Ann., Sec. 408.397.)

Persons with Disabilities Civil Rights Act. The *Persons with Disabilities Civil Rights Act* applies to any employer with four or more employees and prohibits discrimination in employment against anyone because of the person's mental or physical handicap. The act only applies if the handicap is *unrelated to the individual's ability to perform the duties of a particular job or position.* Even if the handicap does relate to the job, the employer must use any available adaptive aids or devices that would allow the handicapped person to perform the job, unless the employer can show it would create an *undue hardship*.

NOTE: *Persons with AIDS and who are HIV positive are covered.*

The act also prohibits the use of any physical or mental examinations that do not relate to the job duties. It also prohibits the use of advertisements, applications, or inquiries that indicate or tend to discriminate against persons with handicaps. The act prohibits the employer from keeping records of employees' handicaps. (Mich. Comp. Laws Ann., beginning with Sec. 37.1101.)

SEXUAL HARASSMENT

In today's employment climate, any employer must pay attention to state and federal laws regarding sexual harassment in the workplace.

Federal Law In the 1980s, the Equal Employment Opportunity Commission (EEOC) interpreted *Title VII* of the *Civil Rights Act of 1964* to forbid sexual harassment. After that, the courts took over and reviewed all types of conduct in the workplace. The numerous lawsuits that followed revealed a definite trend toward expanding the definition of sexual harassment and favoring employees.

The EEOC has held the following in sexual harassment cases.

- ✪ The victim as well as the harasser may be a woman or a man.

- ✪ The victim does not have to be of the opposite sex.

- ✪ The harasser can be the victim's supervisor, an agent of the employer, a supervisor in another area, a coworker, or a nonemployee.

- ✪ The victim does not have to be the person harassed but could be anyone affected by the offensive conduct.

- ✪ Unlawful sexual harassment may occur without economic injury to or discharge of the victim.

- ✪ The harasser's conduct must be unwelcome.

✪ An employer can be held liable for sexual harassment of an employee by a supervisor, even if the employer was unaware of the supervisor's conduct.

Some of the actions that have been considered harassment are:

✪ displaying sexually explicit posters in the workplace;

✪ requiring female employees to wear revealing uniforms;

✪ rating sexual attractiveness of female employees as they passed male employees' desks;

✪ continued sexual jokes and innuendos;

✪ demands for sexual favors from subordinates;

✪ unwelcomed sexual propositions or flirtation;

✪ unwelcomed physical contact; and,

✪ whistling or leering at members of the opposite sex.

The law in the area of sexual harassment is still developing, so it is difficult to make clear rules of conduct.

Some things a business can do to protect against claims of sexual harassment include the following.

✪ Distribute a written policy against all kinds of sexual harassment to all employees.

✪ Encourage employees to report all incidents of sexual harassment.

✪ Ensure there is no retaliation against those who complain.

✪ Make clear that your policy is *zero tolerance.*

✪ Explain that sexual harassment includes both requests for sexual favors and a work environment that some employees may consider hostile.

✪ Allow employees to report harassment to someone other than their immediate supervisor in case that person is involved in the harassment.

✪ Promise as much confidentiality as possible to complainants.

Michigan Law The *Elliot-Larsen Civil Rights Act* has been determined to give individuals the right to sue their employer for sexual harassment. Suits under this law are not as broad as under federal law. Under this Michigan law:

✪ the employee must have been sexually harassed by a supervisor and there must have been a decision that affected his or her employment;

✪ there must have been sexual conduct, communication which was intended to, or did, substantially interfere with the employee's employment; or,

✪ there must have been communication that created an intimidating, hostile, or offensive work environment.

WAGE AND HOUR LAWS

There are state and federal laws governing wages paid to workers and the hours employees work. Some of these laws apply to all employers, while some only apply to certain employers.

Federal Law The federal *Fair Labor Standards Act* (FLSA) applies to all employers who are engaged in *interstate commerce* or in the production of goods for interstate commerce (anything that will cross a state line). It also applies to all employees of hospitals, schools, residential facilities for the disabled or aged, or public agencies. It also applies to all employees of enterprises that gross $500,000 or more per year. While many small businesses might not think they are engaged in interstate commerce, the laws have been interpreted broadly so that nearly any use of the mails, interstate telephone service, or other interstate services, however minor, is enough to bring a business under the law.

Minimum wage. The federal wage and hour laws are contained in the FLSA. In 2007, Congress passed and President Bush signed the *Fair Minimum Wage Act of 2007*, raising the minimum wage to $5.85 an hour beginning July 24, 2007. It also provides that the minimum wage will rise to $6.55 per hour on July 24,

2008, and to $7.25 per hour on July 24, 2009. The current federal minimum wage is $5.15 per hour. In certain circumstances, a wage of $3.62 may be paid to employees under 20 years of age for a ninety-day training period.

For employees who regularly receive more than $30 a month in tips, the minimum wage is $2.13 per hour. But if the employee's tips do not bring him or her up to the full $5.85 minimum wage, then the employer must make up the difference.

Overtime. The general rule is that employees who work more than forty hours a week must be paid time-and-a-half for hours worked over forty. But there are many exemptions to this general rule based on salary and position. These exceptions were completely revised in 2004 and an explanation of the changes, including a tutorial video, are available at **www.dol.gov/esa**. For answers to questions about the law, you can call the Department of Labor at 866-487-9243.

Exempt employees. While nearly all businesses are covered, certain employees are exempt from the FLSA. Exempt employees include employees that are considered executives, administrative and managerial, professionals, computer professionals, and outside sales people.

Whether one of these exceptions applies to a particular employee is a complicated legal question. Thousands of court cases have been decided on this issue but they have given no clear answers. In one case a person could be determined to be exempt because of his or her duties, but in another, a person with the same duties could be found not exempt.

One thing that is clear is that the determination of exemption status is made on the employee's function, and not just the job title. You cannot make a secretary exempt by calling him or her a manager if most of his or her duties are clerical. For more information, contact:

U. S. Department of Labor
Wage and Hour Division
200 Constitution Avenue, NW
Washington, DC 20210
www.dol.gov/esa

Or call a local office:

Department of Labor and Economic Growth
P.O. Box 30004
Lansing, MI 48909
517-373-1820
www.michigan.gov/dleg

You can obtain information on the Department of Labor's *Employment Law Guide* (ELG) at:

www.dol.gov/asp/gils/records/000025.htm

Michigan Law   *Minimum Wage Law of 1964.* This law currently provides for a minimum wage of $7.15 per hour, with a further increase on July 1, 2008, to $7.40 per hour. The law also requires the payment of overtime at the rate of one and one-half times the nonovertime hourly rate. Overtime is considered work in excess of forty hours per week or in excess of 216 hours in twenty-eight consecutive days. Violation of the law gives the employee a cause of action for the difference between actual pay and the amount required by law, plus the same amount as additional liquidated damages, plus attorney's fees and court costs. (Mich. Comp. Laws Ann., beginning with Sec. 408.382.)

The law does not apply to a temporary employee, defined as one who is employed for less than ten weeks. However, a consistent pattern of discharging employees within the first ten weeks of employment will be deemed to show an intent to violate the law, which is a misdemeanor punishable by a fine of from $5.00 to $50.00 per offense.

The law also tells when employees must be paid. Unless there is a properly established schedule, employees must be paid on or before the first day of the month for wages earned during the first fifteen days of the preceding month and on or before the 15th day of the month for wages earned during the second half of the preceding month. (For persons employed in the hand harvesting of crops, wages for a particular week must be paid on or before the second day after the end of the work week, unless another method is agreed to in a written contract.)

A regularly scheduled weekly or biweekly payday is acceptable if wages are paid on the established payday and the payday occurs on or before the 14th day after the end of the pay period. A monthly payday is acceptable if wages for a calendar month are paid on or before the first day of the following calendar month.

In the event of either voluntary or involuntary termination of employment, wages due must be paid *as soon as the amount can, with due diligence, be determined.* In the case of a person employed in the hand harvesting of crops, this may not be later than three days after the date of termination.

Other restrictions on wages include the following.

✪ Wages must be paid in U.S. currency, or by check or other draft payable in U.S. currency.

✪ No direct deposit may be made without the free and written consent of the employee.

✪ No deductions can be made from wages without the written consent of the employee (except for deductions required by law or a collective bargaining agreement).

PENSION AND BENEFIT LAWS

There are no laws requiring small businesses to provide any types of special benefits to employees. Such benefits are given to attract and keep good employees. With pension plans, the main concern is if you do start one, it must comply with federal tax laws.

There are no federal or Michigan laws requiring that employees be given holidays off. You can require them to work Thanksgiving and Christmas and dock their pay or fire them for failing to show up. Of course, you will not have much luck keeping employees.

Holidays   Most companies give full-time employees a certain number of paid holidays, such as New Year's Day (January 1), Memorial Day (last Monday in May), Fourth of July, Labor Day (first Monday in September), Thanksgiving (fourth Thursday in November) and Christmas (December 25). Some, but not many, employers include other holidays such as Martin Luther King, Jr. Day (third Monday in January), Lincoln's birthday (February 12), Washington's birthday (third Monday in February), Columbus Day (second Monday in October), and Veterans Day (November 11). If one of the holidays falls on a Saturday or Sunday, some employers give the preceding Friday or following Monday off.

Michigan law says that statewide legal holidays include all of those in the previous paragraph as well as Mrs. Rosa L. Parks Day (first Monday after February 4). However, the fact that these are designated state holidays does not mean anything. In fact, the state government is not even closed on all of these days.

Sick Leave

There is no federal or Michigan law mandating that an employee be paid for time that he or she is home sick. The situation seems to be that the larger the company, the more paid sick leave is allowed. Part-time workers rarely get sick leave and small business sick leave is usually limited for the simple reason that such businesses cannot afford to pay for time that employees do not work.

Some small companies have an official policy of no paid sick leave, but when an important employee misses a day because he or she is clearly sick, it is paid.

Lunch and Coffee Breaks

There are no federal or Michigan laws requiring coffee breaks or lunch breaks. However, it is common sense that employees will be more productive if they have reasonable breaks for nourishment or to use the toilet facilities.

Pension Plans and Retirement Accounts

Few small new businesses can afford to provide pension plans for their employees. The first concern of a small business is usually how the owner can shelter income in a pension plan without having to set up a pension plan for an employee. Under most pension plans this is not allowed.

IRA. Anyone with $3,000 of earnings can put up to that amount in an individual retirement account (IRA). Unless the person or his or her spouse is covered by a company pension plan and has income over a certain amount, the amount put into the account is tax deductible.

SEP/IRA. With a SEP/IRA a person can put a much greater amount into a retirement plan and deduct it. Employees must also be covered by such a plan, but certain employees are exempt so it is sometimes possible to use these for the owners alone. The best source for more information is a mutual fund company (such as Vanguard, Fidelity, Dreyfus, etc.) or a local bank, which can set up the plan and provide you with all of the rules. These have an advantage over qualified plans (discussed next) since they do not have the high annual fees.

Qualified Retirement Plans. Qualified retirement plans are 401(k) plans, Keough plans, and corporate retirement plans. These are covered by ERISA, the *Employee Retirement Income Security Act,* which is a complicated law meant to protect employee pension plans. Congress did not want employees who contributed to pension plans all their lives ending up with nothing if the plan went bankrupt.

The law is complicated and the penalties for violations are severe. However, many banks and mutual funds have created *canned plans* that can be used instead of drafting one from scratch. Still, the fees for administering them are steep. Check with a bank or mutual fund for details.

FAMILY AND MEDICAL LEAVE LAW

To assist business owners in deciding what type of leave to offer their employees, Congress passed the *Family and Medical Leave Act of 1993* (FMLA). This law requires an employee to be given up to twelve weeks of unpaid leave when:

- ✪ the employee or employee's spouse has a child;

- ✪ the employee adopts a child or takes in a foster child;

- ✪ the employee needs to care for an ill spouse, child, or parent; or,

- ✪ the employee becomes seriously ill.

The law only applies to employers with fifty or more employees. Also, the top 10% of an employer's salaried employees can be denied this leave because of the disruption in business their loss could cause.

NOTE: *There is no Michigan law requiring family or medical leave.*

CHILD LABOR LAWS

If you intend to employ any children, you will need to pay close attention to the federal and state child labor laws.

Federal Law The federal *Fair Labor Standards Act* also contains rules regarding the hiring of children. The basic rules are that children under 16 years old may not be hired at all except in a few jobs such as acting and newspaper delivery. Those under 18 may not be hired for dangerous jobs. Children may not work more than three hours a day/eighteen hours a week in a school week or more than eight hours a day/forty hours a week in a nonschool week. If you plan to hire children you should check the federal Fair Labor Standards Act found in the United States Code (U.S.C.), Title 29 and its related regulations, found in Chapter 29 of the Code of Federal Regulations (C.F.R.).

Michigan Law   The *Michigan Youth Employment Standards Act* has numerous rules governing the employment of children. (Mich. Comp. Laws Ann., Sec. 409.101.) It applies to all employees under the age of 18. The following is a summary of the main provisions of this act.

✪   No child under the age of 14 may work, except:

- children age 11 and older may work as golf caddies, bridge caddies at officially sanctioned events, youth athletic program referees, or as umpires (under certain circumstances); and,

- children age 13 and older may work in family farming operations or setting traps for formal or informal trap, skeet, and sporting clays shooting events.

✪   No child may be employed in a hazardous or injurious occupation.

✪   In order to work, a minor must obtain a work permit from the school district by submitting an application along with a statement from the prospective employer indicating the intent to employ the child and stating the nature of the job.

✪   If the child is under the age of 16, work is limited as follows:

- no more than six days per week;

- no more than a weekly average of eight hours per day;

- no more than forty-eight hours per week total;

- no more than ten hours in any single day;

- no work between the hours of 9:00 p.m. and 7:00 a.m.; and,

- if the child is a student, the number of hours in work and school combined may not exceed forty-eight hours per week while school is in session. (In other words, this limitation does not apply during summer, Christmas, and other vacations from school.)

✪ If the child is at least 16, the same restrictions apply, except:

- no work between the hours of 10:30 p.m. and 6:00 a.m. while school is in session and 11:30 p.m. and 6:00 a.m. during school vacations.

✪ The child must be given at least a thirty-minute rest and lunch period after no more than five hours of work.

✪ If the child is working in cash transactions at a fixed location (such as a convenience store), he or she may not work after sunset or 8:00 p.m., whichever is earlier, unless there is an adult present.

✪ No child may be employed in a business that deals in alcoholic beverages unless the sale of food and other goods is at least 50% of the gross receipts. Exceptions are:

- 14- and 15-year-olds may work in the nonalcohol-related part of the business if the sale of food and other goods in the alcohol-related part is at least 50% of gross receipts;

- 16-year-olds may work if they have completed the requirements for high school graduation (in which case the employer must obtain and keep on file a certificate from the school);

- 17-year-olds who have passed the GED may work (the employer must obtain proof of passing); and,

- any legally emancipated minor may work (the employer must obtain proof of emancipation).

✪ There are several exceptions to this act for such jobs as domestic work in a private residence, selling newspapers, shining shoes, and family businesses.

Poster. Anyone employing a minor must display a poster explaining the child labor laws. This poster is available from:

Michigan Department of Labor and Economic Growth
P.O. Box 30004
Lansing, MI 48909
517-373-1820
www.michigan.gov/dleg

IMMIGRATION LAWS

If you intend to hire even one employee, you need to be aware of certain immigration laws. At least some of these laws will apply to you even if you will only be hiring U.S. citizens.

Federal Law   Under federal law, you must verify both the identity and the employment eligibility of anyone you hire by using the **EMPLOYMENT ELIGIBILITY (IRS FORM I-9)**. (see form 4, p.205.) Both you and the employee must fill out the form and you must check the employee's identification cards or papers.

Fines for hiring illegal aliens range from $250 to $2,000 for the first offense and up to $10,000 for the third offense. Failure to maintain the proper paperwork may result in a fine of up to $1,000. The law does not apply to independent contractors with whom you may contract and it does not penalize you if the employee used fake identification.

There are also penalties that apply to employers of four or more persons for discriminating against eligible applicants because they appear foreign or because of their national origin or citizenship status.

In Appendix B there is a sample, filled-in **IRS FORM I-9**. A blank form, along with instructions and a list of acceptable documentation, may be found in Appendix C. (see form 4, p.205.) For more information, call the U.S. Citizenship and Immigration Services (in Michigan at 800-357-2099 or in Washington, D.C. at 800-375-5283) and ask for the *Handbook for Employers: Instructions for Completing the Form I-9.* You can also check the USCIS website at **www.uscis.gov/files/nativedocuments/m-274.pdf** or write to the following address:

U.S. Citizenship and Immigration Services
425 I Street, NW
Washington, D.C. 20536

The *Illegal Immigration Reform and Immigrant Responsibility Act of 1996* (IIRIRA) required changes in the rules on how to complete Form I-9. But as of 2004 the USCIS had not yet promulgated final versions of the rules. The interim rule made the following changes to the requirements:

✪   remove documents 2, 3, 8, and 9 from column A;

✪   allow document 4 only for aliens authorized to work for a specific employer; and,

✪   new rules for employees who do not have their original documents.

However, no new forms or instructions have been made available and employers are not yet being prosecuted for violations of these changes. Employers can receive updates to these laws by fax. To receive them, send your name, address, and fax number to 202-305-2523.

Foreign employees. If you wish to hire employees who are foreign citizens and are not able to provide the documentation previously explained, they must first obtain a work visa from the U.S. Citizenship and Immigration Services (USCIS). Work visas for foreigners are not easy to get. Millions of people around the globe would like to come to the United States to work and the laws are designed to keep most of them out to protect the jobs of American citizens.

Whether or not a person can get a work visa depends on whether there is a shortage of U.S. workers available to fill the job. For jobs requiring few or no skills, it is practically impossible to get a visa. For highly skilled jobs, such as nurses and physical therapists, and for those persons of exceptional ability, such as Nobel Prize winners and Olympic medalists, obtaining a visa is fairly easy.

There are several types of visas and different rules for different countries. For example, the North American Free Trade Agreement (NAFTA) has made it easier for some types of workers to enter the United States from Canada and Mexico. For some positions, the shortage of workers is assumed by the USCIS. For others, a business must first advertise a position available in the United

States. Only after no qualified persons apply can it hire someone from another country.

The visa system is complicated and subject to regular change. If you wish to hire a foreign worker, consult with an immigration specialist or a book on the subject.

Michigan Law   There are no Michigan laws relating to the hiring of aliens, other than allowing the licensing of aliens legally permitted to work in the United States.

HIRING OFF THE BOOKS

Because of the taxes, insurance, and red tape involved with hiring employees, some new businesses hire people *off the books*. They pay them in cash and never admit they are employees. While the cash paid in wages would not be tax-deductible, they consider this a smaller cost than compliance. Some even use off-the-books receipts to cover it.

Except when your spouse or child is giving you some temporary help, this is a terrible idea. Hiring people off the books can result in civil fines, loss of insurance coverage, and even criminal penalties. When engaged in dangerous work, such as roofing or anything using power tools, you are risking millions of dollars in potential damages if a worker is killed or seriously injured.

It may be more costly and time-consuming to comply with the employment laws, but if you are concerned about long-term growth with less risk, it is the wiser way to go.

FEDERAL CONTRACTS

Companies that do work for the federal government are subject to several laws. In the event you plan to bid on government contracts, you will need to be aware of these laws, which include the following.

✪   The *Davis-Bacon Act* requires contractors engaged in U.S. government construction projects to pay wages and benefits that are equal to or better than the prevailing wages in the area.

✪ The *McNamara-O'Hara Service Contract Act* sets wages and other labor standards for contractors furnishing services to agencies of the U.S. government.

✪ The *Walsh-Healey Public Contracts Act* requires the Department of Labor to settle disputes regarding manufacturers supplying products to the U.S. government.

MISCELLANEOUS LAWS

It is nearly impossible to list every single state and federal law that may apply in some way to every business. However, this section discusses a few of the more common laws that do not fit into any of the specific categories already mentioned.

Federal Law   *Affirmative action.* In most cases, the federal government does not yet tell employers whom they must hire. This is especially true for small new businesses. The only situation where a small business would need to comply with affirmative action requirements would be if it accepted federal contracts or subcontracts. These requirements could include the hiring of minorities or Vietnam veterans.

Layoffs. Companies with one hundred or more full-time employees at one location are subject to the *Worker Adjustment and Retraining Notification Act*. This law requires a sixty-day notification prior to certain layoffs and has other strict provisions.

Unions. The *National Labor Relations Act of 1935* gives employees the right to organize or join a union. (29 USC Sec. 151.) There are things employers can do to protect themselves, but you should consult a labor attorney or a book on the subject before taking action that might be illegal and result in fines.

Poster Laws. In addition to any poster laws previously discussed in this chapter, there are other laws that require certain posters to be displayed to inform employees of their rights.

All employers must display the minimum wage poster and the employee polygraph protection notice poster. Employers with fifteen or more employees for twenty weeks of the year must display the sex, race, religion, and ethnic discrimination poster and the age discrimination poster. Employers with federal contracts or subcontracts of $10,000 or more must also display a poster regarding Vietnam Era Veterans. Employers with government contracts subject to the Davis-Bacon Act or the Service Contract Act must display notices to employees working on government contracts. If you employ fifty or more employees for twenty weeks of the year, you must display the poster titled "Your Rights Under the Family and Medical Leave Act."

All of these posters, and more that relate to specific employment situations, can be obtained from:

U.S. Department of Labor
Employment Standards Administration
Washington, DC 20210
888-972-7332
Contact-OSBP@dol.gov
www.dol.gov/osbp/sbrefa/poster/matrix.htm

Michigan Law

Personnel file. The *Bullard-Plawecki Employee Right to Know Act* relates to an employee's rights with respect to his or her personnel file kept by an employer. It applies to all businesses with four or more employees. Basically, it gives the employee the right to review his or her personnel record at least two times per year. If the employee disagrees with anything, he or she can submit a written statement, which must be disclosed to any third party seeking information about the employee if any other information is given. If the employer intends to disclose information in any disciplinary reports, letters of reprimand, etc., the employer must notify the employee in writing on or before the date of disclosure. Disciplinary reports, letters of reprimand, etc., must be deleted after four years. (Mich. Comp. Laws Ann., beginning with Sec. 423.501.)

Polygraph Protection Act of 1981. The *Polygraph Protection Act* applies to anyone employing one or more people and prohibits an employer from requiring a polygraph examination of an employee or applicant for employment. It does permit an examination at the request of the employee or applicant, but still puts limitations and requirements on the employer. Violation of the act allows the employee or applicant to sue for an injunction and damages (including double wages lost if the person was discharged), and is also a misdemeanor subjecting the employer to a fine of up to $1,000 and up to ninety days in jail. (Mich. Comp. Laws Ann., Sec. 37.201.)

Whistleblowers' Protection Act. The *Whistleblowers' Protection Act* prohibits an employer from taking any retaliatory action against an employee for reporting a violation of a law or regulation. It applies to any employer with one or more employees. Violation subjects the employer to a fine of up to $500. It also allows the employee to sue the employer for an injunction, damages (including attorney's fees), and reinstatement with full back pay. The act also requires the employer to post notices and use other appropriate means to keep his or her employees informed of their protections and obligations under this act. (Mich. Comp. Laws Ann., Sec. 15.361.)

Prohibited requirements of employment. It is a misdemeanor to require an employee or prospective employee to do any of the following things as a condition of hiring, continued employment, promotion, etc.:

✪   make a contribution to a charity (Mich. Comp. Laws Ann., Sec. 750.353);

✪   purchase or contribute toward the purchase of a life or accident insurance policy (Mich. Comp. Laws Ann., Sec. 750.354);

✪   pay for all or part of a medical examination, photographing, or fingerprinting (Mich. Comp. Laws Ann., Sec. 750.354a); or,

✪   pay any money to anyone in consideration of employment, except to an employment agency (Mich. Comp. Laws Ann., Sec. 750.351).

Molesting or disturbing employees. It is a misdemeanor to use threats, intimidation, or otherwise interfere with, or in any way molest, attempt to interfere with, or disturb any person in the quiet and peaceable pursuit of his or her lawful occupation, vocation, or avocation, or on the way to and from such occupation, vocation, or avocation. (Mich. Comp. Laws Ann., Sec. 750.352.)

Migrant and farm labor. If you plan to hire or house migrant or farm labor, read the sections in the statutes on wages and child labor and contact the Michigan Commission on Agricultural Employment for more information. (Mich. Comp. Laws Ann., Sec. 333.12401.)

Poster laws. Michigan has its own poster requirements. In addition to the required federal posters, the following should be obtained.

✪ Unemployment Compensation poster:

Unemployment Insurance Agency
3024 West Grand Boulevard, Suite 11-500
Detroit, MI 48202
800-638-3994
313-456-2400
www.michigan.gov/uia

✪ MIOSHA posters:

Michigan Occupational Safety and Health Agency
P.O. Box 30643
Lansing, MI 48909
517-322-1814
www.michigan.gov/cis

✪ ADA poster:

U.S. Equal Employment Opportunity Commission
P.O. Box 12549
Cincinnati, OH 45212
www.eeoc.gov/posterform.html

✪ Discrimination Prohibited poster:

Michigan Department of Civil Rights
Capitol Tower Building, Suite 800
Lansing, MI 48933
517-335-3165

or
Michigan Department of Civil Rights
3024 West Grand Boulevard, Suite 3-600
Detroit, MI 48202
313-456-3700

Advertising and Promotion Laws

Almost every business engages in some forms of advertising and promotion. There are many laws you should consider before you begin any advertising or promotional campaigns.

ADVERTISING LAWS AND RULES

This section discusses various federal and Michigan laws and regulations relating to advertising.

Federal Law The federal government regulates advertising through the Federal Trade Commission (FTC). The rules are contained in the *Code of Federal Regulations* (C.F.R.). You can find these rules in most law libraries and many public libraries. If you plan any advertising that you think may be questionable, you might want to check the rules. As you read the rules discussed you will probably think of many violations you see every day.

Federal rules do not apply to every business. Small businesses that operate only within the state and do not use the postal service may be exempt. However, many of the federal rules have been adopted into law by the state of Michigan. Therefore, a violation could be prosecuted by the state rather than the federal government. Some of the important rules are summarized below. If you wish, you can obtain copies from your library.

Deceptive pricing. When prices are being compared, it is required that actual and not inflated prices are used.

Example:

If an object would usually be sold for $7, one should not first offer it for $10 and then start offering it at 30% off.

It is considered misleading to suggest that a discount from list price is a bargain if the item is seldom actually sold at list price. If most surrounding stores sell an item for $7, it is considered misleading to say it has a *retail value of $10* even if there are some stores elsewhere selling it at that price. (16 C.F.R. Ch. I, Part 233.)

Bait advertising. Bait advertising is placing an ad when you do not really want the respondents to buy the product offered but actually want them to switch to another item. (16 C.F.R. Ch. I, Part 238.)

Use of free, half-off, and similar words. Use of words such as *free, 1¢ sale,* and the like must not be misleading. This means that the *regular price* must not include a markup to cover the *free* item. The seller must expect to sell the product without the free item at some time in the future. (16 C.F.R. Ch. I, Part 251.)

Substantiation of claims. The FTC requires that advertisers be able to substantiate their claims. (16 C.F.R. Sec 3.40; 48 F.R. Page 10471.) Some information on this policy is contained on the Internet at:

www.ftc.gov/bcp/guides/ad3subst.htm

Endorsements. Rules forbid endorsements that are misleading. An example is a quote from a film review that is used in such a way as to change the substance of the review. It is not necessary to use the exact words of the person endorsing the product as long as the opinion is not distorted. If a product is changed, an endorsement that does not apply to the new version cannot be used. For some items, such as drugs, claims cannot be used without scientific proof. Endorsements by organizations cannot be used unless one is sure that the membership holds the same opinion. (16 C.F.R. Ch. I, Part 255.)

Unfairness. Any advertising practices that can be deemed to be *unfair* are forbidden by the FTC. (15 USC Sec. 45.) An explanation of this policy is located on the Internet at:

www.ftc.gov/bcp/policystmt/ad-unfair.htm

Negative option plans. When a seller uses a sales system in which the buyer must notify the seller if he or she does not want the goods, the seller must provide the buyer with a form to decline the sale and at least ten days in which to decline. Bonus merchandise must be shipped promptly and the seller must promptly terminate any who so request after completion of the contract. (16 C.F.R. Ch. I, Part 425.)

Food and dietary supplements. Under the *Nutritional Labeling Education Act of 1990*, the FTC and the FDA regulate the packaging and advertising of food and dietary products. Anyone involved in this area should obtain a copy of these rules. (21 USC Sec. 343.) They are located on the Internet at:

www.ftc.gov/bcp/menus/business/health.shtm

Jewelry and precious metals. The FTC has numerous rules governing the sale and advertising of jewelry and precious metals. Anyone in this business should obtain a copy of these rules. (61 F.R. Page 27212.) They are located on the Internet at:

www.ftc.gov/bcp/menus/business/adv.shtm

Michigan Law   Most of Michigan's advertising laws are in the criminal statutes (Michigan Penal Code). (Mich. Comp. Laws Ann., Secs. 750.33 through 750.42b.) The following discussion summarizes these laws.

False advertising. It is a misdemeanor to issue any advertising that is untrue, deceptive or misleading, or calculated to subject any person to disadvantage or injury. This includes untrue statements as to the motive or purpose of the sale and inaccurate illustrations. Violation is punishable by a fine of up to $500 and up to one year in jail. (Mich. Comp. Laws Ann., Sec. 750.33.)

Misrepresentation of character or extent of business. Any person who states, in an advertisement of goods, that he or she is a producer, manufacturer, processor, wholesaler, or importer, or that he or she owns or controls a factory or other source of supply of goods, when such is not the fact, or in any other manner knowingly misrepresents the character, extent, volume or type of his or her business, is guilty of a misdemeanor. (Mich. Comp. Laws Ann., Sec. 750.33a.)

Advertising of consumer goods. These laws only apply to consumer items for sale at retail. *Consumer items* are those *used or consumed, or bought for use or consumption, primarily for personal, family, or household purposes. For sale at retail means the transfer of an interest in a consumer item by a person regularly and principally engaged in the business of selling consumer items to a buyer for use or consumption and not for resale.* (Mich. Comp. Laws Ann., beginning with Sec. 445.351.)

It is illegal to knowingly advertise a consumer item for sale at retail at a sale, special, or reduced price, unless the advertisement includes the dates the item is available, or the quantity available together with a statement that the item is available at that price only as long as the advertised quantity lasts. Any limitation in availability must be clearly disclosed in the ad. (Mich. Comp. Laws Ann., Sec. 445.355.)

If a consumer item is advertised at a specific price that is not indicated to be a special, sale, or reduced price, you must either:

✪ make the item available at the advertised price for at least five days after the last date of advertisement (unless it is made unavailable by government action, a plant closing, or an act of God, and the reason is conspicuously posted);

✪ indicate in the ad the dates the item is available at that price; or,

✪ indicate in the ad the quantity available and state that the item will only be available at that price for as long as the stated quantity lasts.

If the ad does not state the quantity available and if the item cannot be sold at the advertised price throughout the advertised sales period, the customer must be given a written guarantee that the item will be delivered under the advertised conditions at a future date as agreed upon or upon notification by the merchant (in not more than ninety days). If this is not possible, the merchant may provide a similar item of equal or greater value. After the merchant notifies the customer of the availability of the item, the merchant must hold the item for the customer for at least seven days (two days if it is a perishable item).

NOTE: *None of the above applies to baked goods, fresh fruit, or fresh vegetables.*

According to Michigan law, it is illegal to:

❂ have an advertisement that contains a statement or representation that is untrue, deceptive, or misleading;

❂ issue an ad with the intent not to sell at the price stated; or,

❂ issue an ad that fails to call attention to the fact that the items offered are *substantially defective and therefore not first class, or which consist of articles or units or parts known as seconds or blemished goods, merchandise, or commodities, which goods, merchandise, or commodities have been rejected by the manufacturer…as not being first class….*(Mich. Comp. Laws Ann., Sec. 445.356.)

Unsolicited fax advertising. Under this law, it is unlawful to send advertising by fax without the consent of the person (which includes business entities) to whom it is sent. The mere fact that the other person has a published fax number is not consent to receive unsolicited fax advertising. Violation of this law subjects the sender to a fine of up to $500 per violation and a civil penalty to the receiver of actual damages or $250, whichever is greater. (Mich. Comp. Laws Ann., Secs. 445.1771 through 445.1776.)

If you receive unsolicited fax advertising, report it to the Michigan attorney general's office or your local prosecuting attorney and send the sender a letter stating that the sender did not have your consent to send the advertisement. Be sure to follow up on your complaint to make sure the attorney general takes action, as this is essential to your ability to file suit against the sender if you later receive more unsolicited fax advertising.

The attorney general is to send the sender a *cease and desist order*. This is simply a letter telling the sender to immediately stop sending unsolicited fax advertising. The sender must then send the attorney general a written *assurance of discontinuance*. This is simply a letter telling the attorney general that the sender will not send any more unsolicited fax advertising. If no such assurance is received, the attorney general should take the sender to court and seek an injunction.

You may only file suit after the following events:

✪ the attorney general receives an assurance of discontinuance or an injunction is granted;

✪ you have sent the sender a letter stating you did not consent to the advertising; and,

✪ the sender again sends unsolicited advertising after the first two items listed here have been done.

Immoral advertising. This set of laws prohibits advertising the cure or treatment of any maladies or problems relating to sexual organs, including miscarriage and abortion. (Mich. Comp. Laws Ann., Secs. 750.34 to 750.37.)

Advertisement displaying violence or the human form. This law makes it a misdemeanor to:

> *post, place, or display on any sign board, bill board, fence, building, sidewalk, or other object, or in any street, road, or other public place, any sign, picture, printing, or other representation of murder, assassination, stabbing, fighting, or any personal violence, or of the commission of any crime, or any representation of the human form in an attitude or dress which would be indecent in the case of a living person, if such person so appeared in any public street, square, or highway.*
> (Mich. Comp. Laws Ann., Sec. 750.38.)

Tobacco products advertising. These laws place restrictions and require certain warnings on outdoor signs advertising smokeless tobacco products, and place restrictions on the distribution of tobacco products through the mail or other common carriers (such as UPS). (Mich. Comp. Laws Ann., Secs. 750.42a and 750.42b.)

There are several other Michigan advertising laws that may violate the Constitutional guarantee of free speech. Although these laws are of questionable constitutional validity, it would be very expensive and time-consuming for you to take a case all the way to the United States Supreme Court to try to declare the law unconstitutional and secure your right to continue your advertising.

Therefore, you may want to consider this before you decide to try advertising that may violate one of these laws.

INTERNET SALES LAWS

There are not yet specific laws governing Internet transactions that are different from laws governing other transactions. The FTC feels that its current rules regarding deceptive advertising, substantiation, disclaimers, refunds, and related matters must be followed by Internet businesses and that consumers are adequately protected by them.

For some specific guidelines on Internet advertising, see the FTC's site at:

www.ftc.gov/bcp/conline/pubs/buspubs/ruleroad.htm

HOME SOLICITATION LAWS

There are specific state and federal rules governing personal or telephone solicitation of sales at people's homes.

Federal Law   The Federal Trade Commission has rules governing door-to-door sales. In any such sale it is a deceptive trade practice to fail to furnish a receipt explaining the sale (in the language of the presentation) and giving notice that there is a three-day right of recision. The notice must be supplied in duplicate, must be in at least 10-point type, and must be captioned either "NOTICE OF RIGHT TO CANCEL" or "NOTICE OF CANCELLATION." The notice must be worded as shown on the following page.

NOTICE OF CANCELLATION

_____
Date

YOU MAY CANCEL THIS TRANSACTION, WITHOUT ANY PENALTY OR OBLIGATION, WITHIN THREE BUSINESS DAYS FROM THE ABOVE DATE.

IF YOU CANCEL, ANY PROPERTY TRADED IN, ANY PAYMENTS MADE BY YOU UNDER THE CONTRACT OR SALE, AND ANY NEGOTIABLE INSTRUMENT EXECUTED BY YOU WILL BE RETURNED TO YOU WITHIN 10 BUSINESS DAYS FOLLOWING RECEIPT BY THE SELLER OF YOUR CANCELLATION NOTICE, AND ANY SECURITY INTEREST ARISING OUT OF THE TRANSACTION WILL BE CANCELLED.

IF YOU CANCEL, YOU MUST MAKE AVAILABLE TO THE SELLER AT YOUR RESIDENCE, IN SUBSTANTIALLY AS GOOD CONDITION AS WHEN RECEIVED, ANY GOODS DELIVERED TO YOU UNDER THIS CONTRACT OR SALE; OR YOU MAY IF YOU WISH, COMPLY WITH THE INSTRUCTIONS OF THE SELLER REGARDING THE RETURN SHIPMENT OF THE GOODS AT THE SELLER'S EXPENSE AND RISK.

IF YOU DO MAKE THE GOODS AVAILABLE TO THE SELLER AND THE SELLER DOES NOT PICK THEM UP WITHIN 20 DAYS OF THE DATE OF YOUR NOTICE OF CANCELLATION, YOU MAY RETAIN OR DISPOSE OF THE GOODS WITHOUT ANY FURTHER OBLIGATION. IF YOU FAIL TO MAKE THE GOODS AVAILABLE TO THE SELLER, OR IF YOU AGREE TO RETURN THE GOODS AND FAIL TO DO SO, THEN YOU REMAIN LIABLE FOR PERFORMANCE OF ALL OBLIGATIONS UNDER THE CONTRACT.

TO CANCEL THIS TRANSACTION, MAIL OR DELIVER A SIGNED AND DATED COPY OF THIS CANCELLATION NOTICE OR ANY OTHER WRITTEN NOTICE, OR SEND A TELEGRAM, TO [name of seller], AT [address of seller's place of business] NOT LATER THAN MIDNIGHT OF _____ (date).

I HEREBY CANCEL THIS TRANSACTION.
(DATE) _____

_____
(Buyer's signature)

The seller must complete the notice and orally inform the buyer of the right to cancel. The seller cannot misrepresent the right to cancel, assign the contract until the fifth business day, nor include a confession of judgment in the contract. For more specific details, see the rules contained in the Code of Federal Regulations. (16 C.F.R. Ch. I, Part 429.)

Michigan Law   If you are going to engage in the type of sales governed by the Michigan *Home Solicitation Sales Act*, get a copy and read it. Basically, the act covers the sale of goods or services of more than $25.00, in which the seller engages in personal or telephone solicitation of the sale at the buyer's residence, when the buyer's agreement or offer to purchase occurs in the residence. Insurance agents and real estate sales people are covered by separate laws. (Mich. Comp. Laws Ann., beginning with Sec. 445.111.)

This act prohibits the use of recorded messages in a telephone sales offer and gives the buyer certain cancellation rights. The act requires the following notice to appear on a written offer to purchase, in immediate proximity to the space reserved in the agreement or offer to purchase for the signature of the buyer:

> *You, the buyer, may cancel this transaction at any time prior to midnight of the third business day after the date of this transaction. See the attached notice of cancellation form for an explanation of this right. Additionally, the seller is prohibited from having an independent courier service or other third party pick up your payment at your residence before the end of the 3-business-day period in which you can cancel the transaction.*

The notice is the same as the *Notice of Cancellation* under federal law. It may be attached to the offer or printed on the reverse side.

TELEPHONE SOLICITATION LAWS

Both the federal and Michigan governments have passed laws regarding telephone solicitations, also known as *telemarketing*. If you will be engaging in telephone solicitations, keep alert for any new laws in this area.

In 2003 the Federal Trade Commission issued new rules regulating telephone solicitation calls. The main provision of these rules allows consumers to be listed on a national *Do Not Call* registry and any company that calls those on the list is subject to penalties. Other provisions:

- ✪ require disclosures of specific information;

- ✪ prohibit misrepresentations;

- ✪ limit when telemarketers may call consumers;

- ✪ require transmission of Caller ID information;

- ✪ prohibit abandoned outbound calls, subject to a safe harbor;

- ✪ prohibit unauthorized billing;

- ✪ set payment restrictions for the sale of certain goods and services; and,

- ✪ require that specific business records be kept for two years.

For more information on these rules you can visit **http://telemarketing. donotcall.gov.**

Michigan Law   Michigan has several laws relating to telephone solicitations. It is a misdemeanor to make an unsolicited sales call that includes a recorded message. The use of an automatic dialing system with a recorded message is considered sufficient evidence for conviction, absent any proof to the contrary by the business. Violation is punishable by a fine of up to $1,000 and up to ten days in jail. (Mich. Comp. Laws Ann., Secs. 445.111 and 484.125.)

It is also a misdemeanor (fine of up to $1,000 and up to six months in jail) to make an unsolicited sales call between the hours of 9:00 p.m. and 9:00 a.m. (Mich. Comp. Laws Ann., Sec. 750.540e.)

PRICING, WEIGHTS, AND LABELING

Depending upon the type of business you are in, you may need to be aware of the various federal and Michigan laws relating to pricing, weights, and the labeling of products.

Federal Law   *Food products.* Beginning in 1994, all food products are required to have labels with information on the product's nutritional values such as calories, fat, and protein. For most products, the label must be in the required format so that consumers can easily compare products. However, if such a format will not fit on the product label, the information may be in another format that is easily readable.

Metric measures. In 1994, federal rules requiring metric measurement of products took effect. Under these rules, metric measures do not have to be the first measurement on the container, but they must be included. Food items that are packaged as they are sold (such as delicatessen items) do not have to contain metric labels.

Michigan Law   The *Michigan Weights and Measures Act of 1964* adopts federal weights and measures standards. It also created the office of the Director of Weights and Measures, which maintains the official standards for use in inspections of weights and measures used by businesses in Michigan. Inspection and enforcement powers lie with the Director of Weights and Measures and with the Sealer of Weights and Measures in the various cities and counties.

Basically, the act requires accuracy in weights and measures used in the sale and labeling of goods. The act also provides the requirements for the following commodities. (Mich. Comp. Laws Ann., beginning with Sec. 290.601.)

Weights and measures. Liquid commodities must be sold only by liquid measure or by weight. Nonliquid must be sold only by weight, measure, or count. However, liquids may only be sold by weight and nonliquids may only be sold by count if the measurement used gives accurate information as to the quantity sold. These rules do not apply to commodities sold for immediate consumption on the premises where sold, vegetables sold by the head or bunch, commodities in containers standardized by state or federal law, or commodities packaged in a form generally used by consumers to show quantity in another manner. (Mich. Comp. Laws Ann., Sec. 290.623.)

Labeling. Any commodity in package form must bear on the outside of the packaging:

✪   the identity of the commodity unless it can easily be identified through the wrapper or container;

✪   the net quantity of the contents in terms of weight, measure, or count; and,

✪   the name and place of business of the manufacturer, packer, or distributor if sold at any place other than where it was packed.

Terms that tend to qualify or exaggerate the quantity, such as *when packed, jumbo, giant,* or *full,* are prohibited. The Director of Weights and Measures may make more detailed regulations and exemptions. Some regulations may require the quantity to be stated in more than one unit of measure (e.g., ounces and liters). (Mich. Comp. Laws Ann., Sec. 290.625.) These types of terms may not be used in an ad either. (Mich. Comp. Laws Ann., Sec. 290.627.)

Random weights and measures. If the package bears one selling price and is one of a lot that contains random weights, measures, or counts, it must be labeled as to the price per single unit. (Mich. Comp. Laws Ann., Sec. 290.626.)

Misleading wrappers. Any commodity in package form shall not be so wrapped, nor shall it be in a container so made, formed, or filled as to mislead the purchaser as to the quantity of the contents of the package. (Mich. Comp. Laws Ann., Sec. 290.626.)

Advertisements. Any advertisement for a packaged commodity must include the basic quantity of the package, except for agricultural and horticultural products in which the custom is to state the number of objects or the amount of area that can be treated per package unit (e.g., pesticides and fertilizer). If a regulation requires the package itself to contain more than one unit of measurement, only the smallest unit need be stated in the ad.

Meat, poultry, and seafood. Except for items sold for immediate consumption on the premises where sold (e.g., restaurants), or as part of a ready-to-eat meal sold for consumption elsewhere (e.g., fast-food restaurants), all meat, meat products, poultry, and seafood except shellfish, must be sold by weight. If it is included in a package with other foods (e.g., spaghetti sauce or frozen dinner), only the weight of the entire package need be indicated. (Mich. Comp. Laws Ann., Sec. 290.628a.)

Representation of price. Michigan law states:

> *Whenever any commodity or service is sold...by weight, measure or count, the price shall not be misrepresented, nor shall the price be represented in any manner calculated or tending to mislead or deceive an actual or prospective purchaser. Whenever any advertised, posted, or labeled price per unit of weight, measure, or count included a fraction of a cent, all elements of the fraction shall be prominently displayed and the numeral or numerals expressing the fraction shall be immediately adjacent to, of the same general design and style as, and at least 1/2 the height and width of the numeral representing the whole cents.*
> (Mich. Comp. Laws Ann., Sec. 290.628b.)

UNFAIR OR DECEPTIVE PRACTICES

Unfair and deceptive trade practices are set forth in Michigan law and are part of the *Michigan Consumer Protection Act.* (Mich. Comp. Laws Ann., Sec. 445.903.) This section provides that unfair, unconscionable, or deceptive methods, acts, or practices in the conduct of trade or commerce are unlawful and are defined as follows:

- ✪ causing a probability of confusion or misunderstanding as to the source, sponsorship, approval, or certification of goods or services;

- ✪ using deceptive representations or deceptive designations of geographic origin in connection with goods or services;

- ✪ representing that goods or services have sponsorship, approval, characteristics, ingredients, uses, benefits, or quantities that they do not have or that a person has sponsorship, approval, status, affiliation, or connection that he or she does not have;

- ✪ representing that goods are new if they are deteriorated, altered, reconditioned, used, or secondhand;

- ✪ representing that goods or services are of a particular standard, quality, or grade, or that goods are of a particular style or model, if they are of another;

✪ disparaging the goods, services, business, or reputation of another by false or misleading representation of fact;

✪ advertising goods or services with intent not to dispose of those goods or services as advertised or represented;

✪ advertising goods or services with intent not to supply reasonably expectable public demand, unless the advertisement discloses a limitation of quantity in immediate conjunction with the advertised goods or services;

✪ making false or misleading statements of fact concerning the reasons for, existence of, or amounts of price reductions;

✪ representing that a part, replacement, or repair service is needed when it is not;

✪ representing to a party to whom goods or services are supplied that the goods or services are being supplied in response to a request made by or on behalf of the party, when they are not;

✪ misrepresenting that because of some defect in a consumer's home the health, safety, or lives of the consumer or his or her family are in danger if the product or services are not purchased, when in fact the defect does not exist or the product or services would not remove the danger;

✪ causing a probability of confusion or of misunderstanding with respect to the authority of a salesperson, representative, or agent to negotiate the final terms of a transaction;

✪ causing a probability of confusion or of misunderstanding as to the legal rights, obligations, or remedies of a party to a transaction;

✪ causing a probability of confusion or of misunderstanding as to the terms or conditions of credit if credit is extended in a transaction;

✪ disclaiming or limiting the implied warranty of merchantability and fitness for use, unless a disclaimer is clearly and conspicuously disclosed;

✪   representing or implying that the subject of a consumer transaction will be provided promptly, or at a specified time, or within a reasonable time, if the merchant knows or has reason to know it will not be so provided;

✪   representing that a consumer will receive goods or services *free*, *without charge*, or words of similar import without clearly and conspicuously disclosing with equal prominence in immediate conjunction with the use of those words the conditions, terms, or prerequisites to the use or retention of the goods or services advertised;

✪   failing to reveal a material fact, the omission of which tends to mislead or deceive the consumer, and which fact could not reasonably be known by the consumer;

✪   entering into a consumer transaction in which the consumer waives or purports to waive a right, benefit, or immunity provided by law, unless the waiver is clearly stated and the consumer has specifically consented to it;

✪   failing to promptly return a deposit, down payment, or other payment in a consumer transaction, when the purchaser has rescinded, canceled, or otherwise terminated the agreement as provided in the agreement, an advertisement, or by law;

✪   if a purchaser in a consumer transaction traded in property that is no longer available to return, failing to promptly pay an agreed-upon value or fair market value of the property when the purchaser has rescinded, canceled, or otherwise terminated the agreement as provided in the agreement, an advertisement, or by law;

✪   where a security interest has been acquired in a consumer transaction, failing to cancel the security interest within a specified time or an otherwise reasonable time when the purchaser has rescinded, canceled, or otherwise terminated the agreement as provided in the agreement, an advertisement, or by law;

✪   taking or arranging for the consumer to sign an acknowledgement, certificate, or other writing affirming acceptance, delivery, compliance with a requirement of law, or other performance, if the merchant knows or has reason to know that the statement is not true;

✪ representing that a consumer will receive a rebate, discount, or other benefit as an inducement for entering into a transaction, if the benefit is contingent on an event to occur subsequent to the consummation of the transaction;

✪ taking advantage of the consumer's inability to reasonably protect his or her interests by reason of disability, illiteracy, or inability to understand the language of an agreement presented by the other party to the transaction who knows or reasonably should know of the consumer's inability;

✪ gross discrepancies between the oral representations of the seller and the written agreement covering the same transaction or failure of the other party to the transaction to provide the promised benefits;

✪ charging the consumer a price that is grossly in excess of the price at which similar property or services are sold;

✪ causing coercion and duress as the result of the time and nature of a sales presentation;

✪ making a representation of fact or statement of fact material to the transaction such that a person reasonably believes the represented or suggested state of affairs to be other than it actually is; and,

✪ failing to reveal facts that are material to the transaction in light of representations of fact made in a positive manner.

Additional rules are made by the attorney general.

Payment and Collection

Depending on the business you are in, you may be paid by cash, checks, credit cards, or some sort of financing arrangement such as a promissory note or mortgage. Both state and federal laws affect the type of payments you collect and failure to follow the laws can cost you considerably.

CASH

Cash is probably the easiest form of payment and it is subject to few restrictions. The most important one is that you keep an accurate accounting of your cash transactions and that you report all of your cash income on your tax return.

Recent efforts to stop the drug trade have resulted in some serious penalties for failing to report cash transactions and for money laundering. The laws are so sweeping that even if you deal in cash in an ordinary business you may violate the law and face huge fines and imprisonment.

The most important law to be concerned with is the one requiring the filing of **REPORT OF CASH PAYMENTS OVER $10,000 (IRS FORM 8300)** for cash transactions of $10,000 or more. (see form 10, p.235.) A transaction does not have to happen in one day. If a person brings you smaller amounts of cash that add up to $10,000 and the government can construe them as one transaction, the form must be filed. Under this law *cash* also includes travelers' checks and money orders, but does not include cashier's checks or bank checks.

CHECKS

It is important to accept checks in your business. While there is a small percentage that will be bad, most checks will be good, and you will be able to accommodate more customers by accepting checks. To avoid having problems, observe the following rules.

Accepting Checks

Most major credit card companies forbid a business to require a customer to provide his or her credit card number in order to pay by or cash a check.

Bad Checks

It is a crime in Michigan to give someone a bad check. If a bad check is given on an existing account, there are increasing penalties based upon the amount of the check and number of times the person has been convicted of the offense. Fines range from $100 to $2,000, and jail terms range from ninety-three days to two years. If a check is written on a closed account, the penalties are a fine of up to $500 and up to two years in jail. (Mich. Comp. Laws Ann., Secs. 750.131 and 750.131a.)

Refunds after Accepting a Check

Anyone giving you a bad check should be notified in writing that the check has been dishonored by the bank and that he or she has five days in which to make payment (including any bank charges and other costs). To aid in prosecution, you should be able to identify the person who gave you the check. To do this you should require identification and write down the sources of identification on the face of the check.

Do not accept postdated checks. If you are going to be accepting a lot of checks, talk to the prosecuting attorney's office in your county about what you will need to do to obtain prosecution of those giving you bad checks.

A popular scam is for a person to purchase something by using a check and then come back the next day demanding a cash refund. After making the refund, the business discovers the initial check bounced. Do not make refunds until checks clear.

CREDIT CARDS

In our buy-now, pay-later society, credit cards can add greatly to your sales potential, especially with large, discretionary purchases. For MasterCard, Visa, and Discover, the fees are about 2% and this amount is easily paid for by the extra purchases that the cards allow.

American Express charges 4% to 5% and you may decide this is not worth paying, since almost everyone who has an American Express card also has another card. You will find that affluent purchasers prefer to use American Express.

For businesses that have a retail outlet, there is usually no problem getting merchant status. Most commercial banks can handle it. Discover can also set you up to accept their card as well as MasterCard and Visa. They will wire the money into your bank account daily.

For mail-order businesses, especially those operating out of the home, it is much harder to get merchant status. This is because of the number of scams in which large amounts are charged, no products are shipped, and the company folds. One good thing about American Express is that it will accept mail-order companies operating out of the home. However, not as many people have its cards as others.

Some companies open a small storefront (or share one) to get merchant status, then process mostly mail orders. The processors usually do not want to accept you if you will do more than 50% of mail orders; but if you do not have many complaints, you may be allowed to process mostly mail orders. Whatever you do, keep your credit customers happy so that they do not complain.

You might be tempted to try to run your charges through another business. This may be okay if you actually sell your products through it, but if you run your business charges through its account, the other business may lose its merchant status. People who bought a book by mail from you and then have a charge on their statement from a florist shop will probably call the credit card company saying that they never bought anything from the florist shop. Too many of these complaints, and the account will be closed.

FINANCING LAWS

Some businesses can more easily make sales if they finance the purchases themselves. If the business has enough capital to do this, it can earn extra profits on the financing terms. However, because of abuses, many consumer protection laws have been passed by both the federal and state governments.

Federal Law   Two important federal laws regarding financing are called the *Truth in Lending Act* and the *Fair Credit Billing Act*. These are implemented by what is called *Regulation Z* (commonly known as *Reg. Z*), issued by the Board of Governors of the Federal Reserve System. It is contained in Volume 12 of the Code of Federal Regulations, page 226. This is a very complicated law and some have said that no business can be sure to be in compliance.

The regulation covers all transactions in which four conditions are met:

1.   credit is offered;

2.   the offering of credit is done regularly;

3.   there is a finance charge for the credit or there is a written agreement with more than four payments; or,

4.   the credit is for personal, family, or household purposes.

It also covers credit card transactions in which only the first two conditions are met. It applies to leases if the consumer ends up paying the full value and keeping the item leased. It does not apply to the following transactions:

✪   transactions with businesses or agricultural purposes;

✪   transactions with organizations such as corporations or the government;

✪   transactions of over $25,000 that are not secured by the consumer's dwelling;

✪   credit involving public utilities;

✪   credit involving securities or commodities; or,

✪   home fuel budget plans.

The way for a small business to avoid Reg. Z violations is to avoid transactions that meet the conditions or to make sure all transactions fall under the exceptions. For many businesses this is easy. Instead of extending credit to customers, accept credit cards and let the credit card company extend the credit. However, if your customers usually do not have credit cards or if you are in a business, such as used car sales, that often extends credit, you should consult a lawyer knowledgeable about Reg. Z.

Michigan Law Michigan also has laws regarding financing arrangements. Anyone engaged in installment sales in Michigan should carefully review the latest versions of the following statutes:

✦ *Retail Installment Sales Act.* (Mich. Comp. Laws Ann., Sec. 445.851.)

✦ *Home Improvement Finance Act.* (Mich. Comp. Laws Ann., Sec. 445.1101.)

✦ *Rental-Purchase Agreement Act.* (Mich. Comp. Laws Ann., Sec. 445.951.)

USURY

Charging an illegally high rate of interest is *usury*. In Michigan, the maximum rate of interest you may charge is 7%. (Mich. Comp. Laws Ann., Sec. 438.31.) However, there are exceptions, such as for credit cards and mortgages. Also, if the borrower is a business, any rate may be charged if agreed to in writing. (Mich. Comp. Laws Ann., Sec. 438.61.)

The penalty for charging in excess of the legal rate is that the borrower does not have to pay any interest or other penalties such as late payment charges and the lender has to pay the borrower's attorney's fees and court costs. (Mich. Comp. Laws Ann., Sec. 438.32.) Anyone charging or receiving interest at a rate of over 25% is guilty of a misdemeanor carrying a penalty of a fine up to $10,000 and up to five years in jail. Possession of usurious loan records carries a penalty of a fine up to $1,000 and up to one year in jail. (Mich. Comp. Laws Ann., Secs. 438.41 and 438.42.)

COLLECTIONS

When trying to collect money you are owed, you need to be careful not to violate any state or federal laws regarding collection practices.

Federal Law   The *Fair Debt Collection Practices Act of 1977* bans the use of deception, harassment, and other unreasonable acts in the collection of debts.

The Federal Trade Commission has issued some rules that prohibit deceptive representations such as pretending to be in the motion picture industry, the government, or a credit bureau, and/or using questionnaires that do not say that they are for the purpose of collecting a debt. (16 C.F.R. Ch. I, Part 237.)

Michigan Law   Debt collection practices are controlled by the provisions of Michigan law. (Mich. Comp. Laws Ann., beginning with Sec. 445.251.) This law forbids:

✪   communicating with a debtor in a misleading or deceptive manner, such as using the stationery of an attorney or credit bureau, unless the person is an attorney or a credit bureau and discloses it is the collection department of the credit bureau;

✪   using forms or instruments that simulate the appearance of a judicial process;

✪   using seals or printed forms of a government agency or instrumentality;

✪   using forms that may otherwise induce the belief that they have judicial or official sanction;

✪   making an inaccurate, misleading, untrue, or deceptive statement or claim in a communication to collect a debt or concealing or not revealing the purpose of a communication when it is made in connection with collecting a debt;

✪   misrepresenting in a communication with a debtor one or more of the following:

• the legal status of a legal action being taken or threatened;

• the legal rights of the creditor or debtor;

• that the nonpayment of a debt will result in the debtor's arrest or imprisonment, or the seizure, garnishment, attachment, or sale of the debtor's property; or,

- that accounts have been turned over to an innocent purchaser for value.

✪ communicating with a debtor without accurately disclosing the caller's identity or causing expenses to the debtor for a long-distance telephone call, telegram, or other charge;

✪ communicating with a debtor, except through billing procedure, when the debtor is actively represented by an attorney, the attorney's name and address are known, and the attorney has been contacted in writing by the credit grantor or the credit grantor's representative or agent, unless the attorney representing the debtor fails to answer written communication or fails to discuss the claim on its merits within thirty days after receipt of the written communication;

✪ communicating information relating to a debtor's indebtedness to an employer or an employer's agent unless the communication is specifically authorized in writing by the debtor subsequent to the forwarding of the claim for collection, the communication is in response to an inquiry initiated by the debtor's employer or the employer's agent, or the communication is for the purpose of acquiring location information about the debtor;

✪ using or employing, in connection with collection of a claim, a person acting as a peace or law enforcement officer or any other officer authorized to serve legal papers;

✪ using or threatening to use physical violence in connection with collection of a claim;

✪ publishing, causing to be published, or threatening to publish lists of debtors, except for credit reporting purposes, when in response to a specific inquiry from a prospective credit grantor about a debtor;

✪ using a shame card, shame automobile, or otherwise bringing to public notice that the consumer is a debtor, except with respect to a legal proceeding that is instituted;

✪ using a harassing, oppressive, or abusive method to collect a debt, including causing a telephone to ring or engaging a person in a telephone conversation repeatedly, continuously, or at unusual times or places that are known to be inconvenient to the debtor. All communications shall be made from 8 a.m. to 9 p.m. unless the debtor expressly agrees in writing to communications at another time. All telephone communications made from 9 p.m. to 8 a.m. shall be presumed to be made at an inconvenient time in the absence of facts to the contrary;

✪ using profane or obscene language;

✪ using a method contrary to a postal law or regulation to collect an account;

✪ failing to implement a procedure designed to prevent a violation by an employee;

✪ communicating with a consumer regarding a debt by postcard; and,

✪ employing a person required to be licensed under the Occupational Code (Mich. Comp. Laws Ann., Sec. 339.901 to 339.916) to collect a claim, unless that person is licensed under the Occupational Code.

The attorney general may issue a *cease and desist order* for violations. An administrative hearing may be requested within thirty days of the effective date of the cease and desist order. Failure to cease and desist can result in a circuit court action, filed by the attorney general, that may result in a fine of up to $500 for each violation. The attorney general may also ask the circuit court to issue an *injunction* (an order that the business stop the illegal activity).

Business Relations Laws

This chapter discusses the numerous federal and Michigan laws governing relations between businesses.

THE UNIFORM COMMERCIAL CODE

The *Uniform Commercial Code* (UCC) is a set of laws regulating numerous aspects of doing business. To avoid having a patchwork of different laws around the fifty states, a national group drafted this set of uniform laws.

Although some states modified some sections of the laws, the code is basically the same in most of the states. In Michigan, the UCC is contained in the statutes. (Mich. Comp. Laws Ann., beginning with Sec. 440.1101.) The UCC is divided into chapters, each of which is concerned with a different aspect of commercial relations such as sales, warranties, bank deposits, commercial paper, and bulk transfers.

Businesses that wish to know their rights in all types of transactions should obtain a copy of the UCC and become familiar with it. It is especially useful in transactions between merchants. However, the meaning is not always clear from a reading of the statutes. In law school, students usually spend a full semester studying each chapter of this law.

UNLAWFUL BUSINESS PRACTICES

While competition between businesses is generally considered healthy and desirable for the economy, certain activities designed to get an advantage over your competition are illegal.

Federal Law   *Robinson-Patman Act of 1936.* This act prohibits businesses from injuring competition by offering the same goods at different prices to different buyers. It also requires that promotional allowances must be made on proportionally the same terms to all buyers.

Sherman Antitrust Act of 1890. This is one of the earliest federal laws affecting business. The purpose of the law was to protect competition in the marketplace by prohibiting monopolies.

Examples of some things that are prohibited are:

  ✪   agreements between competitors to sell at the same prices;

  ✪   agreements between competitors on how much will be sold or produced;

  ✪   agreements between competitors to divide up a market;

  ✪   refusing to sell one product without a second product; or,

  ✪   exchanging information among competitors that results in similarity of prices.

As a new business, you probably will not be in a position to violate the Sherman Antitrust Act, but you should be aware of it in case a larger competitor tries to put you out of business.

Michigan Law   Under the *Michigan Antitrust Reform Act* (beginning with Mich. Comp. Laws Ann., beginning with Sec. 445.771), it is unlawful to have any contract, combination, or conspiracy to restrain trade or to monopolize trade or commerce in a relevant market controlling, fixing, or maintaining prices. The penalty for violation is up to two years in jail and a fine of up to $10,000 for an individual and up to $1,000,000 for other entities. However, no prosecution under this law will be allowed if there is already a prosecution under the federal Sherman Antitrust Act for the same transactions.

INTELLECTUAL PROPERTY PROTECTION

As a business owner you should know enough about intellectual property law to protect your own creations and to keep from violating the rights of others. *Intellectual property* is that which is the product of human creativity, such as writings, designs, inventions, melodies, and processes. They are things that can be stolen without being physically taken. For example, if you write a book, someone can steal the words from your book without stealing a physical copy of it.

As the Internet grows, intellectual property is becoming more valuable. Business owners should take the action necessary to protect their company's intellectual property. Additionally, business owners should know intellectual property law to be sure that they do not violate the rights of others. Even an unknowing violation of the law can result in stiff fines and penalties.

The following are the types of intellectual property and the ways to protect them.

Patent   A *patent* is protection given to new and useful inventions, discoveries, and designs. To be entitled to a patent, a work must be completely *new* and *unobvious*. A patent is granted to the first inventor who files for the patent. Once an invention is patented, no one else can make use of that invention, even if they discover it independently after a lifetime of research. A patent protects an invention for twenty years (for designs it is three-and-a-half, seven, or fourteen years). Patents cannot be renewed. The patent application must clearly explain how to make the invention so that when the patent expires, others will be able to freely make and use the invention. Patents are registered with the United States Patent and Trademark Office (USPTO). Examples of things that would be patentable would be mechanical devices or new drug formulas.

Copyright   A *copyright* is protection given to *original works of authorship*, such as written works, musical works, visual works, performance works, or computer software programs. A copyright exists from the moment of creation, but one cannot register a copyright until it has been fixed in tangible form. Also, one cannot copyright titles, names, or slogans. A copyright currently gives the author and his or her heirs exclusive right to his or her work for the life of the author plus seventy years.

Copyrights first registered before 1978 last for ninety-five years. (This was previously seventy-five years but was extended twenty years to match the European system.) Copyrights are registered with the Register of Copyrights at the Library of Congress. Examples of works that would be copyrightable are books, paintings, songs, poems, plays, drawings, and films.

Trademark

A *trademark* is protection given to a name or symbol that is used to distinguish one person's goods or services from those of others. It can consist of letters, numerals, packaging, labeling, musical notes, colors, or a combination of these. If a trademark is used on services as opposed to goods, it is called a *service mark*.

A trademark lasts indefinitely if it is used continuously and renewed properly. Trademarks are registered with the United States Patent and Trademark Office and with individual states. (This is explained further in Chapter 3.) Examples of trademarks are the *Chrysler* name on automobiles, the red border on TIME Magazine, and the shape of a Coca-Cola bottle.

Trade Secrets

A *trade secret* is information or a process that provides a commercial advantage that is protected by keeping it a secret. Examples of trade secrets may be a list of successful distributors, the formula for Coca-Cola, or some unique source code in a computer program. Trade secrets are not registered anywhere—they are protected by the fact that they are not disclosed. They are protected only for as long as they are kept secret. If you independently discover the formula for Coca-Cola tomorrow, you can freely market it. (But you cannot use the trademark *Coca-Cola* on your product to market it.)

Nonprotectable Creations

Some things are just not protectable. Such things as ideas, systems, and discoveries are not allowed any protection under any law. If you have a great idea, such as selling packets of hangover medicine in bars, you cannot stop others from doing the same thing. If you invent a new medicine, you can patent it; if you pick a distinctive name for it, you can register it as a trademark; if you create a unique picture and instructions for the package, you can copyright them. But you cannot stop others from using your basic business idea of marketing hangover medicine in bars.

Notice the subtle differences between the protective systems available. If you invent something two days after someone else does, you cannot even use it yourself if the other person has patented it. But if you write the same poem as someone else and neither of you copied the other, both of you can copyright the poem. If you patent something, you can have the exclusive rights to it for the term of the patent, but you must disclose how others can make it after the patent expires. However, if you keep it a trade secret, you have exclusive rights as long as no one learns the secret.

We are in a time of transition of the law of intellectual property. Every year new changes are made in the laws and new forms of creativity win protection. For more information, you should consult a new edition of a book on these types of property.

Endless Laws

The state of Michigan and the federal government have numerous laws and rules that apply to every aspect of every type of business. There are laws governing even such things as fence posts, hosiery, rabbit raising, refund policies, frozen desserts, and advertising. Every business is affected by one or another of these laws.

Some activities are covered by both state and federal laws. In such cases you must obey the stricter of the rules. In addition, more than one agency of the state or federal government may have rules governing your business. Each of these may have the power to investigate violations and impose fines or other penalties.

Penalties for violations of these laws can range from a warning to a criminal fine and even jail time. In some cases, employees can sue for damages. Since *ignorance of the law is no excuse*, it is your duty to learn which laws apply to your business, or to risk these penalties.

Very few people in business know the laws that apply to their business. If you take the time to learn them, you can become an expert in your field and avoid problems with regulators. You can also fight back if one of your competitors uses some illegal method to compete with you.

No one could possibly know all the rules that affect business, much less comply with them all. But if you keep up with the important rules, you will stay out of trouble and have more chance of success.

FEDERAL LAWS

The federal laws that are most likely to affect small businesses are rules of the Federal Trade Commission (FTC). The FTC has some rules that affect many businesses such as the rules about labeling, warranties, and mail-order sales. Other rules affect only certain industries.

If you sell goods by mail, send for the booklet *A Business Guide to the Federal Trade Commission's Mail or Telephone Order Merchandise Rule*. If you are going to be involved in a certain industry such as those listed below, or using warranties or your own labeling, you should ask for its latest information on the subject. The address is:

Federal Trade Commission
Washington, DC 20580

The rules of the FTC are contained in the *Code of Federal Regulations* (C.F.R.) in Chapter 16. Some of the industries covered are:

INDUSTRY	PART
Adhesive Compositions	235
Aerosol Products Used for Frosting Cocktail Glasses	417
Automobiles (New car fuel economy advertising)	259
Barber Equipment and Supplies	248
Binoculars	402
Business Opportunities and Franchises	436
Cigarettes	408
Decorative Wall Paneling	243
Dog and Cat Food	241
Dry Cell Batteries	403
Extension Ladders	418
Fallout Shelters	229
Feather and Down Products	253
Fiber Glass Curtains	413
Food (Games of Chance)	419

<u>INDUSTRY</u>	<u>PART</u>
Funerals	453
Gasoline (Octane posting)	306
Gasoline	419
Greeting Cards	244
Home Entertainment Amplifiers	432
Home Insulation	460
Hosiery	22
Household Furniture	250
Jewelry	23
Ladies' Handbags	247
Law Books	256
Light Bulbs	409
Luggage and Related Products	24
Mail Order Insurance	234
Mail Order Merchandise	435
Men's and Boys' Tailored Clothing	412
Metallic Watch Band	19
Mirrors	21
Nursery	18
Ophthalmic Practices	456
Photographic Film and Film Processing	242
Private Vocational and Home Study Schools	254
Radiation Monitoring Instruments	232
Retail Food Stores (Advertising)	424
Shell Homes	230
Shoes	231
Sleeping Bags	400
Tablecloths and Related Products	404
Television Sets	410
Textile Wearing Apparel	423
Textiles	236
Tires	228
Used Automobile Parts	20
Used Lubricating Oil	406
Used Motor Vehicles	455
Waist Belts	405
Watches	245
Wigs and Hairpieces	252

Some other federal laws that affect businesses are as follows:

- ✪ *Alcohol Administration Act*

- ✪ *Americans with Disabilities Act* (see Chapter 11)

- ✪ *Child Protection and Toy Safety Act* (1969)

- ✪ *Clean Water Act*

- ✪ *Comprehensive Smokeless Tobacco Health Education Act* (1986)

- ✪ *Consumer Credit Protection Act* (1968)

- ✪ *Consumer Product Safety Act* (1972)

- ✪ *Energy Policy and Conservation Act*

- ✪ *Environmental Pesticide Control Act of 1972*

- ✪ *Fair Credit Reporting Act* (1970)

- ✪ *Fair Packaging and Labeling Act* (1966)

- ✪ *Flammable Fabrics Act* (1953)

- ✪ *Food, Drug, and Cosmetic Act*

- ✪ *Food Safety Enforcement Enhancement Act of 1997*

- ✪ *Fur Products Labeling Act* (1951)

- ✪ *Hazardous Substances Act* (1960)

- ✪ *Hobby Protection Act*

- ✪ *Insecticide, Fungicide, and Rodenticide Act*

- ✪ *Magnuson-Moss Warranty Act*

- ✪ *Nutrition Labeling and Education Act of 1990*

- ✪ *Poison Prevention Packaging Act of 1970*

- ✪ *Solid Waste Disposal Act*

- ✪ *Textile Fiber Products Identification Act*

- ✪ *Toxic Substance Control Act*

- ✪ *Wool Products Labeling Act* (1939)

MICHIGAN LAWS

Michigan has numerous laws regulating specific types of professions, businesses, or certain activities of businesses. Many of these are listed in Chapter 6. Even if your profession or business is not regulated, as a part of your business operation you may engage in some kind of activity that is regulated or subject to some kind of legal restrictions. The three best sources of information to avoid problems are the trade organization for your type of business, the various state and local governmental agencies with whom you come in contact, and the index to the *Michigan Compiled Laws Annotated*.

Bookkeeping and Accounting

It is beyond the scope of this book to explain all the intricacies of setting up a business's bookkeeping and accounting systems. However, if you do not set up an understandable bookkeeping system, your business will undoubtedly fail.

Without accurate records of where your income is coming from and where it is going, you will be unable to increase your profits, lower your expenses, obtain needed financing, or make the right decisions in all areas of your business. The time to decide how you will handle your bookkeeping is when you open your business, not a year later when it is tax time.

INITIAL BOOKKEEPING

If you do not understand business taxation, you should pick up a good book on the subject as well as the IRS tax guide for your type of business (proprietorship, partnership, or corporation). The IRS tax book for small businesses is Publication 334, *Tax Guide for Small Business*. There are also instruction booklets for each type of business's form: Schedule C for proprietorships, Form 1120 or 1120S for C corporations and S corporations, and 1165 for partnerships and businesses that are taxed like partnerships (LLCs and LLPs).

Keep in mind that the IRS does not give you the best advice for saving on taxes and does not give you the other side of contested issues. For that you need a private tax guide or advisor.

The most important thing to do is to set up your bookkeeping so that you can easily fill out your monthly, quarterly, and annual tax returns. The best way to do this is to get copies of the returns, note the totals that you will need to supply, and set up your bookkeeping system to group those totals.

For example, for a sole proprietorship you will use Schedule C to report business income and expenses to the IRS at the end of the year. Use the categories on that form to sort your expenses. To make your job especially easy, every time you pay a bill, put the category number on the check.

ACCOUNTANTS

Most likely your new business will not be able to afford hiring an accountant to handle your books, but that is good. Doing them yourself will force you to learn about business accounting and taxation. The worst way to run a business is to know nothing about the tax laws and turn everything over to an accountant at the end of the year to find out what is due.

You should know the basics of tax law before making basic decisions such as whether to buy or rent equipment or a premises. You should understand accounting so you can time your financial affairs appropriately. If you were a boxer who only needed to win fights, you could turn everything over to an accountant. If your business needs to buy supplies, inventory, or equipment and provides goods or services throughout the year, you need to at least have a basic understanding of the system you are working within.

Once you can afford an accountant, weigh the cost against your time and the risk that you will make an error. Even if you think you know enough to do your own corporate tax return, you might take it to an accountant one year to see if you have been missing any deductions that you did not know about. You might decide that the money saved is worth the cost of the accountant's services.

COMPUTER PROGRAMS

Today, every business should keep its books by computer. There are inexpensive programs such as Quicken that can instantly provide you with reports of your income and expenses and the right figures to plug into your tax returns. Most programs offer a tax program each year that will take all of your information and print it out on the current year's tax forms.

TAX TIPS

Here are a few tax tips that may help businesses save money.

- ✪ Usually when you buy equipment for a business you must *amortize* the cost over several years. That is, you do not deduct the entire cost when you buy it, but take, say, 25% of the cost off your taxes each year for four years. (The time is determined by the theoretical usefulness of the item.) However, small businesses are allowed to write off the entire cost of a limited amount of items under Internal Revenue Code, Section 179. If you have income to shelter, use it.

- ✪ Owners of S corporations do not have to pay Social Security or Medicare taxes on the part of their profits that is not considered salary. As long as you pay yourself a reasonable salary, other money you take out is not subject to these taxes.

- ✪ Do not neglect to deposit withholding taxes for your own salary or profits. Besides being a large sum to come up with at once in April, there are penalties that must be paid for failure to do so.

- ✪ Be sure to keep track of, and remit, your employees' withholding. You will be personally liable for them even if your business is a corporation.

- ✪ If you keep track of your use of your car for business, you can deduct mileage (see IRS guidelines for the amount, as it can change each year). If you use your car for business a considerable amount of the time, you may be able to depreciate it.

✪ If your business is a corporation and if you designate the stock as *section 1244 stock*, then if the business fails you are able to get a much better deduction for the loss.

✪ By setting up a retirement plan you can exempt up to 20% of your salary from income tax. But do not use money you might need later. There are penalties for taking it out of the retirement plan.

✪ When you buy things that will be resold or made into products that will be resold (i.e., you are buying from a wholesaler), you do not have to pay sales tax on those purchases.

chapter 17

Paying Federal Taxes

All businesses need to be concerned with one or more types of federal taxes. In this chapter we will discuss the federal income tax, withholding of taxes from employee paychecks, federal excise taxes, and federal unemployment compensation taxes.

FEDERAL INCOME TAX

The manner in which each type of business pays taxes is as follows.

Proprietorship   An individual reports profits and expenses on Schedule C attached to the usual Form 1040 and pays tax on all of the net income of the business. Each quarter, Form ES-1040 must be filed along with payment of one-quarter of the amount of income tax and Social Security taxes estimated to be due for the year.

Partnership   A partnership files a return showing the income and expenses but pays no tax. Each partner is given a form showing his or her share of the profits or losses and reports these on Schedule E of Form 1040. Each quarter, Form ES-1040 must be filed by each partner along with payment of one-quarter of the amount of income tax and Social Security taxes estimated to be due for the year.

C Corporation   A regular corporation is a separate taxpayer and pays tax on its profits after deducting all expenses, including officers' salaries. If dividends are distributed, they are paid out of after-tax dollars and the shareholders pay tax a second time when they receive the dividends. If a corporation needs to accumulate money for investment, it may be able to do so at lower tax rates than the shareholders. But if all profits will be distributed to shareholders, the double-taxation may be excessive unless all income is paid as salaries. A C corporation files Form 1120.

S Corporation

A small corporation has the option of being taxed like a partnership. If Form 2553 is filed by the corporation and accepted by the Internal Revenue Service, the S corporation will only file an informational return listing profits and expenses. Then each shareholder will be taxed on a proportional share of the profits (or be able to deduct a proportional share of the losses). Unless a corporation will make a large profit that will not be distributed, S status is usually best in the beginning.

An S corporation files Form 1120S and distributes Form K-1 to each shareholder. If any money is taken out by a shareholder that is not listed as wages subject to withholding, then the shareholder will usually have to file Form ES-1040 each quarter, along with payment of the estimated withholding on the withdrawals.

Limited Liability Company

Limited liability companies will, in most cases, be taxed as partnerships, passing on their income and losses to the owners. However, if the entity has too many corporate attributes, it may be taxed as a corporation.

Tax Workshops and Booklets

The IRS offers publications, recorded information, online workshops, and occasionally conducts live workshops to inform businesses about the tax laws. (Do not expect an in-depth study of the loopholes.) Publications may be obtained by calling 800-829-3676. You may want to obtain some of the following publications.

PUBLICATION	TITLE
334	Tax Guide for Small Business
505	Tax Withholding and Estimated Tax
541	Partnerships
542	Corporations
583	Starting a Business and Keeping Records
910	IRS Guide to Free Tax Services

To find out about live workshops or to utilize online workshops, go to **www.irs.gov/businesses/small/index.html**. You can speak with an IRS representative at 800-829-1040, however, it can be difficult to get through at times. You may also want to visit or contact one of the following local IRS offices. Office hours are 8:30 a.m. to 4:30 p.m., Monday through Friday, unless otherwise indicated. The phone numbers will give recorded information.

IRS LOCAL OFFICES

Detroit:
477 Michigan Avenue
Detroit, MI 48226
313-628-3722

Flint:
815 South Saginaw
Flint, MI 48502
810-342-6190

Grand Rapids:
678 Front Avenue NW
Grand Rapids, MI 49504
616-235-2390

Marquette:
1055 West Baraga Avenue
Marquette, MI 49855
906-228-7845
(Closed for lunch from 12:30 p.m. to 1:30 p.m.)

Saginaw:
4901 Town Centre
Saginaw, MI 48604
989-797-8560

Traverse City:
2040 North US-31 South
Traverse City, MI 49684
231-932-2192
(Closed for lunch from 12:30 p.m. to 1:30 p.m.)

FEDERAL WITHHOLDING, SOCIAL SECURITY, AND MEDICARE TAXES

If you need basic information on business tax returns, the IRS publishes a rather large booklet that answers most questions and is available for free. Call, write, or go online and obtain Publication No. 334, *Tax Guide for Small Business.* You should be able to find an IRS toll-free number in the phone book under U. S. Government/Internal Revenue Service. If you want more creative answers and tax saving information, find a good local accountant or tax attorney. To get started you will need the following.

Employer Identification Number

If you are a sole proprietor with no employees, you can use your Social Security number for your business. If you have employees or are a corporation or partnership, you must obtain an *employer identification number* by filing **APPLICATION FOR EMPLOYER IDENTIFICATION NUMBER (IRS FORM SS-4)**. (see form 2, p.191.) In about three weeks you will get your number, which you will need to open bank accounts for the business. A sample filled-in form may be found in Appendix B. A blank form with instructions is in Appendix C.

If you need a number quickly, you may obtain one by calling 800-829-4933, Monday through Friday, between 7:30 a.m. and 5:30 p.m. local time. You must have your **IRS FORM SS-4** filled out before you call and you will still need to mail or fax the form with your number on it. You can fax it to 800-669-5760 between 10:00 a.m. and 5:30 p.m. If you mail it in, send it to:

Internal Revenue Service
Cincinnati Accounts Management Campus
Attn: EIN Operations
Cincinnati, OH 45999

You can also get your EIN immediately online at the following IRS website:

https://sa1.www4.irs.gov/modiein/individual/index.jsp

Employee's Withholding Allowance Certificate

You must have each employee fill out an **EMPLOYEE'S WITHHOLDING ALLOWANCE CERTIFICATE (IRS FORM W-4)** to calculate the amount of federal taxes to be deducted and to obtain their Social Security numbers. (The number of allowances on this form is used with IRS Circular E, Publication 15, to figure out the exact deductions.) A sample filled-in form may be found in Appendix B. A blank form is in Appendix C. (see form 5, p.209.)

Federal Tax Deposit Coupon

After taking withholdings from employees' wages, you must deposit them at a bank that is authorized to accept such funds. If, at the end of any month, you have over $1,000 in withheld taxes (including your contribution to FICA), you must make a deposit prior to the 15th of the following month. If, on the 3rd, 7th, 11th, 19th, 22nd, or 25th of any month, you have over $3,000 in withheld taxes, you must make a deposit within three banking days. The deposit is made using the coupons in the Form 8109 booklet supplied by the IRS.

Estimated Tax Payment Voucher

Sole proprietors and partners often take money from their businesses without the formality of withholding. However, they are still required to make deposits of income and FICA taxes each quarter. If more than $500 is due in April on a person's 1040 form, then not enough money was withheld each quarter and a penalty is assessed unless the person falls into an exception.

The quarterly withholding is submitted on Form 1040-ES on the 15th of April, June, September, and January of each year. If these days fall on a weekend, then the due date is the following Monday. The worksheet with Form 1040-ES can be used to determine the amount to pay.

NOTE*: One of the exceptions to the rule is that if you withhold the same amount as last year's tax bill, you do not have to pay a penalty. This is usually a lot easier than filling out the 1040-ES worksheet.*

Employer's Quarterly Tax Return

Each quarter you must file Form 941, reporting your federal withholding and FICA taxes. If you owe more than $1,000 at the end of the quarter, you are required to make a deposit at the end of the month in which you have $1,000 in withholding. The deposits are made to the Federal Reserve Bank or an authorized financial institution on Form 501. Most banks are authorized to accept deposits. If you owe more than $3,000 for any month, you must make a deposit at any point in the month in which you owe $3,000. After you file **IRS FORM SS-4**, the 941 forms will be sent to you automatically if you checked the box saying that you expect to have employees.

Wage and Tax Statement

At the end of each year, you are required to issue a W-2 form to each employee. This form shows the amount of wages paid to the employee during the year, as well as the amounts withheld for taxes, Social Security, Medicare, and other deductions.

Miscellaneous Income

If you pay at least $600 to a person other than an employee (such as an independent contractor), you must file a Form 1099 for that person, along with Form 1096, which is a summary sheet. Many people are not aware of this law and fail to file these forms, but they are required for such things as services, royalties, rents, awards, and prizes that you pay to individuals (but not to corporations). The rules for this are quite complicated, so either obtain *Package 1099* from the IRS or consult your accountant.

Earned Income Credit

Persons who are not liable to pay income tax may have the right to a check from the government because of the *Earned Income Credit*. You are required to notify your employees of this. You can satisfy this requirement with one of the following:

- ✪ a W-2 Form with the notice on the back;

- ✪ a substitute for the W-2 with a notice on it;

- ✪ a copy of Notice 797; or,

- ✪ a written statement with the wording from Notice 797.

A Notice 797 can be obtained by calling 800-829-3676.

FEDERAL EXCISE TAXES

Excise taxes are taxes on certain activities or items. Most federal excise taxes have been eliminated since World War II, but a few remain. Some things that are subject to federal excise taxes are tobacco, alcohol, gasoline, tires and inner tubes, some trucks and trailers, firearms, ammunition, bows, arrows, fishing equipment, the use of highway vehicles over 55,000 pounds, aircraft, wagering, telephone and teletype services, coal, hazardous wastes, and vaccines. If you are involved in any of these, you should obtain the IRS Publication 510, *Excise Taxes*.

UNEMPLOYMENT COMPENSATION TAXES

You must pay federal unemployment taxes if you paid wages of $1,500 or more in any quarter, or if you had at least one employee for twenty calendar weeks. The federal tax amount is 0.8% of the first $7,000 of wages paid each employee. If more than $100 is due by the end of any quarter (if you paid $12,500 in wages for the quarter), then IRS Form 508 must be filed with an authorized financial institution or the Federal Reserve Bank in your area. You will receive IRS Form 508 when you obtain your employer identification number.

You must file Form 940 or Form 940EZ at the end of each year as your annual report of federal unemployment taxes. The IRS will send you the form. For more information, call the IRS at 800-829-1040.

NOTE: *There are also state unemployment compensation taxes that are discussed in the next chapter.*

Paying Michigan Taxes

Depending upon the details of your particular business, you may need to be concerned with several types of Michigan taxes (i.e., sales, use, single business, motor fuel, and tobacco products taxes). You will need to complete a **REGISTRATION FOR MICHIGAN TAXES** form if any of these taxes apply to your business. (see form 6, p.211.) A copy of the registration form, completed for a fictional business, may be found in Appendix B, and a blank form with instructions is contained in Appendix C.

Approximately four to six weeks after you file your registration form, you will receive your tax license and any necessary reporting forms. The Michigan Department of Treasury has forms available by calling 800-367-6263, and can provide general information at 517-636-4660 or treasReg@michigan.gov. You can also obtain information through the Department of Treasury websites at **www.michigan.gov/taxes** and **www.michigan.gov/treasury**.

If you have employees, you will also need to be concerned with the Michigan unemployment tax and withholding state income tax from your employees' paychecks. This chapter provides you with a summary of information about each of these taxes.

Finally, if you receive income that is not wages, you will need to file quarterly tax estimates of both Michigan and federal income taxes.

SALES AND USE TAX

If you will be selling goods at retail, you must register and collect Michigan Sales Tax. This applies to personal property sold to the end user from a location in Michigan.

You will need to register and collect Michigan Use Tax if you:

- ✪ lease tangible personal property in Michigan;

- ✪ sell telecommunication services;

- ✪ provide transient hotel or motel room rentals;

- ✪ buy goods for your own use from an out-of-state unlicensed vendor; or,

- ✪ launder or clean textiles under a sole rental or service agreement with a term of at least five days.

If the Use Tax applies to you, the Sales Tax does not. At the time of the publication of this book, the system of taxing businesses in Michigan is being re-evaluated because of the expiration of the Michigan Single Business Tax law on December 31, 2007.

For more information on the sales and use tax, visit **www.michigan.gov/taxes**; email treasSUW@michigan.gov; or, call 517-636-4730.

MICHIGAN BUSINESS TAX

Michigan has just instituted a new tax scheme for businesses, effective January 1, 2008, which replaces the old *Michigan Single Business Tax* (SBT). The new tax is called the *Michigan Business Tax* (MBT); however, just like the old SBT, it only applies to businesses with gross receipts in excess of $350,000. The MBT is actually made up of several different taxes. These are a business income tax, a modified gross receipts tax, and specific separate taxes for insurance companies and financial institutions. The business income tax is imposed on the business income of all taxpayers (not just corporations) with business activity in Michigan, subject to the limitations of federal law. Business income is defined as "that part of federal taxable income derived from business activity."

Of course, there are numerous credits, exclusions, apportionments, and limitations to complicate things. If you expect gross receipts in excess of $350,000, you definitely need an accountant. Your accountant can determine if you need to be concerned about this tax. For more information about the Michigan Business Tax, or the current status of any new tax legislation, visit the Michigan Department of Treasury websites at **www.michigan.gov/treasury** or **www.michigan.gov/taxes**, or call 517-636-4700.

MOTOR FUEL TAX

You will need to register to the Michigan Motor Fuel Tax if you:

- ✪ operate a terminal or refinery for gasoline, diesel, or aviation fuel, or import from a foreign country;

- ✪ transport fuel across a Michigan border for hire;

- ✪ are a position holder in a fuel terminal;

- ✪ sell diesel fuel for use in watercraft;

- ✪ sell liquefied propane gas (LPG) for highway use;

- ✪ sell aviation fuel for resale; or,

- ✪ operate a diesel-powered vehicle for transport across Michigan's borders having three or more axles, or having two axles and a gross vehicle weight of over 26,000 pounds.

For more information on the Motor Fuel Tax, visit **www.michigan.gov/taxes**; email TreasMotFuel@michigan.gov; or, call 517-636-4600.

TOBACCO PRODUCTS TAX

You will need to register for the Michigan Tobacco Products Tax if you:

- ✪ sell cigarettes or other tobacco products for resale (i.e., as a wholesaler);

- ✪ purchase any tobacco products from unlicensed out-of-state sources; or,

- ✪ sell cigarettes or other tobacco products in a vending machine.

For more information on the Tobacco Products Tax, visit **www.michigan.gov/ taxes**; email treas_TobaccoTaxes@michigan.gov; or, call 517-636-4630.

MICHIGAN UNEMPLOYMENT TAX

You will need to register for the Michigan Unemployment Tax if you:

- ✪ have employees performing services in Michigan;

- ✪ plan to have employees working in Michigan; or,

- ✪ have acquired all or any part of the assets, organization, or trade of an existing business having employees in Michigan.

For more information on the Unemployment Tax, visit the Department of Treasury's website at **www.michigan.gov/treasury**.

MICHIGAN INCOME TAX WITHHOLDING

You must register for withholding of Michigan income tax from the paychecks of your employees, just as you withhold federal income tax and Social Security. For information about registering, contact one of the field offices listed below; call the Department of Treasury's main office at 517-636-4730; email them at treasSUW@michigan.gov; or, visit **www.michigan.gov/taxes**.

Michigan Department of Treasury Tax Offices

The Department of Treasury maintains several local offices, although they only provide limited services. It is suggested that you call first, to be sure you can get the services you seek. The local offices are at the following locations:

Detroit:
Cadillac Plaza, Suite 2-200
3060 West Grand Boulevard
Detroit, MI 48202
313-456-4340

Escanaba:
State Office Building, Room 7
305 Ludington Street
Escanaba, MI 49829
906-786-6339
(open 8 a.m.–12 noon)

Flint:
State Office Building, 7th Floor
125 E. Union Street
Flint, MI 48502
810-760-2782

Grand Rapids:
State Office Building
350 Ottawa Street, NW
Grand Rapids, MI 49503
616-356-0300

Lansing Operations Center:
7285 Parsons Drive
Dimondale, MI 48821
517-636-5265
(need appointment)

Sterling Heights:
41300 Dequindre, Suite 200
Sterling Heights, MI 48314
586-997-0801

Traverse City:
701 South Elmwood Avenue, Suite 1
Traverse City, MI 49684
231-922-5244
(open 8 a.m.–12 noon)

Local Income Tax Withholding   A few Michigan cities and counties (such as Detroit and Wayne County) have their own income tax, so be sure to check with your city or county government.

Out-of-State Taxes

In addition to federal and Michigan taxes, you may also need to be concerned with taxes that other states, and Canada, seek to impose in certain circumstances.

STATE SALES TAXES

In 1992, the United States Supreme Court struck a blow for the rights of small businesses by ruling that state tax authorities cannot force them to collect sales taxes on interstate mail orders (*Quill Corporation v. North Dakota*). Unfortunately, the court left open the possibility that Congress could allow interstate taxation of mail-order sales, and since then several bills have been introduced that would do so.

At present, companies are only required to collect sales taxes for states in which they *do business*. Exactly what amount of business is enough to trigger taxation is a legal question and some states try to define it as broadly as possible.

If you have an office in a state, clearly you are doing business there and any goods shipped to consumers in the state are subject to sales taxes. If you have a full-time employee working in the state much of the year, many states will consider you to be doing business there. In some states, attending a two-day trade show is enough business to trigger taxation for the entire year for every order shipped to the state. One loophole that often works is to be represented at shows by persons who are not your employees.

Because the laws are different in each state, you will have to do some research on a state-by-state basis to find out how much business you can do in a state without being subject to its taxation. You can request a state's rules from its department of revenue, but keep in mind that what a department of revenue wants the law to be is not always what the courts will rule that it is.

BUSINESS TAXES

Even worse than being subject to a state's sales taxes is to be subject to its income or other business taxes. For example, California charges every company doing business in the state a minimum $800 a year fee and charges income tax on a portion of the company's worldwide income. Doing a small amount of business in the state is clearly not worth getting mired in California taxation.

For this reason, some trade shows have been moved from the state, which has resulted in a review of the tax policies and some *safe-harbor* guidelines to advise companies on what they can do without becoming subject to taxation.

Write to the department of revenue of any state in which you have business contacts to see what might trigger your taxation.

INTERNET TAXES

State revenue departments are drooling at the prospect of taxing commerce on the Internet. Theories have already been proposed that websites available to state residents mean a company is doing business in a state. Fortunately, Congress has passed a moratorium on taxation of the Internet.

CANADIAN TAXES

The Canadian government expects American companies that sell goods by mail order to Canadians to collect taxes for them and file returns with Revenue Canada, its tax department. Those who receive an occasional unsolicited order are not expected to register and Canadian customers who order things from the United States pay the tax plus a $5 fee upon receipt of the goods. But companies that solicit Canadian orders are expected to be registered if their worldwide income is $30,000 or more per year. In some cases a company may be required to post a bond and to pay for the cost of Canadian auditors visiting its premises and auditing its books. For these reasons, you may notice that some companies decline to accept orders from Canada.

The End...and the Beginning

If you have read through this whole book, you know more about the rules and laws for operating a Michigan business than most people in business today. But after learning about all of the governmental regulations you may become discouraged. You are probably wondering how you can keep track of all the laws and how you will have any time left to make money after complying with the laws. But it is not that bad. People are starting businesses every day and they are making money.

With this book as your guide, you should be able to navigate business law and make your business thrive.

Glossary

A

acceptance. Agreeing to the terms of an offer and creating a contract.

articles of incorporation. A legal document filed with the state government to set up a corporation.

articles of organization. A legal document filed with the state government to set up a limited liability company.

assumed name. A name under which a person, corporation, or other business entity conducts business.

B

bait and switch. An illegal business practice in which one item is advertised for sale to entice a customer into the store, then the customer is told that product is no longer available and the store tries to sell the customer a different (usually more expensive) product.

blue sky laws. A common name for laws regulating investments and securities.

bulk sales. Selling substantially all of a company's inventory.

C

C corporation. A corporation that pays taxes on its profits.

certificate of limited partnership. A legal document filed with the state government to register a limited partnership.

collections. The collection of money owed to a business.

common law. Laws that are determined in court cases rather than statutes.

consideration. The exchange of value or promises in a contract.

contract. A legally binding agreement between two or more parties.

copyright. Legal protection given to original works of authorship.

corporation. An artificial person that is set up to conduct a business owned by shareholders and run by officers and directors.

D

d/b/a. Abbreviation for *doing business as.*

deceptive pricing. Pricing goods or services in a manner intended to deceive the customers.

discrimination. The choosing among various options based on their characteristics.

domain name. A name used and registered for conducting business on the Internet.

E

employee. A person who works for another under that person's control and direction.

endorsements. Positive statements about goods or services.

excise tax. A tax paid on the sale or consumption of goods or services.

express warranty. A specific guarantee of a product or service.

F

fictitious name. *See* assumed name.

G

general partner. A partner in a limited partnership who has authority to engage in operating the business.

goods. Items of personal property.

guarantee. A promise of the quality of a good or service.

H

home solicitation. When a salesperson comes to a customer's home seeking to sell products or services.

I

implied warranty. A guarantee of a product or service that is not specifically made, but can be implied from the circumstances of the sale.

independent contractor. A person who works for another as a separate business, not as an employee.

intellectual property. Legal rights to the products of the mind, such as writings, musical compositions, formulas, and designs.

L

liability. The legal responsibility to pay for an injury.

limited liability company. An entity recognized as a legal person that is set up to conduct a business owned and run by members.

limited liability partnership. An entity recognized as a legal person that is set up to conduct a business owned and run by members that is set up for professionals such as attorneys or doctors.

limited partner. A partner in a limited partnership who is in the position of an investor and has no authority to engage in operating the business.

limited warranty. A guarantee covering certain aspects of a good or service.

M

merchant. A person who is in business.

merchant's firm offer. An offer by a business made under specific terms.

N

nonprofit corporation. An entity recognized as a legal person that is set up to run an operation in which none of the profits are distributed to controlling members.

O

occupational license. A government-issued permit to transact business.

offer. A proposal to enter into a contract.

P

partnership. A business formed by two or more persons.

patent. Protection given to inventions, discoveries, and designs.

personal property. Any type of property other than land and the structures attached to it.

R

real property. Land and the structures attached to it.

Regulation Z (Reg. Z). A complex federal regulation governing interest rate disclosures by lenders to borrowers.

S

sale on approval. Selling an item with the agreement that it may be brought back and the sale cancelled.

service mark. A mark used to identify the provider of certain services.

SCORE. Acronym for *Service Corps of Retired Executives*, which is a group of retired business executives who volunteer to give advice to new small business owners.

S corporation. A corporation that is taxed as a partnership under IRS rules.

securities. Interests in a business such as stocks or bonds.

sexual harassment. Activity that causes an employee to feel or be sexually threatened.

shares. Units of stock in a corporation.

sole proprietorship. A business owned by an individual.

statute of frauds. Laws requiring that certain types of contracts be in writing in order to be binding on the parties.

sublease. An agreement to rent premises from an existing tenant.

T

trade name. A name used to identify the manufacturer of a product or group of products.

trademark. A distinguishing mark used to identify the manufacturer of a product or group of products.

U

unemployment compensation. Payments to a former employee who was terminated from a job for a reason not based on his or her fault.

Uniform Commercial Code (UCC). A set of laws that apply to commercial business transactions.

usury. An illegally high rate of interest charged on a loan.

W

whistleblower. An employee who reports a violation of law or regulation by his or her employer to a government agency.

withholding. Money taken out of an employee's salary and remitted to the government.

workers' compensation. A system of compensating employees for job-related injuries.

Business Start-Up Checklist

This checklist will help you to organize your start-up procedures. Refer to the text of the chapters if you have any questions on the items appearing here.

BUSINESS START-UP CHECKLIST

❑ Make your plan
    ❑ Obtain and read all relevant publications on your type of business
    ❑ Obtain and read all laws and regulations affecting your business
    ❑ Calculate a plan to produce a profit
    ❑ Plan sources of capital
    ❑ Plan sources of goods or services
    ❑ Plan marketing efforts
❑ Choose the form of your business
    ❑ Prepare and file organizational papers (incorporation, LLC, etc.)
    ❑ Prepare and file assumed name registration
❑ Choose your business name
    ❑ Check other business names and trademarks
    ❑ Register your business name, trademark, etc.
❑ Choose the location
    ❑ Check competitors
    ❑ Check zoning
❑ Obtain necessary licenses
    ❑ City   ❑ County   ❑ State   ❑ Federal
❑ Arrange for telephone service
❑ Choose a bank
    ❑ Checking account
    ❑ Credit card processing
    ❑ Loans
❑ Obtain necessary or desired insurance
    ❑ Workers' compensation   ❑ Automobile
    ❑ Liability   ❑ Health
    ❑ Hazard   ❑ Life/disability
❑ File necessary federal and state tax registrations
❑ Set up bookkeeping system
❑ Plan your hiring
    ❑ Obtain required posters
    ❑ Prepare employment application
    ❑ Prepare employment policies
    ❑ Determine compliance with health and safety laws
❑ Plan your opening
    ❑ Obtain necessary equipment and supplies
    ❑ Obtain necessary inventory
    ❑ Marketing and publicity
    ❑ Obtain necessary forms, agreements, etc.
    ❑ Prepare company policies on refunds, exchanges, returns, etc.

Sample, Filled-In Forms

The following forms are samples of *some* of the forms that appear in Appendix C.

Form **SS-4**
(Rev. July 2007)
Department of the Treasury
Internal Revenue Service

Application for Employer Identification Number

(For use by employers, corporations, partnerships, trusts, estates, churches, government agencies, Indian tribal entities, certain individuals, and others.)

▶ See separate instructions for each line.   ▶ Keep a copy for your records.

OMB No. 1545-0003

EIN

1 Legal name of entity (or individual) for whom the EIN is being requested	
Doe Company	

2 Trade name of business (if different from name on line 1)		**3** Executor, administrator, trustee, "care of" name	
123 Main Street			

4a Mailing address (room, apt., suite no. and street, or P.O. box)		**5a** Street address (if different) (Do not enter a P.O. box.)	
Lansing, MI 48910			
4b City, state, and ZIP code (if foreign, see instructions)		**5b** City, state, and ZIP code (if foreign, see instructions)	
Lansing, Michigan			

6 County and state where principal business is located
John Doe

7a Name of principal officer, general partner, grantor, owner, or trustor	**7b** SSN, ITIN, or EIN	
	123-45-6789	

8a Is this application for a limited liability company (LLC) (or a foreign equivalent)? . . . . ☐ Yes ☒ No   **8b** If 8a is "Yes," enter the number of LLC members . . . . . ▶

8c If 8a is "Yes," was the LLC organized in the United States? . . . . ☐ Yes ☐ No

9a **Type of entity** (check only one box). **Caution.** If 8a is "Yes," see the instructions for the correct box to check.

☐ Sole proprietor (SSN) _____
☒ Partnership
☐ Corporation (enter form number to be filed) ▶ _____
☐ Personal service corporation
☐ Church or church-controlled organization
☐ Other nonprofit organization (specify) ▶ _____
☐ Other (specify) ▶

☐ Estate (SSN of decedent) _____
☐ Plan administrator (TIN) _____
☐ Trust (TIN of grantor) _____
☐ National Guard   ☐ State/local government
☐ Farmers' cooperative   ☐ Federal government/military
☐ REMIC   ☐ Indian tribal governments/enterprises
Group Exemption Number (GEN) if any ▶

9b If a corporation, name the state or foreign country (if applicable) where incorporated	State	Foreign country

10 **Reason for applying** (check only one box)

☒ Started new business (specify type) ▶ _____
   clothing manufacturing
☐ Hired employees (Check the box and see line 13.)
☐ Compliance with IRS withholding regulations
☐ Other (specify) ▶

☐ Banking purpose (specify purpose) ▶ _____
☐ Changed type of organization (specify new type) ▶ _____
☐ Purchased going business
☐ Created a trust (specify type) ▶ _____
☐ Created a pension plan (specify type) ▶ _____

11 Date business started or acquired (month, day, year). See instructions.	**12** Closing month of accounting year December	
07-01-07	**14** Do you expect your employment tax liability to be $1,000 or less in a full calendar year? ☐ Yes ☐ No (If you expect to pay $4,000 or less in total wages in a full calendar year, you can mark "Yes.")	

13 Highest number of employees expected in the next 12 months (enter -0- if none).

Agricultural	Household	Other
		3

15 First date wages or annuities were paid (month, day, year). **Note.** If applicant is a withholding agent, enter date income will first be paid to nonresident alien (month, day, year) . . . . ▶ 07-15-07

16 Check **one** box that best describes the principal activity of your business.

☐ Construction   ☐ Rental & leasing   ☐ Transportation & warehousing   ☐ Health care & social assistance   ☐ Wholesale-agent/broker
☐ Real estate   ☒ Manufacturing   ☐ Finance & insurance   ☐ Accommodation & food service   ☐ Wholesale-other   ☐ Retail
☐ Other (specify)

17 Indicate principal line of merchandise sold, specific construction work done, products produced, or services provided.
clothing

18 Has the applicant entity shown on line 1 ever applied for and received an EIN? ☐ Yes ☐ No
If "Yes," write previous EIN here ▶

Third Party Designee	Complete this section **only** if you want to authorize the named individual to receive the entity's EIN and answer questions about the completion of this form.	
	Designee's name	Designee's telephone number (include area code) ( )
	Address and ZIP code	Designee's fax number (include area code) ( )

Under penalties of perjury, I declare that I have examined this application, and to the best of my knowledge and belief, it is true, correct, and complete.

	Applicant's telephone number (include area code)
Name and title (type or print clearly) ▶ John Doe, Partner	( )
	Applicant's fax number (include area code)
Signature ▶ Date ▶	( )

For Privacy Act and Paperwork Reduction Act Notice, see separate instructions.   Cat. No. 16055N   Form **SS-4** (Rev. 7-2007)

Do I Need an EIN?

File Form SS-4 if the applicant entity does not already have an EIN but is required to show an EIN on any return, statement, or other document.[1] See also the separate instructions for each line on Form SS-4.

IF the applicant...	AND...	THEN...
Started a new business	Does not currently have (nor expect to have) employees	Complete lines 1, 2, 4a–8a, 8b–c (if applicable), 9a, 9b (if applicable), and 10–14 and 16–18.
Hired (or will hire) employees, including household employees	Does not already have an EIN	Complete lines 1, 2, 4a–6, 7a–b (if applicable), 8a, 8b–c (if applicable), 9a, 9b (if applicable), 10–18.
Opened a bank account	Needs an EIN for banking purposes only	Complete lines 1–5b, 7a–b (if applicable), 8a, 8b–c (if applicable), 9a, 9b (if applicable), 10, and 18.
Changed type of organization	Either the legal character of the organization or its ownership changed (for example, you incorporate a sole proprietorship or form a partnership)[2]	Complete lines 1–18 (as applicable).
Purchased a going business[3]	Does not already have an EIN	Complete lines 1–18 (as applicable).
Created a trust	The trust is other than a grantor trust or an IRA trust[4]	Complete lines 1–18 (as applicable).
Created a pension plan as a plan administrator[5]	Needs an EIN for reporting purposes	Complete lines 1, 3, 4a–5b, 9a, 10, and 18.
Is a foreign person needing an EIN to comply with IRS withholding regulations	Needs an EIN to complete a Form W-8 (other than Form W-8ECI), avoid withholding on portfolio assets, or claim tax treaty benefits[6]	Complete lines 1–5b, 7a–b (SSN or ITIN optional), 8a, 8b–c (if applicable), 9a, 9b (if applicable), 10, and 18.
Is administering an estate	Needs an EIN to report estate income on Form 1041	Complete lines 1–6, 9a, 10–12, 13–17 (if applicable), and 18.
Is a withholding agent for taxes on non-wage income paid to an alien (i.e., individual, corporation, or partnership, etc.)	Is an agent, broker, fiduciary, manager, tenant, or spouse who is required to file Form 1042, Annual Withholding Tax Return for U.S. Source Income of Foreign Persons	Complete lines 1, 2, 3 (if applicable), 4a–5b, 7a–b (if applicable), 8a, 8b–c (if applicable), 9a, 9b (if applicable), 10 and 18.
Is a state or local agency	Serves as a tax reporting agent for public assistance recipients under Rev. Proc. 80-4, 1980-1 C.B. 581[7]	Complete lines 1, 2, 4a–5b, 9a, 10 and 18.
Is a single-member LLC	Needs an EIN to file Form 8832, Classification Election, for filing employment tax returns, **or** for state reporting purposes[8]	Complete lines 1–18 (as applicable).
Is an S corporation	Needs an EIN to file Form 2553, Election by a Small Business Corporation[9]	Complete lines 1–18 (as applicable).

[1] For example, a sole proprietorship or self-employed farmer who establishes a qualified retirement plan, or is required to file excise, employment, alcohol, tobacco, or firearms returns, must have an EIN. A partnership, corporation, REMIC (real estate mortgage investment conduit), nonprofit organization (church, club, etc.), or farmers' cooperative must use an EIN for any tax-related purpose even if the entity does not have employees.

[2] However, do not apply for a new EIN if the existing entity only (a) changed its business name, (b) elected on Form 8832 to change the way it is taxed (or is covered by the default rules), or (c) terminated its partnership status because at least 50% of the total interests in partnership capital and profits were sold or exchanged within a 12-month period. The EIN of the terminated partnership should continue to be used. See Regulations section 301.6109-1(d)(2)(iii).

[3] Do not use the EIN of the prior business unless you became the "owner" of a corporation by acquiring its stock.

[4] However, grantor trusts that do not file using Optional Method 1 and IRA trusts that are required to file Form 990-T, Exempt Organization Business Income Tax Return, must have an EIN. For more information on grantor trusts, see the Instructions for Form 1041.

[5] A plan administrator is the person or group of persons specified as the administrator by the instrument under which the plan is operated.

[6] Entities applying to be a Qualified Intermediary (QI) need a QI-EIN even if they already have an EIN. See Rev. Proc. 2000-12.

[7] See also *Household employer* on page 4 of the instructions. **Note.** State or local agencies may need an EIN for other reasons, for example, hired employees.

[8] Most LLCs do not need to file Form 8832. See *Limited liability company (LLC)* on page 4 of the instructions for details on completing Form SS-4 for an LLC.

[9] An existing corporation that is electing or revoking S corporation status should use its previously-assigned EIN.

OMB No. 1615-0047; Expires 06/30/08

Department of Homeland Security
U.S. Citizenship and Immigration Services

Form I-9, Employment
Eligibility Verification

Please read instructions carefully before completing this form. The instructions must be available during completion of this form.

ANTI-DISCRIMINATION NOTICE: It is illegal to discriminate against work eligible individuals. Employers CANNOT specify which document(s) they will accept from an employee. The refusal to hire an individual because the documents have a future expiration date may also constitute illegal discrimination.

Section 1. Employee Information and Verification. To be completed and signed by employee at the time employment begins.

Print Name: Last	First	Middle Initial	Maiden Name
Reddenbacher	Mary	J.	Hassenfuss

Address (Street Name and Number)	Apt. #	Date of Birth (month/day/year)
1234 Liberty Lane		1/26/69

City	State	Zip Code	Social Security #
Lansing	MI	12345	123-45-6789

I am aware that federal law provides for imprisonment and/or fines for false statements or use of false documents in connection with the completion of this form.

I attest, under penalty of perjury, that I am (check one of the following):

☐ A citizen or national of the United States
☐ A lawful permanent resident (Alien #) _____
☐ An alien authorized to work until _____

(Alien # or Admission #) _____

Employee's Signature	Date (month/day/year)

Preparer and/or Translator Certification. *(To be completed and signed if Section 1 is prepared by a person other than the employee.)* I attest, under penalty of perjury, that I have assisted in the completion of this form and that to the best of my knowledge the information is true and correct.

Preparer's/Translator's Signature	Print Name

Address (Street Name and Number, City, State, Zip Code)	Date (month/day/year)

Section 2. Employer Review and Verification. To be completed and signed by employer. Examine one document from List A OR examine one document from List B and one from List C, as listed on the reverse of this form, and record the title, number and expiration date, if any, of the document(s).

List A	OR	List B	AND	List C
Document title: PASSPORT		_____		_____
Issuing authority: PASSPORT AGENCY NYC		_____		_____
Document #: 123456789		_____		_____
Expiration Date (if any): 10 5 08		_____		
Document #: _____				
Expiration Date (if any): _____				

CERTIFICATION - I attest, under penalty of perjury, that I have examined the document(s) presented by the above-named employee, that the above-listed document(s) appear to be genuine and to relate to the employee named, that the employee began employment on *(month/day/year)* _____ **and that to the best of my knowledge the employee is eligible to work in the United States. (State employment agencies may omit the date the employee began employment.)**

Signature of Employer or Authorized Representative	Print Name	Title

Business or Organization Name and Address (Street Name and Number, City, State, Zip Code)	Date (month/day/year)

Section 3. Updating and Reverification. To be completed and signed by employer.

A. New Name (if applicable)	B. Date of Rehire (month/day/year) (if applicable)

C. If employee's previous grant of work authorization has expired, provide the information below for the document that establishes current employment eligibility.

Document Title: _____	Document #: _____	Expiration Date (if any): _____

I attest, under penalty of perjury, that to the best of my knowledge, this employee is eligible to work in the United States, and if the employee presented document(s), the document(s) I have examined appear to be genuine and to relate to the individual.

Signature of Employer or Authorized Representative	Date (month/day/year)

Form I-9 (Rev. 06/05/07) N

Form W-4 (2007)

Purpose. Complete Form W-4 so that your employer can withhold the correct federal income tax from your pay. Because your tax situation may change, you may want to refigure your withholding each year.

Exemption from withholding. If you are exempt, complete **only** lines 1, 2, 3, 4, and 7 and sign the form to validate it. Your exemption for 2007 expires February 16, 2008. See Pub. 505, Tax Withholding and Estimated Tax.

Note. You cannot claim exemption from withholding if (a) your income exceeds $850 and includes more than $300 of unearned income (for example, interest and dividends) and (b) another person can claim you as a dependent on their tax return.

Basic instructions. If you are not exempt, complete the **Personal Allowances Worksheet** below. The worksheets on page 2 adjust your withholding allowances based on

itemized deductions, certain credits, adjustments to income, or two-earner/multiple job situations. Complete all worksheets that apply. However, you may claim fewer (or zero) allowances.

Head of household. Generally, you may claim head of household filing status on your tax return only if you are unmarried and pay more than 50% of the costs of keeping up a home for yourself and your dependent(s) or other qualifying individuals.

Tax credits. You can take projected tax credits into account in figuring your allowable number of withholding allowances. Credits for child or dependent care expenses and the child tax credit may be claimed using the **Personal Allowances Worksheet** below. See Pub. 919, How Do I Adjust My Tax Withholding, for information on converting your other credits into withholding allowances.

Nonwage income. If you have a large amount of nonwage income, such as interest or dividends, consider making estimated tax payments using Form 1040-ES, Estimated Tax

for Individuals. Otherwise, you may owe additional tax. If you have pension or annuity income, see Pub. 919 to find out if you should adjust your withholding on Form W-4 or W-4P.

Two earners/Multiple jobs. If you have a working spouse or more than one job, figure the total number of allowances you are entitled to claim on all jobs using worksheets from only one Form W-4. Your withholding usually will be most accurate when all allowances are claimed on the Form W-4 for the highest paying job and zero allowances are claimed on the others.

Nonresident alien. If you are a nonresident alien, see the Instructions for Form 8233 before completing this Form W-4.

Check your withholding. After your Form W-4 takes effect, use Pub. 919 to see how the dollar amount you are having withheld compares to your projected total tax for 2007. See Pub. 919, especially if your earnings exceed $130,000 (Single) or $180,000 (Married).

Personal Allowances Worksheet (Keep for your records.)

A	Enter "1" for **yourself** if no one else can claim you as a dependent	A _____
B	Enter "1" if: { You are single and have only one job; or / You are married, have only one job, and your spouse does not work; or / Your wages from a second job or your spouse's wages (or the total of both) are $1,000 or less. } . .	B _____
C	Enter "1" for your **spouse**. But, you may choose to enter "-0-" if you are married and have either a working spouse or more than one job. (Entering "-0-" may help you avoid having too little tax withheld.)	C _____
D	Enter number of **dependents** (other than your spouse or yourself) you will claim on your tax return	D _____
E	Enter "1" if you will file as **head of household** on your tax return (see conditions under **Head of household** above) .	E _____
F	Enter "1" if you have at least $1,500 of **child or dependent care expenses** for which you plan to claim a credit . .	F _____
	(**Note.** Do **not** include child support payments. See Pub. 503, Child and Dependent Care Expenses, for details.)	
G	**Child Tax Credit** (including additional child tax credit). See Pub 972, Child Tax Credit, for more information.	
	If your total income will be less than $57,000 ($85,000 if married), enter "2" for each eligible child.	
	If your total income will be between $57,000 and $84,000 ($85,000 and $119,000 if married), enter "1" for each eligible child plus "1" **additional** if you have 4 or more eligible children.	G _____
H	Add lines A through G and enter total here. (**Note.** This may be different from the number of exemptions you claim on your tax return.)	H _____

For accuracy, complete all worksheets that apply.	{	If you plan to **itemize or claim adjustments to income** and want to reduce your withholding, see the **Deductions and Adjustments Worksheet** on page 2.
		If you have **more than one job** or are **married and you and your spouse both work** and the combined earnings from all jobs exceed $40,000 ($25,000 if married) see the **Two-Earners/Multiple Jobs Worksheet** on page 2 to avoid having too little tax withheld.
		If **neither** of the above situations applies, **stop here** and enter the number from line H on line 5 of Form W-4 below.

- **Cut here and give Form W-4 to your employer. Keep the top part for your records.** -

Form **W-4** Department of the Treasury Internal Revenue Service	**Employee's Withholding Allowance Certificate** Whether you are entitled to claim a certain number of allowances or exemption from withholding is subject to review by the IRS. Your employer may be required to send a copy of this form to the IRS.	OMB No. 1545-0074 2007

1 Type or print your first name and middle initial. John A.	Last name Doe	2 Your social security number 123 ¦ 45 ¦ 6789

Home address (number and street or rural route) 123 Main Street	3 ☒ Single ☐ Married ☐ Married, but withhold at higher Single rate. **Note.** If married, but legally separated, or spouse is a nonresident alien, check the "Single" box.
City or town, state, and ZIP code Lansing, MI 48910	4 **If your last name differs from that shown on your social security card,** check here. You must call 1-800-772-1213 for a replacement card. . ☐

5	Total number of allowances you are claiming (from line **H** above **or** from the applicable worksheet on page 2)	5	1
6	Additional amount, if any, you want withheld from each paycheck	6	$ 0
7	I claim exemption from withholding for 2007, and I certify that I meet **both** of the following conditions for exemption.		
	Last year I had a right to a refund of **all** federal income tax withheld because I had **no** tax liability **and**		
	This year I expect a refund of **all** federal income tax withheld because I expect to have **no** tax liability.		
	If you meet both conditions, write "Exempt" here	7	

Under penalties of perjury, I declare that I have examined this certificate and to the best of my knowledge and belief, it is true, correct, and complete.

Employee's signature
(Form is not valid
unless you sign it.) ▶ _Doe_   **Date** 07/30/07

8 Employer's name and address (Employer: Complete lines 8 and 10 only if sending to the IRS.)	9 Office code (optional)	10 Employer identification number (EIN)

For Privacy Act and Paperwork Reduction Act Notice, see page 2.	Cat. No. 10220Q	Form **W-4** (2007)

Deductions and Adjustments Worksheet

Note. Use this worksheet *only* if you plan to itemize deductions, claim certain credits, or claim adjustments to income on your 2007 tax return.

1	Enter an estimate of your 2007 itemized deductions. These include qualifying home mortgage interest, charitable contributions, state and local taxes, medical expenses in excess of 7.5% of your income, and miscellaneous deductions. (For 2007, you may have to reduce your itemized deductions if your income is over $156,400 ($78,200 if married filing separately). See *Worksheet 2* in Pub. 919 for details.)	**1** $ _____

2 Enter: { $10,700 if married filing jointly or qualifying widow(er) / $ 7,850 if head of household / $ 5,350 if single or married filing separately } **2** $ _____

3 **Subtract** line 2 from line 1. If zero or less, enter "-0-" **3** $ _____

4 Enter an estimate of your 2007 adjustments to income, including alimony, deductible IRA contributions, and student loan interest **4** $ _____

5 **Add** lines 3 and 4 and enter the total. (Include any amount for credits from *Worksheet 8* in Pub. 919) **5** $ _____

6 Enter an estimate of your 2007 nonwage income (such as dividends or interest) **6** $ _____

7 **Subtract** line 6 from line 5. If zero or less, enter "-0-" **7** $ _____

8 **Divide** the amount on line 7 by $3,400 and enter the result here. Drop any fraction **8** _____

9 Enter the number from the **Personal Allowances Worksheet,** line H, page 1 **9** _____

10 **Add** lines 8 and 9 and enter the total here. If you plan to use the **Two-Earners/Multiple Jobs Worksheet,** also enter this total on line 1 below. Otherwise, **stop here** and enter this total on Form W-4, line 5, page 1 **10** _____

Two-Earners/Multiple Jobs Worksheet (See *Two earners/multiple jobs* on page 1.)

Note. Use this worksheet *only* if the instructions under line H on page 1 direct you here.

1 Enter the number from line H, page 1 (or from line 10 above if you used the **Deductions and Adjustments Worksheet**) **1** _____

2 Find the number in **Table 1** below that applies to the **LOWEST** paying job and enter it here. **However,** if you are married filing jointly and wages from the highest paying job are $50,000 or less, do not enter more than "3." **2** _____

3 If line 1 is **more than or equal to** line 2, subtract line 2 from line 1. Enter the result here (if zero, enter "-0-") and on Form W-4, line 5, page 1. **Do not** use the rest of this worksheet **3** _____

Note. If line 1 is *less than* line 2, enter "-0-" on Form W-4, line 5, page 1. Complete lines 4–9 below to calculate the additional withholding amount necessary to avoid a year-end tax bill.

4 Enter the number from line 2 of this worksheet **4** _____

5 Enter the number from line 1 of this worksheet **5** _____

6 **Subtract** line 5 from line 4 **6** _____

7 Find the amount in **Table 2** below that applies to the **HIGHEST** paying job and enter it here **7** $ _____

8 **Multiply** line 7 by line 6 and enter the result here. This is the additional annual withholding needed **8** $ _____

9 Divide line 8 by the number of pay periods remaining in 2007. For example, divide by 26 if you are paid every two weeks and you complete this form in December 2006. Enter the result here and on Form W-4, line 6, page 1. This is the additional amount to be withheld from each paycheck **9** $ _____

Table 1

Married Filing Jointly		All Others	
If wages from **LOWEST** paying job are—	Enter on line 2 above	If wages from **LOWEST** paying job are—	Enter on line 2 above
$0 - $4,500	0	$0 - $6,000	0
4,501 - 9,000	1	6,001 - 12,000	1
9,001 - 18,000	2	12,001 - 19,000	2
18,001 - 22,000	3	19,001 - 26,000	3
22,001 - 26,000	4	26,001 - 35,000	4
26,001 - 32,000	5	35,001 - 50,000	5
32,001 - 38,000	6	50,001 - 65,000	6
38,001 - 46,000	7	65,001 - 80,000	7
46,001 - 55,000	8	80,001 - 90,000	8
55,001 - 60,000	9	90,001 - 120,000	9
60,001 - 65,000	10	120,001 and over	10
65,001 - 75,000	11		
75,001 - 95,000	12		
95,001 - 105,000	13		
105,001 - 120,000	14		
120,001 and over	15		

Table 2

Married Filing Jointly		All Others	
If wages from **HIGHEST** paying job are—	Enter on line 7 above	If wages from **HIGHEST** paying job are—	Enter on line 7 above
$0 - $65,000	$510	$0 - $35,000	$510
65,001 - 120,000	850	35,001 - 80,000	850
120,001 - 170,000	950	80,001 - 150,000	950
170,001 - 300,000	1,120	150,001 - 340,000	1,120
300,001 and over	1,190	340,001 and over	1,190

Privacy Act and Paperwork Reduction Act Notice. We ask for the information on this form to carry out the Internal Revenue laws of the United States. The Internal Revenue Code requires this information under sections 3402(f)(2)(A) and 6109 and their regulations. Failure to provide a properly completed form will result in your being treated as a single person who claims no withholding allowances; providing fraudulent information may also subject you to penalties. Routine uses of this information include giving it to the Department of Justice for civil and criminal litigation, to cities, states, and the District of Columbia for use in administering their tax laws, and using it in the National Directory of New Hires. We may also disclose this information to other countries under a tax treaty, to federal and state agencies to enforce federal nontax criminal laws, or to federal law enforcement and intelligence agencies to combat terrorism.

You are not required to provide the information requested on a form that is subject to the Paperwork Reduction Act unless the form displays a valid OMB control number. Books or records relating to a form or its instructions must be retained as long as their contents may become material in the administration of any Internal Revenue law. Generally, tax returns and return information are confidential, as required by Code section 6103.

The average time and expenses required to complete and file this form will vary depending on individual circumstances. For estimated averages, see the instructions for your income tax return.

If you have suggestions for making this form simpler, we would be happy to hear from you. See the instructions for your income tax return.

Michigan Department of Treasury
518 (Rev. 7-06)

Registration for Michigan Taxes

Check the box that best describes the reason for this application.

☐ Started a New Business   ☐ Aquired/Transferred All/Part of a Business
☐ Reinstated an Existing Account(s)   ☐ Added a New Location(s)   ▶ **1. Federal Employer Identification Number, if known**
☐ Hired Employee / Hired Michigan Resident   ☐ Flow-thru Entity Withholding
☐ Incorporated / Purchased an Existing Business   ☐ Other (explain) | 1 | 2 | – | 3 | 4 | 5 | 6 | 7 | 8 | 9 |

▶ **2. Company Name or Owner's Full Name** (include, if applicable, Corp, Inc, PC, LC, LLC, LLP, etc.). **Required.**

Doe Company, Inc.

▶ **3. Business Name, Assumed Name or DBA** (as registered with the county)

Legal Address (Required)	▶ **4. Address for all legal contacts** (street and number - no PO boxes)		Business Telephone	
	123 Main Street			
	City	State	ZIP Code	
	Lansing	MI	48910	
Mailing Address	▶ **5. Address, if different from Box 4, where all tax forms will be sent,** unless otherwise instructed		**If this address is for an accountant or other representative, attach Form 151, Power of Attorney.**	
	City	State	ZIP Code	
Physical Address	▶ **6. Address of the actual Michigan location of the business,** if different from above (street and number--no PO boxes). See instructions.			
	City	State	ZIP Code	

▶ **7.** Enter the Business Ownership Type code from Page 4 (Required) .... ▶ **7.** | 4 | 1 |

   If your business is a limited partnership, you must name all general partners beginning on line 27.

   ☐ Check this box if you are an Employee Leasing Company (Professional Employer Organization (PEO)). Attach a list of your clients.

▶ **8.** If you are a Michigan entity **and** line 7 is 34, 40, 41 or 42, enter your Michigan
   Department of Labor and Economic Growth (DLEG) Corporate ID Number .... ▶ **8.** | 1 | 2 | 3 | 4 | 5 | 6 |

   ☐ Check this box if you have applied for and not yet received your ID number.

   Date of Incorporation _____   State of Incorporation_____

▶ **9.** Enter Business Code (SIC) that best describes your business from the list in this booklet .... ▶ **9.** | 3 | 4 | 5 |

10. Define your business activity	11. What products, if any, do you sell (sold to final consumer)?

Check the tax(es) below for which you are registering. At least one box (12-15) must be checked.	**Date that liability will begin** for each box checked at left.			**Estimated monthly payment for each tax** Required if box at left is checked.
	Month	Day	Year	
▶ **12.** ☒ Sales Tax .... ▶ **12a.**	7 1	5	0 8	▶ **12b.** ☐ Up to $65 ☒ Up to $300 ☐ Over $300
▶ **13.** ☐ Use Tax .... ▶ **13a.**				▶ **13b.** ☐ Up to $65 ☐ Up to $300 ☐ Over $300
▶ **14.** ☒ Income Tax Withholding (See line 22.) .... ▶ **14a.**	7 1	5	0 8	▶ **14b.** ☐ Up to $65 ☒ Up to $300 ☐ Over $300
▶ **15.** ☐ Annual Gross Receipts over $350,000 (SBT) .... ▶ **15a.**				**Single Business Tax is required only if annual gross receipts in Michigan exceed $350,000.**

Check the box if these other taxes also apply:

▶ **16.** ☐ Unemployment Insurance Tax. Attach UIA Schedule A and UIA Schedule B. Corporations, LLCs, LLPs: Enclose a copy of your Articles of Incorporation or Organization. **You must complete all items on this form accurately and completely. Failure to do so may subject you to the penalties provided under the Michigan Employment Security (MES) Act.**

▶ **17.** ☐ Motor Fuel/IFTA Tax. Complete line 25. Treasury will review your registration and send any necessary tax application forms.

▶ **18.** ☐ Tobacco Tax. Complete line 26. Treasury will review your registration and send any necessary tax application forms.

▶ **19.** Enter the number of business locations you will operate in Michigan (Required) .... ▶ **19.** ____1____
   If more than 1, attach a list of names and addresses.

Continued on reverse side.

518, Page 2

▶ **20.** Enter the month, numerically, that you close your tax books (for example, enter 08 for August) .... ▶ **20.**

1	2

▶ **21. Seasonal Only:** (Your business is not open continuously for the entire year)

   a. Enter the month, numerically, this seasonal business opens .... ▶ **21a.**

   b. Enter the month, numerically, this seasonal business closes .... ▶ **21b.**

   Note: If you are registering to sell at only one or two events in Michigan per year, do not submit this registration form. Instead, file a *Concessionaire's Sales Tax Return and Payment* (Form 2271). This form can be obtained on Treasury's Web site at **www.michigan.gov/treasurynewbusiness, or by calling toll-free 1-800-367-6263.**

▶ **22.** ☐ Check this box if you use a payroll service that produces your payroll checks and sends income tax withholding payments to the State and Federal Governments. Attach a *Payroll Service Provider Combined Power of Attorney Authorization and Corporate Officer Liability (COL) Certificate for Business* (Form 3683). This form can be obtained on Treasury's Web site at **www.michigan.gov/treasurynewbusiness, or by calling toll-free 1-800-367-6263.**

   Enter the name of your payroll service provider: _____

▶ **23.** If you are incorporating an existing business, or if you purchased an existing business, list previous business names and addresses, if known.

Previous Business Name and Address
Previous Business Name and Address

24. If you purchased an existing business, what assets did you acquire? Check all that apply.

☐ Land ☐ Building ☐ Furniture and Fixtures ☐ Equipment ☐ Inventory ☐ Accounts Payable ☐ Goodwill ☐ None

25. Motor Fuel/IFTA Tax:

                                                         Yes No

   a. Will you operate a terminal or refinery? .... 25a. ☐ ☐

   b. Do you own a diesel-powered vehicle used for transport across Michigan's borders with three or more axles or two axles and a gross vehicle weight over 26,000 lbs? .... 25b. ☐ ☐

   c. Will you transport fuel across Michigan's borders? .... 25c. ☐ ☐

26. Tobacco Tax:

   a. Will you sell tobacco products to someone who will offer them for sale? .... 26a. ☐ ☐

   b. Will you operate a tobacco products vending machine? .... 26b. ☐ ☐

     (1) If yes, do you supply tobacco products for the machine? .... 26b1. ☐ ☐

     (2) If you do not supply the tobacco products, name the supplier _____

Complete all the information for each owner or partner. For limited partnership you must list all general partners. For limited liability companies you must list all members. For corporations you must list all officers, but do not include shareholders who are not officers. Attach a separate list if necessary.

I certify that the information provided on this form is true, correct and complete to the best of my knowledge and belief.

▶ **27.** Name (Last, First, Middle, Jr/Sr/III)		Title	Date of Birth	Phone Number
Doe, John A.		President	06-12-79	
Driver License / MI Identification No.	Social Security Number	Signature		
Q123-2345-6789	123-45-6789			

▶ **28.** Name (Last, First, Middle, Jr/Sr/III)		Title	Date of Birth	Phone Number
Driver License / MI Identification No.	Social Security Number	Signature		

▶ **29.** Name (Last, First, Middle, Jr/Sr/III)		Title	Date of Birth	Phone Number
Driver License / MI Identification No.	Social Security Number	Signature		

▶ **30.** Name (Last, First, Middle, Jr/Sr/III)		Title	Date of Birth	Phone Number
Driver License / MI Identification No.	Social Security Number	Signature		

Questions regarding this form should be directed to the Department at 517-636-4660. Submit this form six weeks before you intend to start your business.

MAIL TO: Michigan Department of Treasury
P.O. Box 30778
Lansing, MI 48909-8278

FAX TO: 517-636-4520

BCS/CD-600 (Rev. 12/03)

MICHIGAN DEPARTMENT OF LABOR & ECONOMIC GROWTH
BUREAU OF COMMERCIAL SERVICES

Date Received	(FOR BUREAU USE ONLY)
This registration will expire 10 years from the stamped registration date.	

| MARK IDENTIFICATION NUMBER | **M** | | | **-** | | | |

APPLICATION FOR REGISTRATION OF TRADEMARK/SERVICE MARK
(Please read information and instructions on last page)

Pursuant to the provisions of Act 242, Public Acts of 1969, as amended, the undersigned executes the following Application:

1. This Application is for the purpose of registering a: (check one)

    [X] Trademark   [ ] Service mark

2. The mark: (Complete only one of the following)

    a) **WORDS ONLY:**
       If the mark is only words, the words in the mark are: (Include type style if it is an inherent part of the mark)
       Doe Dough

    b) **DESIGN ONLY:**
       If the mark is a design only, describe the design: (Include colors if they are an inherent part of the mark)

    c) **WORDS AND DESIGN:**
       Describe the design and list the words in the mark: (Include color and type style if they are an inherent part of the mark)

Please note: Complete either Item 3 **or** Item 4. Designate only one mark and one classification code per application.

Trademarks only

3. a) List the goods in connection with which the mark is used.
      Baked goods

   b) The mode or manner in which the trademark is used in connection with the goods.
      Goods are sold in wrappers or boxes displaying the marking.

   c) Numerical classification of goods: 46

Service marks only

4. a) List the services in connection with which the mark is used.

   b) The mode or manner in which the mark is used in connection with the services.

   c) Numerical classification of services: _____

5. a) The mark was first used in Michigan by the applicant, or a predecessor, in_____ Detroit _____
      on_____ 12-15-07 _____ .   (city)
         (month / day / year)
   b) The mark was first used in the United States by the applicant, or a predecessor, in_____ Detroit _____
                                                                                              (city)
      _____ Michigan _____ on _____ 12-15-07 _____ .
          (state)   (month / day / year)

6. a) The name of the individual or other entity applying for the registration is:
      John Doe

   b) The business name of the applicant, if different than 6(a):
      Doe Dough Bakery

   c) The business address of the applicant is:
      123 Main Street, Detroit, MI   48277

7. a) The applicant is a: (check one)
      ☐ Corporation   ☐ Partnership   ☒ Individual   ☐ Limited Liability Company   ☐ Other

   b) If a corporation, the state where incorporated: _____

8. Two copies, photographs, facsimiles or specimens of the mark, as actually in use must accompany this Application. The sample should be 8.5 x 11 inches or smaller so it may be scanned to optical disk media.

State of _____ Michigan _____

County of _____ Wayne _____ } ss

I, being first sworn, hereby depose and say that I have read the above application, including any attached papers, and the facts set out therein are true; the applicant is the owner of the mark and none other has the right to use the mark in Michigan either in the identical form or in a form which so nearly resembles the mark as to be likely to deceive or to be mistaken for the mark; the specimens of the mark as filed herewith are true and correct. FURTHER, the Bureau of Commercial Services, Michigan Department of Labor & Economic Growth is hereby appointed as the applicant's agent for service of process only in actions relating to the registration or the application for registration of this mark.

Signature	Type or Print Name	Type or Print Title
	John Doe	owner

Subscribed and sworn to before me this _____ 27th _____ day of _____ June _____ , _____ 2008 _____ .

_____
(Signature of Notary)

M.R. Witness
(Type or Print Name of Notary)

Notary Public for _____ Wayne _____ County,

State of _____ Michigan _____

(Notary Seal)   My Commission expires _____ 12-30-11 _____

Preparer's name_____

Business telephone number _____

INFORMATION AND INSTRUCTIONS

1. This application must be used to register a Trademark/Service Mark. A document required or permitted to be filed under this act cannot be filed unless it contains the minimum information required by the act. This is a legal document and agency staff cannot provide legal advice.

2. Submit one original of this document. Upon filing, a Certificate of Registration will be mailed to the applicant or his/her representative to the address provided on this Application.

   Since this application will be maintained on electronic format, it is important that the filing be legible. Documents with poor black and white contrast, or otherwise illegible, will be rejected.

3. This Application is to be used pursuant to Section 3(1) of Act 242, P.A. of 1969 for the purpose of registering a trademark or service mark. A trademark is any word, name, symbol, or device, or any combination thereof, other than a trade name in its entirety, adopted and used by a person to identify goods made or sold by him or her and to distinguish them from similar goods made or sold by others. Similarly, a service mark is a mark used by a person in the sale or advertising of services to identify his or her services and distinguish them from the similar services of others. The term person, as used above, means an individual, firm, partnership, corporation, association, union, or other organization. A mark is not registrable until it has actually been adopted and used in Michigan. The registration is effective for ten years and is renewable for successive terms of 10 years upon the filing of an application for renewal, on a form provided by the Bureau, within six months prior to the expiration date.

4. The Department of Labor and Economic Growth, Bureau of Commercial Services is appointed as the applicant's agent for service of process in actions relating to the registration or application for registration if: (1) the applicant is or becomes a nonresident individual, partnership or association, (2) the applicant is or becomes a foreign corporation or limited liability company without a certificate of authority to transact business in Michigan, or (3) the applicant cannot be found in Michigan.

5. Item 2 - Complete section (a), (b) or (c) depending on the type of mark that is being registered.

6. **Trademarks only:**
   Item 3(a) - List the good(s) on which the mark is used.
   Item 3(b) - List how the mark is used on the good(s) i.e. tag, label, etc.
   Item 3(c) - List the classification of the good, but be aware that only one classification can be designated per application.
     A list of the classification codes can be found on the back of this Application.

7. **Service marks only:**
   Item 4(a) - List the service(s) in connection with which the mark is used.
   Item 4(b) - List how the mark is used i.e. in advertising, signs, letterhead, etc.
   Item 4(c) - List the classification of the good, but be aware that only one classification can be designated per application.
     A list of the classification codes can be found on the back of this Application.

8. Item 5 - A trademark is considered "used in Michigan" when affixed to the product, container, tags or labels and sold in Michigan. For services, the mark must be used or displayed in this state in the sale or advertising of services rendered in Michigan.

9. Item 8 - **Two copies, photographs, facsimiles or specimens of the mark, as actually in use must accompany this Application. The sample should be 8.5 x 11 inches or smaller so it may be maintained on electronic format.**

10. This Application must be signed by:
    Individual - by the applicant
    Corporation - by an authorized officer or agent.
    Limited Liability Company - by a manager if management is vested in one or more managers or by a member if management is reserved for members.
    Partnership - by a partner.

11. **NONREFUNDABLE FEE:** Make remittance payable to the State of Michigan **$50.00**

To submit by mail:	To submit in person:
Michigan Department of Labor & Economic Growth	2501 Woodlake Circle
Bureau of Commercial Services	Okemos, MI
Corporation Division	Telephone: (517) 241-6470
7150 Harris Drive	
P.O. Box 30054	Fees may be paid by VISA or Mastercard when
Lansing, MI 48909	delivered in person to our office.

Preparer's name _____

Business telephone number _____

INFORMATION AND INSTRUCTIONS

1. This application must be used to register a Trademark/Service Mark. A document required or permitted to be filed under this act cannot be filed unless it contains the minimum information required by the act. This is a legal document and agency staff cannot provide legal advice.

2. Submit one original of this document. Upon filing, a Certificate of Registration will be mailed to the applicant or his/her representative to the address provided on this Application.

   Since this application will be maintained on electronic format, it is important that the filing be legible. Documents with poor black and white contrast, or otherwise illegible, will be rejected.

3. This Application is to be used pursuant to Section 3(1) of Act 242, P.A. of 1969 for the purpose of registering a trademark or service mark. A trademark is any word, name, symbol, or device, or any combination thereof, other than a trade name in its entirety, adopted and used by a person to identify goods made or sold by him or her and to distinguish them from similar goods made or sold by others. Similarly, a service mark is a mark used by a person in the sale or advertising of services to identify his or her services and distinguish them from the similar services of others. The term person, as used above, means an individual, firm, partnership, corporation, association, union, or other organization. A mark is not registrable until it has actually been adopted and used in Michigan. The registration is effective for ten years and is renewable for successive terms of 10 years upon the filing of an application for renewal, on a form provided by the Bureau, within six months prior to the expiration date.

4. The Department of Labor and Economic Growth, Bureau of Commercial Services is appointed as the applicant's agent for service of process in actions relating to the registration or application for registration if: (1) the applicant is or becomes a nonresident individual, partnership or association, (2) the applicant is or becomes a foreign corporation or limited liability company without a certificate of authority to transact business in Michigan, or (3) the applicant cannot be found in Michigan.

5. Item 2 - Complete section (a), (b) or (c) depending on the type of mark that is being registered.

6. **Trademarks only:**
   Item 3(a) - List the good(s) on which the mark is used.
   Item 3(b) - List how the mark is used on the good(s) i.e. tag, label, etc.
   Item 3(c) - List the classification of the good, but be aware that only one classification can be designated per application.
      A list of the classification codes can be found on the back of this Application.

7. **Service marks only:**
   Item 4(a) - List the service(s) in connection with which the mark is used.
   Item 4(b) - List how the mark is used i.e. in advertising, signs, letterhead, etc.
   Item 4(c) - List the classification of the good, but be aware that only one classification can be designated per application.
      A list of the classification codes can be found on the back of this Application.

8. Item 5 - A trademark is considered "used in Michigan" when affixed to the product, container, tags or labels and sold in Michigan. For services, the mark must be used or displayed in this state in the sale or advertising of services rendered in Michigan.

9. Item 8 - **Two copies, photographs, facsimiles or specimens of the mark, as actually in use must accompany this Application. The sample should be 8.5 x 11 inches or smaller so it may be maintained on electronic format.**

10. This Application must be signed by:
    Individual - by the applicant
    Corporation - by an authorized officer or agent.
    Limited Liability Company - by a manager if management is vested in one or more managers or by a member if management is reserved for members.
    Partnership - by a partner.

11. **NONREFUNDABLE FEE:** Make remittance payable to the State of Michigan **$50.00**

To submit by mail:	To submit in person:
Michigan Department of Labor & Economic Growth Bureau of Commercial Services Corporation Division 7150 Harris Drive P.O. Box 30054 Lansing, MI 48909	2501 Woodlake Circle Okemos, MI Telephone: (517) 241-6470 Fees may be paid by VISA or Mastercard when delivered in person to our office.

TRADEMARK UNIFORM CLASSIFICATION OF GOODS

1. Raw or partly prepared materials
2. Receptacles
3. Baggage, animal equipments, portfolios and pocketbooks
4. Abrasives and polishing materials
5. Adhesives
6. Chemicals and chemical compositions
7. Cordage
8. Smokers' articles, not including tobacco products
9. Explosives, firearms, equipments and projectiles
10. Fertilizers
11. Inks and inking materials
12. Construction materials
13. Hardware and plumbing and steam fitting supplies
14. Metals and metal castings and forgings
15. Oils and greases
16. Paints and painters' materials
17. Tobacco products
18. Medicines and pharmaceutical preparations
19. Vehicles
20. Linoleum and oiled cloth
21. Electrical apparatus, machines and supplies
22. Games, toys and sporting goods
23. Cutlery, machinery and tools, and parts thereof
24. Laundry appliances and machines
25. Locks and safes
26. Measuring and scientific appliances
27. Horological instruments
28. Jewelry and precious-metal ware
29. Brooms, brushes and dusters
30. Crockery, earthenware and porcelain
31. Filters and refrigerators
32. Furniture and upholstery
33. Glassware
34. Heating, lighting and ventilating apparatus
35. Belting, hose, machinery packing, and non-metallic tires
36. Musical instruments and supplies
37. Paper and stationery
38. Prints and publications
39. Clothing
40. Fancy goods, furnishings and notions
41. Canes, parasols and umbrellas
42. Knitted, netted and textile
43. Thread and yarn
44. Dental, medical and surgical appliances
45. Soft drinks and carbonated waters
46. Foods and ingredients of foods
47. Wines
48. Malt beverages and liquors
49. Distilled alcoholic liquors
50. Merchandise not otherwise classified
51. Cosmetics and toilet preparations
52. Detergents and soaps

SERVICE MARK UNIFORM CLASSIFICATION OF SERVICES

100. Miscellaneous
101. Advertising and business
102. Insurance and financial
103. Construction and repair
104. Communication
105. Transportation and storage
106. Material treatment
107. Education and entertainment

Blank Forms

The following forms may be photocopied or removed from this book and used immediately. Some of the tax forms explained in this book are not included here because you should use original forms provided by the IRS, the Michigan Department of Treasury, or some other agency as explained in the portion of this book where the particular form was discussed.

TAX TIMETABLE

MICHIGAN   FEDERAL

	SUW*	SBT**	Unemploy.	Est. Tax	Est. Tax	Annual Return	Form 941***	Misc.
JAN.	15th		25th	15th	15th		31st	31st 940 W-2 508 1099
FEB.	15th							28th W-3
MAR.	15th					15th		
APR.	15th	30th Ann. Ret.	25th	15th	15th	15th	30th	30th 508
MAY	15th							
JUN.	15th			15th	15th			
JUL.	15th		25th				31st	31st 508
AUG.	15th							
SEP.	15th			15th	15th			
OCT.	15th		25th				31st	31st 508
NOV.	15th							
DEC.	15th							

*   SUW = Sales, Use, and Withholding taxes; a combined return is filed.

**   SBT = Single Business Tax. Based on calendar year. If fiscal year, due 15th day of 4th month after end of fiscal year. Quarterly returns are required if you expect annual liability greater than $600.

***   In addition to Form 941, deposits must be made regularly if withholding exceeds $500 in any month.

This page intentionally blank.

Form SS-4
(Rev. July 2007)
Department of the Treasury
Internal Revenue Service

Application for Employer Identification Number

(For use by employers, corporations, partnerships, trusts, estates, churches, government agencies, Indian tribal entities, certain individuals, and others.)

▶ See separate instructions for each line.   ▶ Keep a copy for your records.

OMB No. 1545-0003

EIN

Type or print clearly.

1 Legal name of entity (or individual) for whom the EIN is being requested

2 Trade name of business (if different from name on line 1)

3 Executor, administrator, trustee, "care of" name

4a Mailing address (room, apt., suite no. and street, or P.O. box)

5a Street address (if different) (Do not enter a P.O. box.)

4b City, state, and ZIP code (if foreign, see instructions)

5b City, state, and ZIP code (if foreign, see instructions)

6 County and state where principal business is located

7a Name of principal officer, general partner, grantor, owner, or trustor

7b SSN, ITIN, or EIN

8a Is this application for a limited liability company (LLC) (or a foreign equivalent)? . . . . ☐ Yes ☐ No

8b If 8a is "Yes," enter the number of LLC members . . . . . ▶

8c If 8a is "Yes," was the LLC organized in the United States? . . . . ☐ Yes ☐ No

9a **Type of entity** (check only one box). **Caution.** If 8a is "Yes," see the instructions for the correct box to check.

☐ Sole proprietor (SSN) _____
☐ Partnership
☐ Corporation (enter form number to be filed) ▶ _____
☐ Personal service corporation
☐ Church or church-controlled organization
☐ Other nonprofit organization (specify) ▶ _____
☐ Other (specify) ▶

☐ Estate (SSN of decedent) _____
☐ Plan administrator (TIN) _____
☐ Trust (TIN of grantor) _____
☐ National Guard   ☐ State/local government
☐ Farmers' cooperative   ☐ Federal government/military
☐ REMIC   ☐ Indian tribal governments/enterprises
Group Exemption Number (GEN) if any ▶

9b If a corporation, name the state or foreign country (if applicable) where incorporated

State

Foreign country

10 **Reason for applying** (check only one box)

☐ Started new business (specify type) ▶ _____
☐ Hired employees (Check the box and see line 13.)
☐ Compliance with IRS withholding regulations
☐ Other (specify) ▶

☐ Banking purpose (specify purpose) ▶ _____
☐ Changed type of organization (specify new type) ▶ _____
☐ Purchased going business
☐ Created a trust (specify type) ▶ _____
☐ Created a pension plan (specify type) ▶ _____

11 Date business started or acquired (month, day, year). See instructions.

12 Closing month of accounting year

14 Do you expect your employment tax liability to be $1,000 or less in a full calendar year? ☐ Yes ☐ No (If you expect to pay $4,000 or less in total wages in a full calendar year, you can mark "Yes.")

13 Highest number of employees expected in the next 12 months (enter -0- if none).

Agricultural	Household	Other

15 First date wages or annuities were paid (month, day, year). **Note.** If applicant is a withholding agent, enter date income will first be paid to nonresident alien (month, day, year) . . . . ▶

16 Check **one** box that best describes the principal activity of your business.
☐ Construction ☐ Rental & leasing ☐ Transportation & warehousing ☐ Health care & social assistance ☐ Wholesale-agent/broker
☐ Real estate ☐ Manufacturing ☐ Finance & insurance ☐ Accommodation & food service ☐ Wholesale-other ☐ Retail
☐ Other (specify)

17 Indicate principal line of merchandise sold, specific construction work done, products produced, or services provided.

18 Has the applicant entity shown on line 1 ever applied for and received an EIN? ☐ Yes ☐ No
If "Yes," write previous EIN here ▶

Third Party Designee

Complete this section **only** if you want to authorize the named individual to receive the entity's EIN and answer questions about the completion of this form.

Designee's name

Designee's telephone number (include area code)
( )

Address and ZIP code

Designee's fax number (include area code)
( )

Under penalties of perjury, I declare that I have examined this application, and to the best of my knowledge and belief, it is true, correct, and complete.

Applicant's telephone number (include area code)
( )

Name and title (type or print clearly) ▶

Applicant's fax number (include area code)
( )

Signature ▶   Date ▶

For Privacy Act and Paperwork Reduction Act Notice, see separate instructions.   Cat. No. 16055N   Form **SS-4** (Rev. 7-2007)

Do I Need an EIN?

File Form SS-4 if the applicant entity does not already have an EIN but is required to show an EIN on any return, statement, or other document.[1] See also the separate instructions for each line on Form SS-4.

IF the applicant...	AND...	THEN...
Started a new business	Does not currently have (nor expect to have) employees	Complete lines 1, 2, 4a–8a, 8b–c (if applicable), 9a, 9b (if applicable), and 10–14 and 16–18.
Hired (or will hire) employees, including household employees	Does not already have an EIN	Complete lines 1, 2, 4a–6, 7a–b (if applicable), 8a, 8b–c (if applicable), 9a, 9b (if applicable), 10–18.
Opened a bank account	Needs an EIN for banking purposes only	Complete lines 1–5b, 7a–b (if applicable), 8a, 8b–c (if applicable), 9a, 9b (if applicable), 10, and 18.
Changed type of organization	Either the legal character of the organization or its ownership changed (for example, you incorporate a sole proprietorship or form a partnership)[2]	Complete lines 1–18 (as applicable).
Purchased a going business[3]	Does not already have an EIN	Complete lines 1–18 (as applicable).
Created a trust	The trust is other than a grantor trust or an IRA trust[4]	Complete lines 1–18 (as applicable).
Created a pension plan as a plan administrator[5]	Needs an EIN for reporting purposes	Complete lines 1, 3, 4a–5b, 9a, 10, and 18.
Is a foreign person needing an EIN to comply with IRS withholding regulations	Needs an EIN to complete a Form W-8 (other than Form W-8ECI), avoid withholding on portfolio assets, or claim tax treaty benefits[6]	Complete lines 1–5b, 7a–b (SSN or ITIN optional), 8a, 8b–c (if applicable), 9a, 9b (if applicable), 10, and 18.
Is administering an estate	Needs an EIN to report estate income on Form 1041	Complete lines 1–6, 9a, 10–12, 13–17 (if applicable), and 18.
Is a withholding agent for taxes on non-wage income paid to an alien (i.e., individual, corporation, or partnership, etc.)	Is an agent, broker, fiduciary, manager, tenant, or spouse who is required to file Form 1042, Annual Withholding Tax Return for U.S. Source Income of Foreign Persons	Complete lines 1, 2, 3 (if applicable), 4a–5b, 7a–b (if applicable), 8a, 8b–c (if applicable), 9a, 9b (if applicable), 10 and 18.
Is a state or local agency	Serves as a tax reporting agent for public assistance recipients under Rev. Proc. 80-4, 1980-1 C.B. 581[7]	Complete lines 1, 2, 4a–5b, 9a, 10 and 18.
Is a single-member LLC	Needs an EIN to file Form 8832, Classification Election, for filing employment tax returns, **or** for state reporting purposes[8]	Complete lines 1–18 (as applicable).
Is an S corporation	Needs an EIN to file Form 2553, Election by a Small Business Corporation[9]	Complete lines 1–18 (as applicable).

[1] For example, a sole proprietorship or self-employed farmer who establishes a qualified retirement plan, or is required to file excise, employment, alcohol, tobacco, or firearms returns, must have an EIN. A partnership, corporation, REMIC (real estate mortgage investment conduit), nonprofit organization (church, club, etc.), or farmers' cooperative must use an EIN for any tax-related purpose even if the entity does not have employees.

[2] However, do not apply for a new EIN if the existing entity only (a) changed its business name, (b) elected on Form 8832 to change the way it is taxed (or is covered by the default rules), or (c) terminated its partnership status because at least 50% of the total interests in partnership capital and profits were sold or exchanged within a 12-month period. The EIN of the terminated partnership should continue to be used. See Regulations section 301.6109-1(d)(2)(iii).

[3] Do not use the EIN of the prior business unless you became the "owner" of a corporation by acquiring its stock.

[4] However, grantor trusts that do not file using Optional Method 1 and IRA trusts that are required to file Form 990-T, Exempt Organization Business Income Tax Return, must have an EIN. For more information on grantor trusts, see the Instructions for Form 1041.

[5] A plan administrator is the person or group of persons specified as the administrator by the instrument under which the plan is operated.

[6] Entities applying to be a Qualified Intermediary (QI) need a QI-EIN even if they already have an EIN. See Rev. Proc. 2000-12.

[7] See also Household employer on page 4 of the instructions. **Note.** State or local agencies may need an EIN for other reasons, for example, hired employees.

[8] Most LLCs do not need to file Form 8832. See Limited liability company (LLC) on page 4 of the instructions for details on completing Form SS-4 for an LLC.

[9] An existing corporation that is electing or revoking S corporation status should use its previously-assigned EIN.

Instructions for Form SS-4

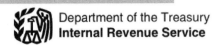

Department of the Treasury
Internal Revenue Service

(Rev. July 2007)

Application for Employer Identification Number

Section references are to the Internal Revenue Code unless otherwise noted.

General Instructions

Use these instructions to complete Form SS-4, Application for Employer Identification Number. Also see *Do I Need an EIN?* on page 2 of Form SS-4.

Purpose of Form

Use Form SS-4 to apply for an employer identification number (EIN). An EIN is a nine-digit number (for example, 12-3456789) assigned to sole proprietors, corporations, partnerships, estates, trusts, and other entities for tax filing and reporting purposes. The information you provide on this form will establish your business tax account.

 An EIN is for use in connection with your business activities only. Do not use your EIN in place of your social security number (SSN).

Reminders

Apply online. Generally, you can apply for and receive an EIN online using the Internet. See *How To Apply* below.

 This is a free service offered by the Internal Revenue Service at www.irs.gov. Beware of websites on the Internet that charge for this free service.

File only one Form SS-4. Generally, a sole proprietor should file only one Form SS-4 and needs only one EIN, regardless of the number of businesses operated as a sole proprietorship or trade names under which a business operates. However, if the proprietorship incorporates or enters into a partnership, a new EIN is required. Also, each corporation in an affiliated group must have its own EIN.

EIN applied for, but not received. If you do not have an EIN by the time a return is due, write "Applied For" and the date you applied in the space shown for the number. Do not show your SSN as an EIN on returns.

If you do not have an EIN by the time a tax deposit is due, send your payment to the Internal Revenue Service Center for your filing area as shown in the instructions for the form that you are filing. Make your check or money order payable to the "United States Treasury" and show your name (as shown on Form SS-4), address, type of tax, period covered, and date you applied for an EIN.

Federal tax deposits. New employers that have a federal tax obligation will be pre-enrolled in the Electronic Federal Tax Payment System (EFTPS). EFTPS allows you to make all of your federal tax payments online at *www.eftps.gov* or by telephone. Shortly after we have assigned you your EIN, you will receive instructions by mail for activating your EFTPS enrollment. You will also receive an EFTPS Personal Identification Number (PIN) that you will use to make your payments, as well as instructions for obtaining an Internet password you will need to make payments online.

If you are not required to make deposits by EFTPS, you can use Form 8109, Federal Tax Deposit (FTD) Coupon, to make deposits at an authorized depositary. If you would like to receive Form 8109, call 1-800-829-4933. Allow 5 to 6 weeks for delivery. For more information on federal tax deposits, see Pub. 15 (Circular E), Employer's Tax Guide.

How To Apply

You can apply for an EIN online, by telephone, by fax, or by mail depending on how soon you need to use the EIN. Use only one method for each entity so you do not receive more than one EIN for an entity.

Online. Taxpayers and authorized third party designees located within the United States and U.S. possessions can receive an EIN online and use it immediately to file a return or make a payment. Go to the IRS website at *www.irs.gov/businesses* and click on *Employer ID Numbers*.

 Taxpayers who apply online have an option to view, print, and save their EIN assignment notice at the end of the session. (Authorized third party designees will receive the EIN but the notice will be mailed to the applicant.)

 Applicants who are not located within the United States or U.S. possessions cannot use the online application to obtain an EIN. Please use one of the other methods to apply.

Telephone. You can receive your EIN by telephone and use it immediately to file a return or make a payment. Call the IRS at 1-800-829-4933. The hours of operation are 7:00 a.m. to 10:00 p.m. local time (Pacific time for Alaska and Hawaii). The person making the call must be authorized to sign the form or be an authorized designee. See *Third Party Designee* and *Signature* on page 6. Also see the *TIP* below.

Note. International applicants must call 215-516-6999.

If you are applying by telephone, it will be helpful to complete Form SS-4 before contacting the IRS. An IRS representative will use the information from the Form SS-4 to establish your account and assign you an EIN. Write the number you are given on the upper right corner of the form and sign and date it. Keep this copy for your records.

If requested by an IRS representative, mail or fax (facsimile) the signed Form SS-4 (including any Third Party Designee authorization) within 24 hours to the IRS address provided by the IRS representative.

 *Taxpayer representatives can apply for an EIN on behalf of their client and request that the EIN be faxed to their client on the same day. **Note.** By using this procedure, you are authorizing the IRS to fax the EIN without a cover sheet.*

Fax. Under the Fax-TIN program, you can receive your EIN by fax within 4 business days. Complete and fax Form SS-4 to the IRS using the Fax-TIN number listed on page 2 for your state. A long-distance charge to callers outside of the local calling area will apply. Fax-TIN numbers can only be used to apply for an EIN. The numbers may change without notice. Fax-TIN is available 24 hours a day, 7 days a week.

Be sure to provide your fax number so the IRS can fax the EIN back to you.

Note. By using this procedure, you are authorizing the IRS to fax the EIN without a cover sheet.

Mail. Complete Form SS-4 at least 4 to 5 weeks before you will need an EIN. Sign and date the application and mail it to

Cat. No. 62736F

the service center address for your state. You will receive your EIN in the mail in approximately 4 weeks. See also *Third Party Designee* on page 6.

Call 1-800-829-4933 to verify a number or to ask about the status of an application by mail.

Where to File or Fax

If your principal business, office or agency, or legal residence in the case of an individual, is located in:	File or fax with the "Internal Revenue Service Center" at:
Connecticut, Delaware, District of Columbia, Florida, Georgia, Maine, Maryland, Massachusetts, New Hampshire, New Jersey, New York, North Carolina, Ohio, Pennsylvania, Rhode Island, South Carolina, Vermont, Virginia, West Virginia	Attn: EIN Operation Holtsville, NY 11742 Fax-TIN: 631-447-8960
Illinois, Indiana, Kentucky, Michigan	Attn: EIN Operation Cincinnati, OH 45999 Fax-TIN: 859-669-5760
Alabama, Alaska, Arizona, Arkansas, California, Colorado, Hawaii, Idaho, Iowa, Kansas, Louisiana, Minnesota, Mississippi, Missouri, Montana, Nebraska, Nevada, New Mexico, North Dakota, Oklahoma, Oregon, South Dakota, Tennessee, Texas, Utah, Washington, Wisconsin, Wyoming	Attn: EIN Operation Philadelphia, PA 19255 Fax-TIN: 859-669-5760
If you have no legal residence, principal place of business, or principal office or agency in any state:	Attn: EIN Operation Philadelphia, PA 19255 Fax-TIN: 215-516-1040

How To Get Forms and Publications

Internet. You can access the IRS website 24 hours a day, 7 days a week at *www.irs.gov* to download forms, instructions, and publications.

Phone. Call 1-800-TAX-FORM (1-800-829-3676) to order forms, instructions, and publications. You should receive your order or notification of its status within 10 workdays.

CD-ROM. For small businesses, return preparers, or others who may frequently need tax forms or publications, a CD-ROM containing over 2,000 tax products (including many prior year forms) can be purchased from the National Technical Information Service (NTIS).

To order Pub. 1796, IRS Tax Products CD, call 1-877-CDFORMS (1-877-233-6767) toll free or connect to *www.irs.gov/cdorders*.

Tax Help for Your Business

IRS-sponsored Small Business Workshops provide information about your federal and state tax obligations. For information about workshops in your area, call 1-800-829-4933.

Related Forms and Publications

The following forms and instructions may be useful to filers of Form SS-4.
- Form 990-T, Exempt Organization Business Income Tax Return.
- Instructions for Form 990-T.
- Schedule C (Form 1040), Profit or Loss From Business.
- Schedule F (Form 1040), Profit or Loss From Farming.
- Instructions for Form 1041 and Schedules A, B, D, G, I, J, and K-1, U.S. Income Tax Return for Estates and Trusts.
- Form 1042, Annual Withholding Tax Return for U.S. Source Income of Foreign Persons.
- Instructions for Form 1065, U.S. Return of Partnership Income.
- Instructions for Form 1066, U.S. Real Estate Mortgage Investment Conduit (REMIC) Income Tax Return.
- Instructions for Forms 1120 and 1120-A.
- Form 2553, Election by a Small Business Corporation.
- Form 2848, Power of Attorney and Declaration of Representative.
- Form 8821, Tax Information Authorization.
- Form 8832, Entity Classification Election.

For more information about filing Form SS-4 and related issues, see:
- Pub. 51 (Circular A), Agricultural Employer's Tax Guide;
- Pub. 15 (Circular E), Employer's Tax Guide;
- Pub. 538, Accounting Periods and Methods;
- Pub. 542, Corporations;
- Pub. 557, Tax-Exempt Status for Your Organization;
- Pub. 583, Starting a Business and Keeping Records;
- Pub. 966, The Secure Way to Pay Your Federal Taxes for Business and Individual Taxpayers;
- Pub. 1635, Understanding Your EIN;
- Package 1023, Application for Recognition of Exemption Under Section 501(c)(3) of the Internal Revenue Code; and
- Package 1024, Application for Recognition of Exemption Under Section 501(a).

Specific Instructions

Print or type all entries on Form SS-4. Follow the instructions for each line to expedite processing and to avoid unnecessary IRS requests for additional information. Enter "N/A" (nonapplicable) on the lines that do not apply.

Line 1. Legal name of entity (or individual) for whom the EIN is being requested. Enter the legal name of the entity (or individual) applying for the EIN exactly as it appears on the social security card, charter, or other applicable legal document. An entry is required.

Individuals. Enter your first name, middle initial, and last name. If you are a sole proprietor, enter your individual name, not your business name. Enter your business name on line 2. Do not use abbreviations or nicknames on line 1.

Trusts. Enter the name of the trust as it appears on the trust instrument.

Estate of a decedent. Enter the name of the estate. For an estate that has no legal name, enter the name of the decedent followed by "Estate."

Partnerships. Enter the legal name of the partnership as it appears in the partnership agreement.

Corporations. Enter the corporate name as it appears in the corporate charter or other legal document creating it.

Plan administrators. Enter the name of the plan administrator. A plan administrator who already has an EIN should use that number.

Line 2. Trade name of business. Enter the trade name of the business if different from the legal name. The trade name is the "doing business as" (DBA) name.

 Use the full legal name shown on line 1 on all tax returns filed for the entity. (However, if you enter a trade name on line 2 and choose to use the trade name instead of the legal name, enter the trade name on all returns you file.) To prevent processing delays and errors, always use the legal name only (or the trade name only) on all tax returns.

Line 3. Executor, administrator, trustee, "care of" name. Trusts enter the name of the trustee. Estates enter the name of the executor, administrator, or other fiduciary. If the entity applying has a designated person to receive tax information, enter that person's name as the "care of" person. Enter the individual's first name, middle initial, and last name.

Lines 4a–b. Mailing address. Enter the mailing address for the entity's correspondence. If the entity's address is outside the United States or its possessions, you must enter the city, province or state, postal code, and the name of the country. Do not abbreviate the country name. If line 3 is completed, enter the address for the executor, trustee or "care of" person. Generally, this address will be used on all tax returns.

If the entity is filing the Form SS-4 only to obtain an EIN for the Form 8832, use the same address where you would like to have the acceptance or nonacceptance letter sent.

 File Form 8822, Change of Address, to report any subsequent changes to the entity's mailing address.

Lines 5a–b. Street address. Provide the entity's physical address only if different from its mailing address shown in lines 4a–b. Do not enter a P.O. box number here. If the entity's address is outside the United States or its possessions, you must enter the city, province or state, postal code, and the name of the country. Do not abbreviate the country name.

Line 6. County and state where principal business is located. Enter the entity's primary physical location.

Lines 7a–b. Name of principal officer, general partner, grantor, owner, or trustor. Enter the first name, middle initial, last name, and SSN of (a) the principal officer if the business is a corporation, (b) a general partner if a partnership, (c) the owner of an entity that is disregarded as separate from its owner (disregarded entities owned by a corporation enter the corporation's name and EIN), or (d) a grantor, owner, or trustor if a trust.

If the person in question is an alien individual with a previously assigned individual taxpayer identification number (ITIN), enter the ITIN in the space provided and submit a copy of an official identifying document. If necessary, complete Form W-7, Application for IRS Individual Taxpayer Identification Number, to obtain an ITIN.

You must enter an SSN, ITIN, or EIN unless the only reason you are applying for an EIN is to make an entity classification election (see Regulations sections 301.7701-1 through 301.7701-3) and you are a nonresident alien or other foreign entity with no effectively connected income from sources within the United States.

Lines 8a–c. Limited liability company (LLC) information. An LLC is an entity organized under the laws of a state or foreign country as a limited liability company. For federal tax purposes, an LLC may be treated as a partnership or corporation or be disregarded as an entity separate from its owner.

By default, a domestic LLC with only one member is disregarded as an entity separate from its owner and must include all of its income and expenses on the owner's tax return (for example, Schedule C (Form 1040)). Also by default, a domestic LLC with two or more members is treated as a partnership. A domestic LLC may file Form 8832 to avoid either default classification and elect to be classified as an association taxable as a corporation. For more information on entity classifications (including the rules for foreign entities), see the instructions for Form 8832.

If the answer to line 8a is "Yes," enter the number of LLC members. If the LLC is owned solely by a husband and wife in a community property state and the husband and wife choose to treat the entity as a disregarded entity, enter "1" on line 8b.

 Do not file Form 8832 if the LLC accepts the default classifications above. If the LLC is eligible to be treated as a corporation that meets certain tests and it will be electing S corporation status, it must timely file Form 2553. The LLC will be treated as a corporation as of the effective date of the S corporation election and does not need to file Form 8832. See the Instructions for Form 2553.

Line 9a. Type of entity. Check the box that best describes the type of entity applying for the EIN. If you are an alien individual with an ITIN previously assigned to you, enter the ITIN in place of a requested SSN.

 This is not an election for a tax classification of an entity. See Limited Liability Company (LLC) on page 4.

Sole proprietor. Check this box if you file Schedule C, C-EZ, or F (Form 1040) and have a qualified plan, or are required to file excise, employment, alcohol, tobacco, or firearms returns, or are a payer of gambling winnings. Enter your SSN (or ITIN) in the space provided. If you are a nonresident alien with no effectively connected income from sources within the United States, you do not need to enter an SSN or ITIN.

Corporation. This box is for any corporation other than a personal service corporation. If you check this box, enter the income tax form number to be filed by the entity in the space provided.

 If you entered "1120S" after the "Corporation" checkbox, the corporation must file Form 2553 no later than the 15th day of the 3rd month of the tax year the election is to take effect. Until Form 2553 has been received and approved, you will be considered a Form 1120 filer. See the Instructions for Form 2553.

Personal service corporation. Check this box if the entity is a personal service corporation. An entity is a personal service corporation for a tax year only if:
• The principal activity of the entity during the testing period (prior tax year) for the tax year is the performance of personal services substantially by employee-owners, and
• The employee-owners own at least 10% of the fair market value of the outstanding stock in the entity on the last day of the testing period.

Personal services include performance of services in such fields as health, law, accounting, or consulting. For more information about personal service corporations, see the Instructions for Forms 1120 and 1120-A and Pub. 542.

 If the corporation is recently formed, the testing period begins on the first day of its tax year and ends on the earlier of the last day of its tax year, or the last day of the calendar year in which its tax year begins.

Other nonprofit organization. Check this box if the nonprofit organization is other than a church or church-controlled organization and specify the type of nonprofit organization (for example, an educational organization).

If the organization also seeks tax-exempt status, you must file either Package 1023 or Package 1024. See Pub. 557 for more information.

If the organization is covered by a group exemption letter, enter the four-digit group exemption number (GEN) in the last entry. (Do not confuse the GEN with the nine-digit EIN.) If you do not know the GEN, contact the parent organization. Get Pub. 557 for more information about group exemption numbers.

If the organization is a section 527 political organization, check the box for *Other nonprofit organization* and specify "section 527 organization" in the space to the right. To be recognized as exempt from tax, a section 527 political organization must electronically file Form 8871, Political Organization Notice of Section 527 Status, within 24 hours of the date on which the organization was established. The organization may also have to file Form 8872, Political Organization Report of Contributions and Expenditures. See *www.irs.gov/polorgs* for more information.

Plan administrator. If the plan administrator is an individual, enter the plan administrator's taxpayer identification number (TIN) in the space provided.

REMIC. Check this box if the entity has elected to be treated as a real estate mortgage investment conduit (REMIC). See the Instructions for Form 1066 for more information.

State/local government. If you are a government employer and you are not sure of your social security and Medicare coverage options, go to *www.ncsssa.org/ssaframes.html* to obtain the contact information for your state's Social Security Administrator.

Other. If not specifically listed, check the "Other" box, enter the type of entity and the type of return, if any, that will be filed (for example, "Common Trust Fund, Form 1065" or "Created a Pension Plan"). Do not enter "N/A." If you are an alien individual applying for an EIN, see the *Lines 7a–b* instructions on page 3.
• **Household employer.** If you are an individual that will employ someone to provide services in your household, check the "Other" box and enter "Household Employer" and your SSN. If you are a trust that qualifies as a household employer, you do not need a separate EIN for reporting tax information relating to household employees; use the EIN of the trust.
• **Household employer agent.** If you are an agent of a household employer that is a disabled individual or other welfare recipient receiving home care services through a state or local program, check the "Other" box and enter "Household Employer Agent." (See Rev. Proc. 80-4, 1980-1 C.B. 581 and Notice 2003-70, 2003-43 I.R.B. 916.) If you are a state or local government also check the box for state/local government.
• **QSub.** For a qualified subchapter S subsidiary (QSub) check the "Other" box and specify "QSub."
• **Withholding agent.** If you are a withholding agent required to file Form 1042, check the "Other" box and enter "Withholding Agent."

Limited Liability Company (LLC). Complete Form SS-4 for LLCs as follows.
• A single-member domestic LLC that accepts the default classification (above) does not need an EIN and generally should not file Form SS-4. Generally, the LLC should use the name and EIN of its owner for all federal tax purposes. However, the reporting and payment of employment taxes for employees of the LLC may be made using the name and EIN of either the owner or the LLC as explained in Notice 99-6. You can find Notice 99-6 on page 12 of Internal Revenue Bulletin 1999-3 at *www.irs.gov/pub/irs-irbs/irb99-03.pdf.*

Note. If the LLC applicant indicates in box 13 that it has employees or expects to have employees, the owner (whether an individual or other entity) of a single-member domestic LLC will also be assigned its own EIN (if it does not already have one) even if the LLC will be filing the employment tax returns.
• A single-member, domestic LLC that accepts the default classification (above) and wants an EIN for filing employment tax returns (see above) or non-federal purposes, such as a state requirement, must check the "Other" box and write "Disregarded Entity" or, when applicable, "Disregarded Entity—Sole Proprietorship" in the space provided.
• A multi-member, domestic LLC that accepts the default classification (above) must check the "Partnership" box.
• A domestic LLC that will be filing Form 8832 to elect corporate status must check the "Corporation" box and write in "Single-Member" or "Multi-Member" immediately below the "form number" entry line.

Line 10. Reason for applying. Check only one box. Do not enter "N/A." A selection is required.

Started new business. Check this box if you are starting a new business that requires an EIN. If you check this box, enter the type of business being started. Do not apply if you already have an EIN and are only adding another place of business.

Hired employees. Check this box if the existing business is requesting an EIN because it has hired or is hiring employees and is therefore required to file employment tax returns. Do not apply if you already have an EIN and are only hiring employees. For information on employment taxes (for example, for family members), see Pub. 15 (Circular E).

 You may have to make electronic deposits of all depository taxes (such as employment tax, excise tax, and corporate income tax) using the Electronic Federal Tax Payment System (EFTPS). See Federal tax deposits on page 1; section 11, Depositing Taxes, of Pub. 15 (Circular E); and Pub. 966.

Banking purpose. Check this box if you are requesting an EIN for banking purposes only, and enter the banking purpose (for example, a bowling league for depositing dues or an investment club for dividend and interest reporting).

Changed type of organization. Check this box if the business is changing its type of organization. For example, the business was a sole proprietorship and has been incorporated or has become a partnership. If you check this box, specify in the space provided (including available space immediately below) the type of change made. For example, "From Sole Proprietorship to Partnership."

Purchased going business. Check this box if you purchased an existing business. Do not use the former owner's EIN unless you became the "owner" of a corporation by acquiring its stock.

Created a trust. Check this box if you created a trust, and enter the type of trust created. For example, indicate if the trust is a nonexempt charitable trust or a split-interest trust.

Exception. Do not file this form for certain grantor-type trusts. The trustee does not need an EIN for the trust if the trustee furnishes the name and TIN of the grantor/owner and the address of the trust to all payors. However, grantor trusts that do not file using Optional Method 1 and IRA trusts that are required to file Form 990-T, Exempt Organization Business Income Tax Return, must have an EIN. For more information on grantor trusts, see the Instructions for Form 1041.

Do not check this box if you are applying for a trust EIN when a new pension plan is established. Check "Created a pension plan."

Created a pension plan. Check this box if you have created a pension plan and need an EIN for reporting purposes. Also, enter the type of plan in the space provided.

 Check this box if you are applying for a trust EIN when a new pension plan is established. In addition, check the "Other" box on line 9a and write "Created a Pension Plan" in the space provided.

Other. Check this box if you are requesting an EIN for any other reason; and enter the reason. For example, a newly-formed state government entity should enter "Newly-Formed State Government Entity" in the space provided.

Line 11. Date business started or acquired. If you are starting a new business, enter the starting date of the business. If the business you acquired is already operating, enter the date you acquired the business. If you are changing the form of ownership of your business, enter the date the new ownership entity began. Trusts should enter the date the trust was funded. Estates should enter the date of death of the decedent whose name appears on line 1 or the date when the estate was legally funded.

Line 12. Closing month of accounting year. Enter the last month of your accounting year or tax year. An accounting or tax year is usually 12 consecutive months, either a calendar year or a fiscal year (including a period of 52 or 53 weeks). A calendar year is 12 consecutive months ending on December 31. A fiscal year is either 12 consecutive months ending on the last day of any month other than December or a 52-53 week year. For more information on accounting periods, see Pub. 538.

Individuals. Your tax year generally will be a calendar year.

Partnerships. Partnerships must adopt one of the following tax years.
• The tax year of the majority of its partners.
• The tax year common to all of its principal partners.
• The tax year that results in the least aggregate deferral of income.
• In certain cases, some other tax year.

See the Instructions for Form 1065 for more information.

REMICs. REMICs must have a calendar year as their tax year.

Personal service corporations. A personal service corporation generally must adopt a calendar year unless it meets one of the following requirements.
• It can establish a business purpose for having a different tax year.
• It elects under section 444 to have a tax year other than a calendar year.

Trusts. Generally, a trust must adopt a calendar year except for the following trusts.
• Tax-exempt trusts.
• Charitable trusts.
• Grantor-owned trusts.

Line 13. Highest number of employees expected in the next 12 months. Complete each box by entering the number (including zero ("-0-")) of "Agricultural," "Household," or "Other" employees expected by the applicant in the next 12 months.

Line 14. Do you expect your employment tax liability to be $1,000 or less in a full calendar year? Check the appropriate box to indicate if you expect your annual tax liability to be $1,000 or less in a full calendar year. Generally, if you pay $4,000 or less in wages subject to social security and Medicare taxes and federal income tax

withholding, you are likely to pay $1,000 or less in employment taxes.

 For employers in the U.S. possessions, generally, if you pay $6,536 or less in wages subject to social security and Medicare taxes, you are likely to pay $1,000 or less in employment taxes.

For more information on employment taxes, see Pub. 15 (Circular E); or Pub. 51 (Circular A) if you have agricultural employees (farmworkers).

Line 15. First date wages or annuities were paid. If the business has employees, enter the date on which the business began to pay wages. If the business does not plan to have employees, enter "N/A."

Withholding agent. Enter the date you began or will begin to pay income (including annuities) to a nonresident alien. This also applies to individuals who are required to file Form 1042 to report alimony paid to a nonresident alien.

Line 16. Check the one box on line 16 that best describes the principal activity of the applicant's business. Check the "Other" box (and specify the applicant's principal activity) if none of the listed boxes applies. You must check a box.

Construction. Check this box if the applicant is engaged in erecting buildings or engineering projects (for example, streets, highways, bridges, tunnels). The term "Construction" also includes special trade contractors (for example, plumbing, HVAC, electrical, carpentry, concrete, excavation, etc. contractors).

Real estate. Check this box if the applicant is engaged in renting or leasing real estate to others; managing, selling, buying, or renting real estate for others; or providing related real estate services (for example, appraisal services). Also check this box for mortgage real estate investment trusts (REITS). Mortgage REITS are engaged in issuing shares of funds consisting primarily of portfolios of real estate mortgage assets with gross income of the trust solely derived from interest earned.

Rental and leasing. Check this box if the applicant is engaged in providing tangible goods such as autos, computers, consumer goods, or industrial machinery and equipment to customers in return for a periodic rental or lease payment. Also check this box for equity real estate investment trusts (REITS). Equity REITS are engaged in issuing shares of funds consisting primarily of portfolios of real estate assets with gross income of the trust derived from renting real property.

Manufacturing. Check this box if the applicant is engaged in the mechanical, physical, or chemical transformation of materials, substances, or components into new products. The assembling of component parts of manufactured products is also considered to be manufacturing.

Transportation & warehousing. Check this box if the applicant provides transportation of passengers or cargo; warehousing or storage of goods; scenic or sight-seeing transportation; or support activities related to transportation.

Finance & insurance. Check this box if the applicant is engaged in transactions involving the creation, liquidation, or change of ownership of financial assets and/or facilitating such financial transactions; underwriting annuities/insurance policies; facilitating such underwriting by selling insurance policies; or by providing other insurance or employee-benefit related services.

Health care & social assistance. Check this box if the applicant is engaged in providing physical, medical, or psychiatric care or providing social assistance activities such as youth centers, adoption agencies, individual/family services, temporary shelters, daycare, etc.

Accommodation & food services. Check this box if the applicant is engaged in providing customers with lodging, meal preparation, snacks, or beverages for immediate consumption.

Wholesale—agent/broker. Check this box if the applicant is engaged in arranging for the purchase or sale of goods owned by others or purchasing goods on a commission basis for goods traded in the wholesale market, usually between businesses.

Wholesale—other. Check this box if the applicant is engaged in selling goods in the wholesale market generally to other businesses for resale on their own account, goods used in production, or capital or durable nonconsumer goods.

Retail. Check this box if the applicant is engaged in selling merchandise to the general public from a fixed store; by direct, mail-order, or electronic sales; or by using vending machines.

Other. Check this box if the applicant is engaged in an activity not described above. Describe the applicant's principal business activity in the space provided.

Line 17. Use line 17 to describe the applicant's principal line of business in more detail. For example, if you checked the "Construction" box on line 16, enter additional detail such as "General contractor for residential buildings" on line 17. An entry is required. For mortgage REITS indicate mortgage REIT and for equity REITS indicate what type of real property is the principal type (residential REIT, nonresidential REIT, miniwarehouse REIT).

Line 18. Check the applicable box to indicate whether or not the applicant entity applying for an EIN was issued one previously.

Third Party Designee. Complete this section only if you want to authorize the named individual to receive the entity's EIN and answer questions about the completion of Form SS-4. The designee's authority terminates at the time the EIN is assigned and released to the designee. You must complete the signature area for the authorization to be valid.

Signature. When required, the application must be signed by (a) the individual, if the applicant is an individual, (b) the president, vice president, or other principal officer, if the applicant is a corporation, (c) a responsible and duly authorized member or officer having knowledge of its affairs, if the applicant is a partnership, government entity, or other unincorporated organization, or (d) the fiduciary, if the applicant is a trust or an estate. Foreign applicants may have any duly-authorized person (for example, division manager) sign Form SS-4.

Privacy Act and Paperwork Reduction Act Notice. We ask for the information on this form to carry out the Internal Revenue laws of the United States. We need it to comply with section 6109 and the regulations thereunder, which generally require the inclusion of an employer identification number (EIN) on certain returns, statements, or other documents filed with the Internal Revenue Service. If your entity is required to obtain an EIN, you are required to provide all of the information requested on this form. Information on this form may be used to determine which federal tax returns you are required to file and to provide you with related forms and publications.

We disclose this form to the Social Security Administration (SSA) for their use in determining compliance with applicable laws. We may give this information to the Department of Justice for use in civil and criminal litigation, and to the cities, states, and the District of Columbia for use in administering their tax laws. We may also disclose this information to other countries under a tax treaty, to federal and state agencies to enforce federal nontax criminal laws, and to federal law enforcement and intelligence agencies to combat terrorism.

We will be unable to issue an EIN to you unless you provide all of the requested information that applies to your entity. Providing false information could subject you to penalties.

You are not required to provide the information requested on a form that is subject to the Paperwork Reduction Act unless the form displays a valid OMB control number. Books or records relating to a form or its instructions must be retained as long as their contents may become material in the administration of any Internal Revenue law. Generally, tax returns and return information are confidential, as required by section 6103.

The time needed to complete and file this form will vary depending on individual circumstances. The estimated average time is:

Recordkeeping	8 hrs., 22 min.
Learning about the law or the form	42 min.
Preparing the form	52 min.
Copying, assembling, and sending the form to the IRS	- - - - -

If you have comments concerning the accuracy of these time estimates or suggestions for making this form simpler, we would be happy to hear from you. You can write to Internal Revenue Service, Tax Products Coordinating Committee, SE:W:CAR:MP:T:T:SP, IR-6406, 1111 Constitution Avenue, NW, Washington, DC 20224. Do not send the form to this address. Instead, see *Where to File or Fax* on page 2.

Form **2553**
(Rev. December 2006)

Department of the Treasury
Internal Revenue Service

Election by a Small Business Corporation

(Under section 1362 of the Internal Revenue Code)

See Parts II and III on back and the separate instructions.

The corporation can fax this form to the IRS (see separate instructions).

OMB No. 1545-0146

Notes: 1. **Do not** file **Form 1120S,** U.S. Income Tax Return for an S Corporation, for any tax year before the year the election takes effect.

2. This election to be an S corporation can be accepted only if all the tests are met under **Who May Elect** on page 1 of the instructions; all shareholders have signed the consent statement; an officer has signed this form; and the exact name and address of the corporation and other required form information are provided.

Part I Election Information

Please Type or Print

Name (see instructions)	**A** Employer identification number
Number, street, and room or suite no. (If a P.O. box, see instructions.)	**B** Date incorporated
City or town, state, and ZIP code	**C** State of incorporation

D Check the applicable box(es) if the corporation, after applying for the EIN shown in **A** above, changed its name ☐ or address ☐

E Election is to be effective for tax year beginning (month, day, year) (see instructions) . . . .   /   /

F Name and title of officer or legal representative who the IRS may call for more information

G Telephone number of officer or legal representative

( )

H If this election takes effect for the first tax year the corporation exists, enter month, day, and year of the **earliest** of the following: (1) date the corporation first had shareholders, (2) date the corporation first had assets, or (3) date the corporation began doing business . . . .   /   /

I Selected tax year: Annual return will be filed for tax year ending (month and day) ....

If the tax year ends on any date other than December 31, except for a 52-53-week tax year ending with reference to the month of December, complete Part II on the back. If the date you enter is the ending date of a 52-53-week tax year, write "52-53-week year" to the right of the date.

J Name and address of each shareholder or former shareholder required to consent to the election. (See the instructions for column K) If more than 100 shareholders are listed, check the box if treating members of a family as one shareholder results in no more than 100 shareholders (see test 2 under **Who May Elect** in the instructions) . . . ☐	**K** Shareholders' Consent Statement. Under penalties of perjury, we declare that we consent to the election of the above-named corporation to be an S corporation under section 1362(a) and that we have examined this consent statement, including accompanying schedules and statements, and to the best of our knowledge and belief, it is true, correct, and complete. We understand our consent is binding and may not be withdrawn after the corporation has made a valid election. (Sign and date below.)		**L** Stock owned or percentage of ownership (see instructions)		**M** Social security number or employer identification number (see instructions)	**N** Share-holder's tax year ends (month and day)
	Signature	Date	Number of shares or percentage of ownership	Date(s) acquired		

Under penalties of perjury, I declare that I have examined this election, including accompanying schedules and statements, and to the best of my knowledge and belief, it is true, correct, and complete.

Signature of officer	Title	Date

For Paperwork Reduction Act Notice, see separate instructions. Cat. No. 18629R Form **2553** (Rev. 12-2006)

200

Part II   Selection of Fiscal Tax Year (see instructions)

Note: *All corporations using this part must complete item O and item P, Q, or R.*

O   Check the applicable box to indicate whether the corporation is:

    1. ☐ A new corporation **adopting** the tax year entered in item I, Part I.

    2. ☐ An existing corporation **retaining** the tax year entered in item I, Part I.

    3. ☐ An existing corporation **changing** to the tax year entered in item I, Part I.

P   Complete item P if the corporation is using the automatic approval provisions of Rev. Proc. 2006-46, 2006-45 I.R.B. 859, to request **(1)** a natural business year (as defined in section 5.07 of Rev. Proc. 2006-46) or **(2)** a year that satisfies the ownership tax year test (as defined in section 5.08 of Rev. Proc. 2006-46). Check the applicable box below to indicate the representation statement the corporation is making.

    1. Natural Business Year   ☐ I represent that the corporation is adopting, retaining, or changing to a tax year that qualifies as its natural business year (as defined in section 5.07 of Rev. Proc. 2006-46) and has attached a statement showing separately for each month the gross receipts for the most recent 47 months (see instructions). I also represent that the corporation is not precluded by section 4.02 of Rev. Proc. 2006-46 from obtaining automatic approval of such adoption, retention, or change in tax year.

    2. Ownership Tax Year   ☐ I represent that shareholders (as described in section 5.08 of Rev. Proc. 2006-46) holding more than half of the shares of the stock (as of the first day of the tax year to which the request relates) of the corporation have the same tax year or are concurrently changing to the tax year that the corporation adopts, retains, or changes to per item I, Part I, and that such tax year satisfies the requirement of section 4.01(3) of Rev. Proc. 2006-46. I also represent that the corporation is not precluded by section 4.02 of Rev. Proc. 2006-46 from obtaining automatic approval of such adoption, retention, or change in tax year.

Note: *If you do not use item P and the corporation wants a fiscal tax year, complete either item Q or R below. Item Q is used to request a fiscal tax year based on a business purpose and to make a back-up section 444 election. Item R is used to make a regular section 444 election.*

Q   Business Purpose—To request a fiscal tax year based on a business purpose, check box Q1. See instructions for details including payment of a user fee. You may also check box Q2 and/or box Q3.

    1. Check here   ☐ if the fiscal year entered in item I, Part I, is requested under the prior approval provisions of Rev. Proc. 2002-39, 2002-22 I.R.B. 1046. Attach to Form 2553 a statement describing the relevant facts and circumstances and, if applicable, the gross receipts from sales and services necessary to establish a business purpose. See the instructions for details regarding the gross receipts from sales and services. If the IRS proposes to disapprove the requested fiscal year, do you want a conference with the IRS National Office?

    ☐ Yes   ☐ No

    2. Check here   ☐ to show that the corporation intends to make a back-up section 444 election in the event the corporation's business purpose request is not approved by the IRS. (See instructions for more information.)

    3. Check here   ☐ to show that the corporation agrees to adopt or change to a tax year ending December 31 if necessary for the IRS to accept this election for S corporation status in the event (1) the corporation's business purpose request is not approved and the corporation makes a back-up section 444 election, but is ultimately not qualified to make a section 444 election, or (2) the corporation's business purpose request is not approved and the corporation did not make a back-up section 444 election.

R   Section 444 Election—To make a section 444 election, check box R1. You may also check box R2.

    1. Check here   ☐ to show that the corporation will make, if qualified, a section 444 election to have the fiscal tax year shown in item I, Part I. To make the election, you must complete **Form 8716,** Election To Have a Tax Year Other Than a Required Tax Year, and either attach it to Form 2553 or file it separately.

    2. Check here   ☐ to show that the corporation agrees to adopt or change to a tax year ending December 31 if necessary for the IRS to accept this election for S corporation status in the event the corporation is ultimately not qualified to make a section 444 election.

Part III   Qualified Subchapter S Trust (QSST) Election Under Section 1361(d)(2)*

Income beneficiary's name and address	Social security number
Trust's name and address	Employer identification number

Date on which stock of the corporation was transferred to the trust (month, day, year) . . . .   /   /

In order for the trust named above to be a QSST and thus a qualifying shareholder of the S corporation for which this Form 2553 is filed, I hereby make the election under section 1361(d)(2). Under penalties of perjury, I certify that the trust meets the definitional requirements of section 1361(d)(3) and that all other information provided in Part III is true, correct, and complete.

_____   _____
Signature of income beneficiary or signature and title of legal representative or other qualified person making the election   Date

*Use Part III to make the QSST election only if stock of the corporation has been transferred to the trust on or before the date on which the corporation makes its election to be an S corporation. The QSST election must be made and filed separately if stock of the corporation is transferred to the trust **after** the date on which the corporation makes the S election.

Instructions for Form 2553

Department of the Treasury
Internal Revenue Service

(Rev. December 2006)

Election by a Small Business Corporation

Section references are to the Internal Revenue Code unless otherwise noted.

General Instructions

Purpose of Form

A corporation or other entity eligible to elect to be treated as a corporation must use Form 2553 to make an election under section 1362(a) to be an S corporation. An entity eligible to elect to be treated as a corporation that meets certain tests discussed below will be treated as a corporation as of the effective date of the S corporation election and does not need to file Form 8832, Entity Classification Election.

The income of an S corporation generally is taxed to the shareholders of the corporation rather than to the corporation itself. However, an S corporation may still owe tax on certain income. For details, see *Tax and Payments* in the instructions for Form 1120S, U.S. Income Tax Return for an S Corporation.

Who May Elect

A corporation or other entity eligible to elect to be treated as a corporation may elect to be an S corporation only if it meets all the following tests.

1. It is (a) a domestic corporation, or (b) a domestic entity eligible to elect to be treated as a corporation, that timely files Form 2553 and meets all the other tests listed below. If Form 2553 is not timely filed, see Rev. Proc. 2004-48, 2004-32 I.R.B. 172.

2. It has no more than 100 shareholders. You can treat a husband and wife (and their estates) as one shareholder for this test. You can also treat all members of a family (as defined in section 1361(c)(1)(B)) and their estates as one shareholder for this test. All others are treated as separate shareholders. For details, see section 1361(c)(1).

3. Its only shareholders are individuals, estates, exempt organizations described in section 401(a) or 501(c)(3), or certain trusts described in section 1361(c)(2)(A).

For information about the section 1361(d)(2) election to be a qualified subchapter S trust (QSST), see the instructions for Part III. For information about the section 1361(e)(3) election to be an electing small business trust (ESBT), see Regulations section 1.1361-1(m). For guidance on how to convert a QSST to an ESBT, see Regulations section 1.1361-1(j)(12). If these elections were not timely made, see Rev. Proc. 2003-43, 2003-23 I.R.B. 998.

4. It has no nonresident alien shareholders.

5. It has only one class of stock (disregarding differences in voting rights). Generally, a corporation is treated as having only one class of stock if all outstanding shares of the corporation's stock confer identical rights to distribution and liquidation proceeds. See Regulations section 1.1361-1(l) for details.

6. It is not one of the following ineligible corporations.

a. A bank or thrift institution that uses the reserve method of accounting for bad debts under section 585.

b. An insurance company subject to tax under subchapter L of the Code.

c. A corporation that has elected to be treated as a possessions corporation under section 936.

d. A domestic international sales corporation (DISC) or former DISC.

7. It has or will adopt or change to one of the following tax years.

a. A tax year ending December 31.

b. A natural business year.

c. An ownership tax year.

d. A tax year elected under section 444.

e. A 52-53-week tax year ending with reference to a year listed above.

f. Any other tax year (including a 52-53-week tax year) for which the corporation establishes a business purpose.

For details on making a section 444 election or requesting a natural business, ownership, or other business purpose tax year, see Part II of Form 2553.

8. Each shareholder consents as explained in the instructions for column K.

See sections 1361, 1362, and 1378, and their related regulations for additional information on the above tests.

A parent S corporation can elect to treat an eligible wholly-owned subsidiary as a qualified subchapter S subsidiary. If the election is made, the subsidiary's assets, liabilities, and items of income, deduction, and credit are treated as those of the parent. For details, see Form 8869, Qualified Subchapter S Subsidiary Election.

When To Make the Election

Complete and file Form 2553:
- No more than two months and 15 days after the beginning of the tax year the election is to take effect, or
- At any time during the tax year preceding the tax year it is to take effect.

For this purpose, the 2 month period begins on the day of the month the tax year begins and ends with the close of the day before the numerically corresponding day of the second calendar month following that month. If there is no corresponding day, use the close of the last day of the calendar month.

Example 1. No prior tax year. A calendar year small business corporation begins its first tax year on January 7. The two month period ends March 6 and 15 days after that is March 21. To be an S corporation beginning with its first tax year, the corporation must file Form 2553 during the period that begins January 7 and ends March 21. Because the corporation had no prior tax year, an election made before January 7 will not be valid.

Example 2. Prior tax year. A calendar year small business corporation has been filing Form 1120 as a C corporation but wishes to make an S election for its next tax year beginning January 1. The two month period ends February 28 (29 in leap years) and 15 days after that is March 15. To be an S corporation beginning with its next tax year, the corporation must file Form 2553 during the period that begins the first day (January 1) of its last year as a C corporation and ends March 15th of the year it wishes to be an S corporation. Because the corporation had a prior tax year, it can make the election at any time during that prior tax year.

Cat. No. 49978N

Example 3. Tax year less than 2 1/2 months. A calendar year small business corporation begins its first tax year on November 8. The two month period ends January 7 and 15 days after that is January 22. To be an S corporation beginning with its short tax year, the corporation must file Form 2553 during the period that begins November 8 and ends January 22. Because the corporation had no prior tax year, an election made before November 8 will not be valid.

A late election generally is effective for the next tax year. However, a late election will be accepted as timely filed if the corporation can show that the failure to file on time was due to reasonable cause.

Relief for late elections. To request relief for a late election, the corporation generally must request a private letter ruling and pay a user fee in accordance with Rev. Proc. 2007-1, 2007-1 I.R.B. 1 (or its successor). However, the ruling and user fee requirements may not apply if the following revenue procedures apply.
- If an entity eligible to elect to be treated as a corporation (a) failed to timely file Form 2553, and (b) has not elected to be treated as a corporation, see Rev. Proc. 2004-48, 2004-32 I.R.B. 172.
- If a corporation failed to timely file Form 2553, see Rev. Proc. 2003-43, 2003-23 I.R.B. 998.
- If Form 1120S was filed without an S corporation election and neither the corporation nor any shareholder was notified by the IRS of any problem with the S corporation status within 6 months after the return was timely filed, see Rev. Proc. 97-48, 1997-43 I.R.B. 19.

Where To File

Send the original election (no photocopies) or fax it to the Internal Revenue Service Center listed below. If the corporation files this election by fax, keep the original Form 2553 with the corporation's permanent records.

If the corporation's principal business, office, or agency is located in:	Use the following Internal Revenue Service Center address or fax number:
Connecticut, Delaware, District of Columbia, Illinois, Indiana, Kentucky, Maine, Maryland, Massachusetts, Michigan, New Hampshire, New Jersey, New York, North Carolina, Ohio, Pennsylvania, Rhode Island, South Carolina, Vermont, Virginia, West Virginia, Wisconsin	Cincinnati, OH 45999 Fax: (859) 669-5748
Alabama, Alaska, Arizona, Arkansas, California, Colorado, Florida, Georgia, Hawaii, Idaho, Iowa, Kansas, Louisiana, Minnesota, Mississippi, Missouri, Montana, Nebraska, Nevada, New Mexico, North Dakota, Oklahoma, Oregon, South Dakota, Tennessee, Texas, Utah, Washington, Wyoming	Ogden, UT 84201 Fax: (801) 620-7116

Acceptance or Nonacceptance of Election

The service center will notify the corporation if its election is accepted and when it will take effect. The corporation will also be notified if its election is not accepted. The corporation should generally receive a determination on its election within 60 days after it has filed Form 2553. If box Q1 in Part II is checked, the corporation will receive a ruling letter from the IRS in Washington, DC, that either approves or denies the selected tax year. When box Q1 is checked, it will generally take an additional 90 days for the Form 2553 to be accepted.

Care should be exercised to ensure that the IRS receives the election. If the corporation is not notified of acceptance or nonacceptance of its election within 2 months of the date of filing (date faxed or mailed), or within 5 months if box Q1 is checked, take follow-up action by calling 1-800-829-4933.

If the IRS questions whether Form 2553 was filed, an acceptable proof of filing is (a) a certified or registered mail receipt (timely postmarked) from the U.S. Postal Service, or its equivalent from a designated private delivery service (see Notice 2004-83, 2004-52 I.R.B. 1030 (or its successor)); (b) Form 2553 with an accepted stamp; (c) Form 2553 with a stamped IRS received date; or (d) an IRS letter stating that Form 2553 has been accepted.

 Do not file Form 1120S for any tax year before the year the election takes effect. If the corporation is now required to file Form 1120, U.S. Corporation Income Tax Return, or any other applicable tax return, continue filing it until the election takes effect.

End of Election

Once the election is made, it stays in effect until it is terminated. IRS consent generally is required for another election by the corporation (or a successor corporation) on Form 2553 for any tax year before the 5th tax year after the first tax year in which the termination took effect. See Regulations section 1.1362-5 for details.

Specific Instructions

Part I

Name and Address

Enter the corporation's true name as stated in the corporate charter or other legal document creating it. If the corporation's mailing address is the same as someone else's, such as a shareholder's, enter "C/O" and this person's name following the name of the corporation. Include the suite, room, or other unit number after the street address. If the Post Office does not deliver to the street address and the corporation has a P.O. box, show the box number instead of the street address. If the corporation changed its name or address after applying for its employer identification number, be sure to check the box in item D of Part I.

Item A. Employer Identification Number (EIN)

Enter the corporation's EIN. If the corporation does not have an EIN, it must apply for one. An EIN can be applied for:
- Online—Click on the EIN link at *www.irs.gov/businesses/small*. The EIN is issued immediately once the application information is validated.
- By telephone at 1-800-829-4933 from 7:00 a.m. to 10:00 p.m. in the corporation's local time zone.
- By mailing or faxing Form SS-4, Application for Employer Identification Number.

If the corporation has not received its EIN by the time the return is due, enter "Applied For" and the date you applied in the space for the EIN. For more details, see the Instructions for Form SS-4.

Line 2. Trade name of business. Enter the trade name of the business if different from the legal name. The trade name is the "doing business as" (DBA) name.

 Use the full legal name shown on line 1 on all tax returns filed for the entity. (However, if you enter a trade name on line 2 and choose to use the trade name instead of the legal name, enter the trade name on all returns you file.) To prevent processing delays and errors, always use the legal name only (or the trade name only) on all tax returns.

Line 3. Executor, administrator, trustee, "care of" name. Trusts enter the name of the trustee. Estates enter the name of the executor, administrator, or other fiduciary. If the entity applying has a designated person to receive tax information, enter that person's name as the "care of" person. Enter the individual's first name, middle initial, and last name.

Lines 4a–b. Mailing address. Enter the mailing address for the entity's correspondence. If the entity's address is outside the United States or its possessions, you must enter the city, province or state, postal code, and the name of the country. Do not abbreviate the country name. If line 3 is completed, enter the address for the executor, trustee or "care of" person. Generally, this address will be used on all tax returns.

If the entity is filing the Form SS-4 only to obtain an EIN for the Form 8832, use the same address where you would like to have the acceptance or nonacceptance letter sent.

 File Form 8822, Change of Address, to report any subsequent changes to the entity's mailing address.

Lines 5a–b. Street address. Provide the entity's physical address only if different from its mailing address shown in lines 4a–b. Do not enter a P.O. box number here. If the entity's address is outside the United States or its possessions, you must enter the city, province or state, postal code, and the name of the country. Do not abbreviate the country name.

Line 6. County and state where principal business is located. Enter the entity's primary physical location.

Lines 7a–b. Name of principal officer, general partner, grantor, owner, or trustor. Enter the first name, middle initial, last name, and SSN of (a) the principal officer if the business is a corporation, (b) a general partner if a partnership, (c) the owner of an entity that is disregarded as separate from its owner (disregarded entities owned by a corporation enter the corporation's name and EIN), or (d) a grantor, owner, or trustor if a trust.

If the person in question is an alien individual with a previously assigned individual taxpayer identification number (ITIN), enter the ITIN in the space provided and submit a copy of an official identifying document. If necessary, complete Form W-7, Application for IRS Individual Taxpayer Identification Number, to obtain an ITIN.

You must enter an SSN, ITIN, or EIN unless the only reason you are applying for an EIN is to make an entity classification election (see Regulations sections 301.7701-1 through 301.7701-3) and you are a nonresident alien or other foreign entity with no effectively connected income from sources within the United States.

Lines 8a–c. Limited liability company (LLC) information. An LLC is an entity organized under the laws of a state or foreign country as a limited liability company. For federal tax purposes, an LLC may be treated as a partnership or corporation or be disregarded as an entity separate from its owner.

By default, a domestic LLC with only one member is disregarded as an entity separate from its owner and must include all of its income and expenses on the owner's tax return (for example, Schedule C (Form 1040)). Also by default, a domestic LLC with two or more members is treated as a partnership. A domestic LLC may file Form 8832 to avoid either default classification and elect to be classified as an association taxable as a corporation. For more information on entity classifications (including the rules for foreign entities), see the instructions for Form 8832.

If the answer to line 8a is "Yes," enter the number of LLC members. If the LLC is owned solely by a husband and wife in a community property state and the husband and wife choose to treat the entity as a disregarded entity, enter "1" on line 8b.

 Do not file Form 8832 if the LLC accepts the default classifications above. If the LLC is eligible to be treated as a corporation that meets certain tests and it will be electing S corporation status, it must timely file Form 2553. The LLC will be treated as a corporation as of the effective date of the S corporation election and does not need to file Form 8832. See the Instructions for Form 2553.

Line 9a. Type of entity. Check the box that best describes the type of entity applying for the EIN. If you are an alien individual with an ITIN previously assigned to you, enter the ITIN in place of a requested SSN.

 This is not an election for a tax classification of an entity. See Limited Liability Company (LLC) *on page 4.*

Sole proprietor. Check this box if you file Schedule C, C-EZ, or F (Form 1040) and have a qualified plan, or are required to file excise, employment, alcohol, tobacco, or firearms returns, or are a payer of gambling winnings. Enter your SSN (or ITIN) in the space provided. If you are a nonresident alien with no effectively connected income from sources within the United States, you do not need to enter an SSN or ITIN.

Corporation. This box is for any corporation other than a personal service corporation. If you check this box, enter the income tax form number to be filed by the entity in the space provided.

 If you entered "1120S" after the "Corporation" checkbox, the corporation must file Form 2553 no later than the 15th day of the 3rd month of the tax year the election is to take effect. Until Form 2553 has been received and approved, you will be considered a Form 1120 filer. See the Instructions for Form 2553.

Personal service corporation. Check this box if the entity is a personal service corporation. An entity is a personal service corporation for a tax year only if:
• The principal activity of the entity during the testing period (prior tax year) for the tax year is the performance of personal services substantially by employee-owners, and
• The employee-owners own at least 10% of the fair market value of the outstanding stock in the entity on the last day of the testing period.

Personal services include performance of services in such fields as health, law, accounting, or consulting. For more information about personal service corporations, see the Instructions for Forms 1120 and 1120-A and Pub. 542.

 If the corporation is recently formed, the testing period begins on the first day of its tax year and ends on the earlier of the last day of its tax year, or the last day of the calendar year in which its tax year begins.

Other nonprofit organization. Check this box if the nonprofit organization is other than a church or church-controlled organization and specify the type of nonprofit organization (for example, an educational organization).

seasonal business test, provide the gross receipts from sales and services (and inventory costs, if applicable) for each month of the short period, if any, and the three immediately preceding tax years. If the corporation has been in existence for less than three tax years, submit figures for the period of existence.

If you check box Q1, you will be charged a user fee of $1,500 (subject to change by Rev. Proc. 2008-1 or its successor). Do not pay the fee when filing Form 2553. The service center will send Form 2553 to the IRS in Washington, DC, who, in turn, will notify the corporation that the fee is due.

Box Q2

If the corporation makes a back-up section 444 election for which it is qualified, then the section 444 election will take effect in the event the business purpose request is not approved. In some cases, the tax year requested under the back-up section 444 election may be different than the tax year requested under business purpose. See Form 8716, Election To Have a Tax Year Other Than a Required Tax Year, for details on making a back-up section 444 election.

Boxes Q3 and R2

If the corporation is not qualified to make the section 444 election after making the item Q2 back-up section 444 election or indicating its intention to make the election in item R1, and therefore it later files a calendar year return, it should write "Section 444 Election Not Made" in the top left corner of the first calendar year Form 1120S it files.

Part III

In Part III, the income beneficiary (or legal representative) of certain qualified subchapter S trusts (QSSTs) may make the QSST election required by section 1361(d)(2). Part III may be used to make the QSST election only if corporate stock has been transferred to the trust on or before the date on which the corporation makes its election to be an S corporation. However, a statement can be used instead of Part III to make the election. If there was an inadvertent failure to timely file a QSST election, see the relief provisions under Rev. Proc. 2003-43.

Note. Use Part III only if you make the election in Part I. Form 2553 cannot be filed with only Part III completed.

The deemed owner of the QSST must also consent to the S corporation election in column K of Form 2553.

Paperwork Reduction Act Notice. We ask for the information on this form to carry out the Internal Revenue laws of the United States. You are required to give us the information. We need it to ensure that you are complying with these laws and to allow us to figure and collect the right amount of tax.

You are not required to provide the information requested on a form that is subject to the Paperwork Reduction Act unless the form displays a valid OMB control number. Books or records relating to a form or its instructions must be retained as long as their contents may become material in the administration of any Internal Revenue law. Generally, tax returns and return information are confidential, as required by section 6103.

The time needed to complete and file this form will depend on individual circumstances. The estimated average time is:

Recordkeeping	9 hr., 19 min.
Learning about the law or the form	3 hr., 9 min.
Preparing, copying, assembling, and sending the form to the IRS	4 hr., 38 min.

If you have comments concerning the accuracy of these time estimates or suggestions for making this form simpler, we would be happy to hear from you. You can write to Internal Revenue Service, Tax Products Coordinating Committee, SE:W:CAR:MP:T:T:SP, 1111 Constitution Ave. NW, IR-6406, Washington, DC 20224. Do not send the form to this address. Instead, see *Where To File* on page 2.

OMB No. 1615-0047; Expires 06/30/08

Department of Homeland Security
U.S. Citizenship and Immigration Services

Form I-9, Employment Eligibility Verification

Please read instructions carefully before completing this form. The instructions must be available during completion of this form.

ANTI-DISCRIMINATION NOTICE: It is illegal to discriminate against work eligible individuals. Employers CANNOT specify which document(s) they will accept from an employee. The refusal to hire an individual because the documents have a future expiration date may also constitute illegal discrimination.

Section 1. Employee Information and Verification. To be completed and signed by employee at the time employment begins.

Print Name: Last	First	Middle Initial	Maiden Name

Address *(Street Name and Number)*	Apt. #	Date of Birth *(month/day/year)*

City	State	Zip Code	Social Security #

I am aware that federal law provides for imprisonment and/or fines for false statements or use of false documents in connection with the completion of this form.

I attest, under penalty of perjury, that I am (check one of the following):

☐ A citizen or national of the United States
☐ A lawful permanent resident (Alien #) _____
☐ An alien authorized to work until _____
(Alien # or Admission #) _____

Employee's Signature	Date *(month/day/year)*

Preparer and/or Translator Certification. *(To be completed and signed if Section 1 is prepared by a person other than the employee.)* I attest, under penalty of perjury, that I have assisted in the completion of this form and that to the best of my knowledge the information is true and correct.

Preparer's/Translator's Signature	Print Name

Address *(Street Name and Number, City, State, Zip Code)*	Date *(month/day/year)*

Section 2. Employer Review and Verification. To be completed and signed by employer. Examine one document from List A OR examine one document from List B and one from List C, as listed on the reverse of this form, and record the title, number and expiration date, if any, of the document(s).

List A	OR	List B	AND	List C
Document title:				
Issuing authority:				
Document #:				
Expiration Date *(if any):*				
Document #:				
Expiration Date *(if any):*				

CERTIFICATION - I attest, under penalty of perjury, that I have examined the document(s) presented by the above-named employee, that the above-listed document(s) appear to be genuine and to relate to the employee named, that the employee began employment on *(month/day/year)* _____ **and that to the best of my knowledge the employee is eligible to work in the United States. (State employment agencies may omit the date the employee began employment.)**

Signature of Employer or Authorized Representative	Print Name	Title

Business or Organization Name and Address *(Street Name and Number, City, State, Zip Code)*	Date *(month/day/year)*

Section 3. Updating and Reverification. To be completed and signed by employer.

A. New Name *(if applicable)*	B. Date of Rehire *(month/day/year) (if applicable)*

C. If employee's previous grant of work authorization has expired, provide the information below for the document that establishes current employment eligibility.

Document Title:	Document #:	Expiration Date (if any):

I attest, under penalty of perjury, that to the best of my knowledge, this employee is eligible to work in the United States, and if the employee presented document(s), the document(s) I have examined appear to be genuine and to relate to the individual.

Signature of Employer or Authorized Representative	Date *(month/day/year)*

Form I-9 (Rev. 06/05/07) N

OMB No. 1615-0047; Expires 06/30/08

Department of Homeland Security
U.S. Citizenship and Immigration Services

Form I-9, Employment Eligibility Verification

Instructions
Please read all instructions carefully before completing this form.

Anti-Discrimination Notice. It is illegal to discriminate against any individual (other than an alien not authorized to work in the U.S.) in hiring, discharging, or recruiting or referring for a fee because of that individual's national origin or citizenship status. It is illegal to discriminate against work eligible individuals. Employers **CANNOT** specify which document(s) they will accept from an employee. The refusal to hire an individual because the documents presented have a future expiration date may also constitute illegal discrimination.

What Is the Purpose of This Form?

The purpose of this form is to document that each new employee (both citizen and non-citizen) hired after November 6, 1986 is authorized to work in the United States.

When Should the Form I-9 Be Used?

All employees, citizens and noncitizens, hired after November 6, 1986 and working in the United States must complete a Form I-9.

Filling Out the Form I-9

Section 1, Employee: This part of the form must be completed at the time of hire, which is the actual beginning of employment. Providing the Social Security number is voluntary, except for employees hired by employers participating in the USCIS Electronic Employment Eligibility Verification Program (E-Verify). **The employer is responsible for ensuring that Section 1 is timely and properly completed.**

Preparer/Translator Certification. The Preparer/Translator Certification must be completed if **Section 1** is prepared by a person other than the employee. A preparer/translator may be used only when the employee is unable to complete **Section 1** on his/her own. However, the employee must still sign **Section 1** personally.

Section 2, Employer: For the purpose of completing this form, the term "employer" means all employers including those recruiters and referrers for a fee who are agricultural associations, agricultural employers or farm labor contractors.

Employers must complete **Section 2** by examining evidence of identity and employment eligibility within three (3) business days of the date employment begins. If employees are authorized to work, but are unable to present the required document(s) within three business days, they must present a receipt for the application of the document(s) within three business days and the actual document(s) within ninety (90) days. However, if employers hire individuals for a duration of less than three business days, **Section 2** must be completed at the time employment begins. **Employers must record:**

1. Document title;
2. Issuing authority;
3. Document number;
4. Expiration date, if any; and
5. The date employment begins.

Employers must sign and date the certification. Employees must present original documents. Employers may, but are not required to, photocopy the document(s) presented. These photocopies may only be used for the verification process and must be retained with the Form I-9. **However, employers are still responsible for completing and retaining the Form I-9.**

Section 3, Updating and Reverification: Employers must complete **Section 3** when updating and/or reverifying the Form I-9. Employers must reverify employment eligibility of their employees on or before the expiration date recorded in **Section 1.** Employers **CANNOT** specify which document(s) they will accept from an employee.

A. If an employee's name has changed at the time this form is being updated/reverified, complete Block A.

B. If an employee is rehired within three (3) years of the date this form was originally completed and the employee is still eligible to be employed on the same basis as previously indicated on this form (updating), complete Block B and the signature block.

C. If an employee is rehired within three (3) years of the date this form was originally completed and the employee's work authorization has expired **or** if a current employee's work authorization is about to expire (reverification), complete Block B and:

1. Examine any document that reflects that the employee is authorized to work in the U.S. (see List A **or** C);
2. Record the document title, document number and expiration date (if any) in Block C, and
3. Complete the signature block.

What Is the Filing Fee?

There is no associated filing fee for completing the Form I-9. This form is not filed with USCIS or any government agency. The Form I-9 must be retained by the employer and made available for inspection by U.S. Government officials as specified in the Privacy Act Notice below.

USCIS Forms and Information

To order USCIS forms, call our toll-free number at **1-800-870-3676**. Individuals can also get USCIS forms and information on immigration laws, regulations and procedures by telephoning our National Customer Service Center at **1-800-375-5283** or visiting our internet website at **www.uscis.gov**.

Photocopying and Retaining the Form I-9

A blank Form I-9 may be reproduced, provided both sides are copied. The Instructions must be available to all employees completing this form. Employers must retain completed Forms I-9 for three (3) years after the date of hire or one (1) year after the date employment ends, whichever is later.

The Form I-9 may be signed and retained electronically, as authorized in Department of Homeland Security regulations at 8 CFR § 274a.2.

Privacy Act Notice

The authority for collecting this information is the Immigration Reform and Control Act of 1986, Pub. L. 99-603 (8 USC 1324a).

This information is for employers to verify the eligibility of individuals for employment to preclude the unlawful hiring, or recruiting or referring for a fee, of aliens who are not authorized to work in the United States.

This information will be used by employers as a record of their basis for determining eligibility of an employee to work in the United States. The form will be kept by the employer and made available for inspection by officials of U.S. Immigration and Customs Enforcement, Department of Labor and Office of Special Counsel for Immigration Related Unfair Employment Practices.

Submission of the information required in this form is voluntary. However, an individual may not begin employment unless this form is completed, since employers are subject to civil or criminal penalties if they do not comply with the Immigration Reform and Control Act of 1986.

Paperwork Reduction Act

We try to create forms and instructions that are accurate, can be easily understood and which impose the least possible burden on you to provide us with information. Often this is difficult because some immigration laws are very complex. Accordingly, the reporting burden for this collection of information is computed as follows: **1)** learning about this form, and completing the form, 9 minutes; **2)** assembling and filing (recordkeeping) the form, 3 minutes, for an average of 12 minutes per response. If you have comments regarding the accuracy of this burden estimate, or suggestions for making this form simpler, you can write to: U.S. Citizenship and Immigration Services, Regulatory Management Division, 111 Massachusetts Avenue, N.W., 3rd Floor, Suite 3008, Washington, DC 20529. OMB No. 1615-0047.

LISTS OF ACCEPTABLE DOCUMENTS

LIST A	LIST B	LIST C
Documents that Establish Both Identity and Employment Eligibility OR	**Documents that Establish Identity** AND	**Documents that Establish Employment Eligibility**
1. U.S. Passport (unexpired or expired)	1. Driver's license or ID card issued by a state or outlying possession of the United States provided it contains a photograph or information such as name, date of birth, gender, height, eye color and address	1. U.S. Social Security card issued by the Social Security Administration *(other than a card stating it is not valid for employment)*
2. Permanent Resident Card or Alien Registration Receipt Card (Form I-551)	2. ID card issued by federal, state or local government agencies or entities, provided it contains a photograph or information such as name, date of birth, gender, height, eye color and address	2. Certification of Birth Abroad issued by the Department of State *(Form FS-545 or Form DS-1350)*
3. An unexpired foreign passport with a temporary I-551 stamp	3. School ID card with a photograph	3. Original or certified copy of a birth certificate issued by a state, county, municipal authority or outlying possession of the United States bearing an official seal
4. An unexpired Employment Authorization Document that contains a photograph (Form I-766, I-688, I-688A, I-688B)	4. Voter's registration card	4. Native American tribal document
4. (cont.)	5. U.S. Military card or draft record	5. U.S. Citizen ID Card *(Form I-197)*
5. An unexpired foreign passport with an unexpired Arrival-Departure Record, Form I-94, bearing the same name as the passport and containing an endorsement of the alien's nonimmigrant status, if that status authorizes the alien to work for the employer	6. Military dependent's ID card	6. ID Card for use of Resident Citizen in the United States *(Form I-179)*
	7. U.S. Coast Guard Merchant Mariner Card	
	8. Native American tribal document	7. Unexpired employment authorization document issued by DHS *(other than those listed under List A)*
	9. Driver's license issued by a Canadian government authority	
	For persons under age 18 who are unable to present a document listed above:	
	10. School record or report card	
	11. Clinic, doctor or hospital record	
	12. Day-care or nursery school record	

Illustrations of many of these documents appear in Part 8 of the Handbook for Employers (M-274)

Form W-4 (2007)

Purpose. Complete Form W-4 so that your employer can withhold the correct federal income tax from your pay. Because your tax situation may change, you may want to refigure your withholding each year.

Exemption from withholding. If you are exempt, complete **only** lines 1, 2, 3, 4, and 7 and sign the form to validate it. Your exemption for 2007 expires February 16, 2008. See Pub. 505, Tax Withholding and Estimated Tax.

Note. You cannot claim exemption from withholding if (a) your income exceeds $850 and includes more than $300 of unearned income (for example, interest and dividends) and (b) another person can claim you as a dependent on their tax return.

Basic instructions. If you are not exempt, complete the **Personal Allowances Worksheet** below. The worksheets on page 2 adjust your withholding allowances based on

itemized deductions, certain credits, adjustments to income, or two-earner/multiple job situations. Complete all worksheets that apply. However, you may claim fewer (or zero) allowances.

Head of household. Generally, you may claim head of household filing status on your tax return only if you are unmarried and pay more than 50% of the costs of keeping up a home for yourself and your dependent(s) or other qualifying individuals.

Tax credits. You can take projected tax credits into account in figuring your allowable number of withholding allowances. Credits for child or dependent care expenses and the child tax credit may be claimed using the **Personal Allowances Worksheet** below. See Pub. 919, How Do I Adjust My Tax Withholding, for information on converting your other credits into withholding allowances.

Nonwage income. If you have a large amount of nonwage income, such as interest or dividends, consider making estimated tax payments using Form 1040-ES, Estimated Tax

for Individuals. Otherwise, you may owe additional tax. If you have pension or annuity income, see Pub. 919 to find out if you should adjust your withholding on Form W-4 or W-4P.

Two earners/Multiple jobs. If you have a working spouse or more than one job, figure the total number of allowances you are entitled to claim on all jobs using worksheets from only one Form W-4. Your withholding usually will be most accurate when all allowances are claimed on the Form W-4 for the highest paying job and zero allowances are claimed on the others.

Nonresident alien. If you are a nonresident alien, see the Instructions for Form 8233 before completing this Form W-4.

Check your withholding. After your Form W-4 takes effect, use Pub. 919 to see how the dollar amount you are having withheld compares to your projected total tax for 2007. See Pub. 919, especially if your earnings exceed $130,000 (Single) or $180,000 (Married).

Personal Allowances Worksheet (Keep for your records.)

A   Enter "1" for **yourself** if no one else can claim you as a dependent . . . . **A** _____

B   Enter "1" if: You are single and have only one job; or

   You are married, have only one job, and your spouse does not work; or   . .   **B** _____

   Your wages from a second job or your spouse's wages (or the total of both) are $1,000 or less.

C   Enter "1" for your **spouse**. But, you may choose to enter "-0-" if you are married and have either a working spouse or more than one job. (Entering "-0-" may help you avoid having too little tax withheld.) . . . . **C** _____

D   Enter number of **dependents** (other than your spouse or yourself) you will claim on your tax return   . . . . . . **D** _____

E   Enter "1" if you will file as **head of household** on your tax return (see conditions under **Head of household** above) . **E** _____

F   Enter "1" if you have at least $1,500 of **child or dependent care expenses** for which you plan to claim a credit . . **F** _____

   (**Note.** Do **not** include child support payments. See Pub. 503, Child and Dependent Care Expenses, for details.)

G   **Child Tax Credit** (including additional child tax credit). See Pub 972, Child Tax Credit, for more information.

   If your total income will be less than $57,000 ($85,000 if married), enter "2" for each eligible child.

   If your total income will be between $57,000 and $84,000 ($85,000 and $119,000 if married), enter "1" for each eligible child plus "1" **additional** if you have 4 or more eligible children.   **G** _____

H   Add lines A through G and enter total here. (**Note.** This may be different from the number of exemptions you claim on your tax return.)   **H** _____

For accuracy, complete all worksheets that apply.
- If you plan to **itemize or claim adjustments to income** and want to reduce your withholding, see the **Deductions and Adjustments Worksheet** on page 2.
- If you have **more than one job** or are **married and you and your spouse both work** and the combined earnings from all jobs exceed $40,000 ($25,000 if married) see the **Two-Earners/Multiple Jobs Worksheet** on page 2 to avoid having too little tax withheld.
- If **neither** of the above situations applies, **stop here** and enter the number from line H on line 5 of Form W-4 below.

- - - - - - - - - - - - -   **Cut here and give Form W-4 to your employer. Keep the top part for your records.**   - - - - - - - - - - - - -

Form **W-4**	**Employee's Withholding Allowance Certificate**	OMB No. 1545-0074
Department of the Treasury Internal Revenue Service	Whether you are entitled to claim a certain number of allowances or exemption from withholding is subject to review by the IRS. Your employer may be required to send a copy of this form to the IRS.	2007

1 Type or print your first name and middle initial.	Last name	2 Your social security number

Home address (number and street or rural route)	3 ☐ Single ☐ Married ☐ Married, but withhold at higher Single rate.
City or town, state, and ZIP code	**Note.** If married, but legally separated, or spouse is a nonresident alien, check the "Single" box.
	4 **If your last name differs from that shown on your social security card, check here. You must call 1-800-772-1213 for a replacement card.** ☐

5	Total number of allowances you are claiming (from line **H** above **or** from the applicable worksheet on page 2)	**5**	
6	Additional amount, if any, you want withheld from each paycheck	**6**	$

7   I claim exemption from withholding for 2007, and I certify that I meet **both** of the following conditions for exemption.

   Last year I had a right to a refund of **all** federal income tax withheld because I had **no** tax liability **and**

   This year I expect a refund of **all** federal income tax withheld because I expect to have **no** tax liability.

   If you meet both conditions, write "Exempt" here **7**

Under penalties of perjury, I declare that I have examined this certificate and to the best of my knowledge and belief, it is true, correct, and complete.

Employee's signature
(Form is not valid unless you sign it.) ▶   **Date** ▶

8 Employer's name and address (Employer: Complete lines 8 and 10 only if sending to the IRS.)	9 Office code (optional)	10 Employer identification number (EIN)

For Privacy Act and Paperwork Reduction Act Notice, see page 2.   Cat. No. 10220Q   Form **W-4** (2007)

Deductions and Adjustments Worksheet

Note. Use this worksheet *only* if you plan to itemize deductions, claim certain credits, or claim adjustments to income on your 2007 tax return.

1   Enter an estimate of your 2007 itemized deductions. These include qualifying home mortgage interest, charitable contributions, state and local taxes, medical expenses in excess of 7.5% of your income, and miscellaneous deductions. (For 2007, you may have to reduce your itemized deductions if your income is over $156,400 ($78,200 if married filing separately). See *Worksheet 2* in Pub. 919 for details.)   .   .   **1** $ _____

2   Enter:
  $10,700 if married filing jointly or qualifying widow(er)
  $ 7,850 if head of household   .   .   .   .   **2** $ _____
  $ 5,350 if single or married filing separately

3   **Subtract** line 2 from line 1. If zero or less, enter "-0-"   .   .   .   .   **3** $ _____

4   Enter an estimate of your 2007 adjustments to income, including alimony, deductible IRA contributions, and student loan interest   **4** $ _____

5   **Add** lines 3 and 4 and enter the total. (Include any amount for credits from *Worksheet 8* in Pub. 919)   .   **5** $ _____

6   Enter an estimate of your 2007 nonwage income (such as dividends or interest)   .   .   .   .   .   .   **6** $ _____

7   **Subtract** line 6 from line 5. If zero or less, enter "-0-"   .   .   .   .   **7** $ _____

8   **Divide** the amount on line 7 by $3,400 and enter the result here. Drop any fraction   .   .   .   .   .   **8**   _____

9   Enter the number from the **Personal Allowances Worksheet,** line H, page 1   .   .   .   .   .   .   **9**   _____

10   **Add** lines 8 and 9 and enter the total here. If you plan to use the **Two-Earners/Multiple Jobs Worksheet,** also enter this total on line 1 below. Otherwise, **stop here** and enter this total on Form W-4, line 5, page 1   **10**   _____

Two-Earners/Multiple Jobs Worksheet (See *Two earners/multiple jobs* on page 1.)

Note. Use this worksheet *only* if the instructions under line H on page 1 direct you here.

1   Enter the number from line H, page 1 (or from line 10 above if you used the **Deductions and Adjustments Worksheet)**   **1**   _____

2   Find the number in **Table 1** below that applies to the **LOWEST** paying job and enter it here. **However,** if you are married filing jointly and wages from the highest paying job are $50,000 or less, do not enter more than "3."   .   .   .   .   **2**   _____

3   If line 1 is **more than or equal to** line 2, subtract line 2 from line 1. Enter the result here (if zero, enter "-0-") and on Form W-4, line 5, page 1. **Do not** use the rest of this worksheet   .   .   .   .   **3**   _____

Note. If line 1 is *less than* line 2, enter "-0-" on Form W-4, line 5, page 1. Complete lines 4–9 below to calculate the additional withholding amount necessary to avoid a year-end tax bill.

4   Enter the number from line 2 of this worksheet   .   .   .   .   **4**   _____

5   Enter the number from line 1 of this worksheet   .   .   .   .   **5**   _____

6   **Subtract** line 5 from line 4   .   .   .   .   **6**   _____

7   Find the amount in **Table 2** below that applies to the **HIGHEST** paying job and enter it here   .   .   .   .   **7** $ _____

8   **Multiply** line 7 by line 6 and enter the result here. This is the additional annual withholding needed   .   .   **8** $ _____

9   Divide line 8 by the number of pay periods remaining in 2007. For example, divide by 26 if you are paid every two weeks and you complete this form in December 2006. Enter the result here and on Form W-4, line 6, page 1. This is the additional amount to be withheld from each paycheck   .   .   .   .   **9** $ _____

Table 1

Married Filing Jointly		All Others	
If wages from **LOWEST** paying job are—	Enter on line 2 above	If wages from **LOWEST** paying job are—	Enter on line 2 above
$0 - $4,500	0	$0 - $6,000	0
4,501 - 9,000	1	6,001 - 12,000	1
9,001 - 18,000	2	12,001 - 19,000	2
18,001 - 22,000	3	19,001 - 26,000	3
22,001 - 26,000	4	26,001 - 35,000	4
26,001 - 32,000	5	35,001 - 50,000	5
32,001 - 38,000	6	50,001 - 65,000	6
38,001 - 46,000	7	65,001 - 80,000	7
46,001 - 55,000	8	80,001 - 90,000	8
55,001 - 60,000	9	90,001 - 120,000	9
60,001 - 65,000	10	120,001 and over	10
65,001 - 75,000	11		
75,001 - 95,000	12		
95,001 - 105,000	13		
105,001 - 120,000	14		
120,001 and over	15		

Table 2

Married Filing Jointly		All Others	
If wages from **HIGHEST** paying job are—	Enter on line 7 above	If wages from **HIGHEST** paying job are—	Enter on line 7 above
$0 - $65,000	$510	$0 - $35,000	$510
65,001 - 120,000	850	35,001 - 80,000	850
120,001 - 170,000	950	80,001 - 150,000	950
170,001 - 300,000	1,120	150,001 - 340,000	1,120
300,001 and over	1,190	340,001 and over	1,190

Form W-4 (2007)

Purpose. Complete Form W-4 so that your employer can withhold the correct federal income tax from your pay. Because your tax situation may change, you may want to refigure your withholding each year.

Exemption from withholding. If you are exempt, complete **only** lines 1, 2, 3, 4, and 7 and sign the form to validate it. Your exemption for 2007 expires February 16, 2008. See Pub. 505, Tax Withholding and Estimated Tax.

Note. You cannot claim exemption from withholding if (a) your income exceeds $850 and includes more than $300 of unearned income (for example, interest and dividends) and (b) another person can claim you as a dependent on their tax return.

Basic instructions. If you are not exempt, complete the **Personal Allowances Worksheet** below. The worksheets on page 2 adjust your withholding allowances based on

itemized deductions, certain credits, adjustments to income, or two-earner/multiple job situations. Complete all worksheets that apply. However, you may claim fewer (or zero) allowances.

Head of household. Generally, you may claim head of household filing status on your tax return only if you are unmarried and pay more than 50% of the costs of keeping up a home for yourself and your dependent(s) or other qualifying individuals.

Tax credits. You can take projected tax credits into account in figuring your allowable number of withholding allowances. Credits for child or dependent care expenses and the child tax credit may be claimed using the **Personal Allowances Worksheet** below. See Pub. 919, How Do I Adjust My Tax Withholding, for information on converting your other credits into withholding allowances.

Nonwage income. If you have a large amount of nonwage income, such as interest or dividends, consider making estimated tax payments using Form 1040-ES, Estimated Tax

for Individuals. Otherwise, you may owe additional tax. If you have pension or annuity income, see Pub. 919 to find out if you should adjust your withholding on Form W-4 or W-4P.

Two earners/Multiple jobs. If you have a working spouse or more than one job, figure the total number of allowances you are entitled to claim on all jobs using worksheets from only one Form W-4. Your withholding usually will be most accurate when all allowances are claimed on the Form W-4 for the highest paying job and zero allowances are claimed on the others.

Nonresident alien. If you are a nonresident alien, see the Instructions for Form 8233 before completing this Form W-4.

Check your withholding. After your Form W-4 takes effect, use Pub. 919 to see how the dollar amount you are having withheld compares to your projected total tax for 2007. See Pub. 919, especially if your earnings exceed $130,000 (Single) or $180,000 (Married).

Personal Allowances Worksheet (Keep for your records.)

A	Enter "1" for **yourself** if no one else can claim you as a dependent .		**A**	_____
		You are single and have only one job; or		
B	Enter "1" if:	You are married, have only one job, and your spouse does not work; or	**B**	_____
		Your wages from a second job or your spouse's wages (or the total of both) are $1,000 or less.		
C	Enter "1" for your **spouse**. But, you may choose to enter "-0-" if you are married and have either a working spouse or more than one job. (Entering "-0-" may help you avoid having too little tax withheld.)		**C**	_____
D	Enter number of **dependents** (other than your spouse or yourself) you will claim on your tax return		**D**	_____
E	Enter "1" if you will file as **head of household** on your tax return (see conditions under **Head of household** above) .		**E**	_____
F	Enter "1" if you have at least $1,500 of **child or dependent care expenses** for which you plan to claim a credit . .		**F**	_____
	(**Note.** Do **not** include child support payments. See Pub. 503, Child and Dependent Care Expenses, for details.)			
G	**Child Tax Credit** (including additional child tax credit). See Pub 972, Child Tax Credit, for more information.			
	If your total income will be less than $57,000 ($85,000 if married), enter "2" for each eligible child.			
	If your total income will be between $57,000 and $84,000 ($85,000 and $119,000 if married), enter "1" for each eligible child plus "1" **additional** if you have 4 or more eligible children.		**G**	_____
H	Add lines A through G and enter total here. (**Note.** This may be different from the number of exemptions you claim on your tax return.)		**H**	_____

For accuracy, complete all worksheets that apply.	If you plan to **itemize or claim adjustments to income** and want to reduce your withholding, see the **Deductions and Adjustments Worksheet** on page 2.
	If you have **more than one job** or are **married and you and your spouse both work** and the combined earnings from all jobs exceed $40,000 ($25,000 if married) see the **Two-Earners/Multiple Jobs Worksheet** on page 2 to avoid having too little tax withheld.
	If **neither** of the above situations applies, **stop here** and enter the number from line H on line 5 of Form W-4 below.

-------------------------- **Cut here and give Form W-4 to your employer. Keep the top part for your records.** --------------------------

Form **W-4**	**Employee's Withholding Allowance Certificate**	OMB No. 1545-0074
Department of the Treasury Internal Revenue Service	Whether you are entitled to claim a certain number of allowances or exemption from withholding is subject to review by the IRS. Your employer may be required to send a copy of this form to the IRS.	**2007**

1	Type or print your first name and middle initial.	Last name		2	Your social security number

Home address (number and street or rural route)	3 ☐ Single ☐ Married ☐ Married, but withhold at higher Single rate. **Note.** If married, but legally separated, or spouse is a nonresident alien, check the "Single" box.
City or town, state, and ZIP code	4 **If your last name differs from that shown on your social security card, check here. You must call 1-800-772-1213 for a replacement card.** ☐

5	Total number of allowances you are claiming (from line **H** above **or** from the applicable worksheet on page 2)	**5**	
6	Additional amount, if any, you want withheld from each paycheck	**6**	$
7	I claim exemption from withholding for 2007, and I certify that I meet **both** of the following conditions for exemption.		
	Last year I had a right to a refund of **all** federal income tax withheld because I had **no** tax liability **and**		
	This year I expect a refund of **all** federal income tax withheld because I expect to have **no** tax liability.		
	If you meet both conditions, write "Exempt" here	**7**	

Under penalties of perjury, I declare that I have examined this certificate and to the best of my knowledge and belief, it is true, correct, and complete.

Employee's signature
(Form is not valid unless you sign it.) ▶ _____   **Date** ▶ _____

8	Employer's name and address (Employer: Complete lines 8 and 10 only if sending to the IRS.)	9 Office code (optional)	10 Employer identification number (EIN)

For Privacy Act and Paperwork Reduction Act Notice, see page 2.   Cat. No. 10220Q   Form **W-4** (2007)

Deductions and Adjustments Worksheet

Note. Use this worksheet *only* if you plan to itemize deductions, claim certain credits, or claim adjustments to income on your 2007 tax return.

1	Enter an estimate of your 2007 itemized deductions. These include qualifying home mortgage interest, charitable contributions, state and local taxes, medical expenses in excess of 7.5% of your income, and miscellaneous deductions. (For 2007, you may have to reduce your itemized deductions if your income is over $156,400 ($78,200 if married filing separately). See *Worksheet 2* in Pub. 919 for details.) . .	**1**	$ _____
2	Enter: $10,700 if married filing jointly or qualifying widow(er) $ 7,850 if head of household $ 5,350 if single or married filing separately	**2**	$ _____
3	**Subtract** line 2 from line 1. If zero or less, enter "-0-"	**3**	$ _____
4	Enter an estimate of your 2007 adjustments to income, including alimony, deductible IRA contributions, and student loan interest	**4**	$ _____
5	**Add** lines 3 and 4 and enter the total. (Include any amount for credits from *Worksheet 8* in Pub. 919) .	**5**	$ _____
6	Enter an estimate of your 2007 nonwage income (such as dividends or interest)	**6**	$ _____
7	**Subtract** line 6 from line 5. If zero or less, enter "-0-"	**7**	$ _____
8	**Divide** the amount on line 7 by $3,400 and enter the result here. Drop any fraction	**8**	_____
9	Enter the number from the **Personal Allowances Worksheet,** line H, page 1	**9**	_____
10	**Add** lines 8 and 9 and enter the total here. If you plan to use the **Two-Earners/Multiple Jobs Worksheet,** also enter this total on line 1 below. Otherwise, **stop here** and enter this total on Form W-4, line 5, page 1	**10**	_____

Two-Earners/Multiple Jobs Worksheet (See *Two earners/multiple jobs* on page 1.)

Note. Use this worksheet *only* if the instructions under line H on page 1 direct you here.

1	Enter the number from line H, page 1 (or from line 10 above if you used the **Deductions and Adjustments Worksheet**)	**1**	_____
2	Find the number in **Table 1** below that applies to the **LOWEST** paying job and enter it here. **However,** if you are married filing jointly and wages from the highest paying job are $50,000 or less, do not enter more than "3."	**2**	_____
3	If line 1 is **more than or equal to** line 2, subtract line 2 from line 1. Enter the result here (if zero, enter "-0-") and on Form W-4, line 5, page 1. **Do not** use the rest of this worksheet	**3**	_____

Note. If line 1 is *less than* line 2, enter "-0-" on Form W-4, line 5, page 1. Complete lines 4–9 below to calculate the additional withholding amount necessary to avoid a year-end tax bill.

4	Enter the number from line 2 of this worksheet **4**		_____
5	Enter the number from line 1 of this worksheet **5**		_____
6	**Subtract** line 5 from line 4	**6**	_____
7	Find the amount in **Table 2** below that applies to the **HIGHEST** paying job and enter it here	**7**	$ _____
8	**Multiply** line 7 by line 6 and enter the result here. This is the additional annual withholding needed . .	**8**	$ _____
9	**Divide** line 8 by the number of pay periods remaining in 2007. For example, divide by 26 if you are paid every two weeks and you complete this form in December 2006. Enter the result here and on Form W-4, line 6, page 1. This is the additional amount to be withheld from each paycheck	**9**	$ _____

Table 1

Married Filing Jointly		All Others	
If wages from **LOWEST** paying job are—	Enter on line 2 above	If wages from **LOWEST** paying job are—	Enter on line 2 above
$0 - $4,500	0	$0 - $6,000	0
4,501 - 9,000	1	6,001 - 12,000	1
9,001 - 18,000	2	12,001 - 19,000	2
18,001 - 22,000	3	19,001 - 26,000	3
22,001 - 26,000	4	26,001 - 35,000	4
26,001 - 32,000	5	35,001 - 50,000	5
32,001 - 38,000	6	50,001 - 65,000	6
38,001 - 46,000	7	65,001 - 80,000	7
46,001 - 55,000	8	80,001 - 90,000	8
55,001 - 60,000	9	90,001 - 120,000	9
60,001 - 65,000	10	120,001 and over	10
65,001 - 75,000	11		
75,001 - 95,000	12		
95,001 - 105,000	13		
105,001 - 120,000	14		
120,001 and over	15		

Table 2

Married Filing Jointly		All Others	
If wages from **HIGHEST** paying job are—	Enter on line 7 above	If wages from **HIGHEST** paying job are—	Enter on line 7 above
$0 - $65,000	$510	$0 - $35,000	$510
65,001 - 120,000	850	35,001 - 80,000	850
120,001 - 170,000	950	80,001 - 150,000	950
170,001 - 300,000	1,120	150,001 - 340,000	1,120
300,001 and over	1,190	340,001 and over	1,190

Michigan Department of Treasury
518 (Rev. 7-06)

Registration for Michigan Taxes

Check the box that best describes the reason for this application.

- ☐ Started a New Business
- ☐ Reinstated an Existing Account(s)
- ☐ Hired Employee / Hired Michigan Resident
- ☐ Incorporated / Purchased an Existing Business
- ☐ Aquired/Transferred All/Part of a Business
- ☐ Added a New Location(s)
- ☐ Flow-thru Entity Withholding
- ☐ Other (explain)

▶ **1. Federal Employer Identification Number, if known**

▶ **2.** Company Name or Owner's Full Name (include, if applicable, Corp, Inc, PC, LC, LLC, LLP, etc.). Required.

▶ **3.** Business Name, Assumed Name or DBA (as registered with the county)

Legal Address (Required)	▶ **4.** Address for all legal contacts (street and number - no PO boxes)		Business Telephone
	City	State	ZIP Code
Mailing Address	▶ **5.** Address, if different from Box 4, where all tax forms will be sent, unless otherwise instructed		**If this address is for an accountant or other representative, attach Form 151, Power of Attorney.**
	City	State	ZIP Code
Physical Address	▶ **6.** Address of the actual Michigan location of the business, if different from above (street and number--no PO boxes). See instructions.		
	City	State	ZIP Code

▶ **7.** Enter the Business Ownership Type code from Page 4 (Required) .... ▶ **7.**

If your business is a limited partnership, you must name all general partners beginning on line 27.

☐ Check this box if you are an Employee Leasing Company (Professional Employer Organization (PEO)). Attach a list of your clients.

▶ **8.** If you are a Michigan entity **and** line 7 is 34, 40, 41 or 42, enter your Michigan
Department of Labor and Economic Growth (DLEG) Corporate ID Number .... ▶ **8.**

☐ Check this box if you have applied for and not yet received your ID number.

Date of Incorporation _____ State of Incorporation_____

▶ **9.** Enter Business Code (SIC) that best describes your business from the list in this booklet .... ▶ **9.**

| 10. Define your business activity | 11. What products, if any, do you sell (sold to final consumer)? |
| | |

Check the tax(es) below for which you are registering. At least one box (12-15) must be checked.	**Date that liability will begin** for each box checked at left.			**Estimated monthly payment for each tax** Required if box at left is checked.		
	Month	Day	Year			
▶ **12.** ☐ Sales Tax .... ▶ **12a.**				▶ **12b.** ☐ Up to $65	☐ Up to $300	☐ Over $300
▶ **13.** ☐ Use Tax .... ▶ **13a.**				▶ **13b.** ☐ Up to $65	☐ Up to $300	☐ Over $300
▶ **14.** ☐ Income Tax Withholding (See line 22.) .... ▶ **14a.**				▶ **14b.** ☐ Up to $65	☐ Up to $300	☐ Over $300
▶ **15.** ☐ Annual Gross Receipts over $350,000 (SBT) .... ▶ **15a.**				**Single Business Tax is required only if annual gross receipts in Michigan exceed $350,000.**		

Check the box if these other taxes also apply:

▶ **16.** ☐ Unemployment Insurance Tax. Attach UIA Schedule A and UIA Schedule B. Corporations, LLCs, LLPs: Enclose a copy of your Articles of Incorporation or Organization. **You must complete all items on this form accurately and completely. Failure to do so may subject you to the penalties provided under the Michigan Employment Security (MES) Act.**

▶ **17.** ☐ Motor Fuel/IFTA Tax. Complete line 25. Treasury will review your registration and send any necessary tax application forms.

▶ **18.** ☐ Tobacco Tax. Complete line 26. Treasury will review your registration and send any necessary tax application forms.

▶ **19.** Enter the number of business locations you will operate in Michigan (Required) _____ ▶ **19.** _____
If more than 1, attach a list of names and addresses.

Continued on reverse side.

518, Page 2

▶ **20.** Enter the month, numerically, that you close your tax books (for example, enter 08 for August) .... ▶ **20.**

▶ **21. Seasonal Only:** (Your business is not open continuously for the entire year)

   a. Enter the month, numerically, this seasonal business opens .... ▶ **21a.**

   b. Enter the month, numerically, this seasonal business closes .... ▶ **21b.**

Note: If you are registering to sell at only one or two events in Michigan per year, do not submit this registration form. Instead, file a *Concessionaire's Sales Tax Return and Payment* (Form 2271). This form can be obtained on Treasury's Web site at **www.michigan.gov/treasurynewbusiness, or by calling toll-free 1-800-367-6263.**

▶ **22.** ☐ Check this box if you use a payroll service that produces your payroll checks and sends income tax withholding payments to the State and Federal Governments. Attach a *Payroll Service Provider Combined Power of Attorney Authorization and Corporate Officer Liability (COL) Certificate for Business* (Form 3683). This form can be obtained on Treasury's Web site at **www.michigan.gov/treasurynewbusiness, or by calling toll-free 1-800-367-6263.**

   Enter the name of your payroll service provider: _____

▶ **23.** If you are incorporating an existing business, or if you purchased an existing business, list previous business names and addresses, if known.

Previous Business Name and Address
Previous Business Name and Address

24. If you purchased an existing business, what assets did you acquire? Check all that apply.

   ☐ Land ☐ Building ☐ Furniture and Fixtures ☐ Equipment ☐ Inventory ☐ Accounts Payable ☐ Goodwill ☐ None

25. **Motor Fuel/IFTA Tax:**

		Yes	No
a. Will you operate a terminal or refinery?	25a.	☐	☐
b. Do you own a diesel-powered vehicle used for transport across Michigan's borders with three or more axles or two axles and a gross vehicle weight over 26,000 lbs?	25b.	☐	☐
c. Will you transport fuel across Michigan's borders?	25c.	☐	☐

26. **Tobacco Tax:**

a. Will you sell tobacco products to someone who will offer them for sale?	26a.	☐	☐
b. Will you operate a tobacco products vending machine?	26b.	☐	☐
(1) If yes, do you supply tobacco products for the machine?	26b1.	☐	☐
(2) If you do not supply the tobacco products, name the supplier _____			

Complete all the information for each owner or partner. For limited partnership you must list all general partners. For limited liability companies you must list all members. For corporations you must list all officers, but do not include shareholders who are not officers. Attach a separate list if necessary.

I certify that the information provided on this form is true, correct and complete to the best of my knowledge and belief.				
▶ **27.** Name (Last, First, Middle, Jr/Sr/III)		Title	Date of Birth	Phone Number
Driver License / MI Identification No.	Social Security Number	Signature		
▶ **28.** Name (Last, First, Middle, Jr/Sr/III)		Title	Date of Birth	Phone Number
Driver License / MI Identification No.	Social Security Number	Signature		
▶ **29.** Name (Last, First, Middle, Jr/Sr/III)		Title	Date of Birth	Phone Number
Driver License / MI Identification No.	Social Security Number	Signature		
▶ **30.** Name (Last, First, Middle, Jr/Sr/III)		Title	Date of Birth	Phone Number
Driver License / MI Identification No.	Social Security Number	Signature		

Questions regarding this form should be directed to the Department at 517-636-4660. Submit this form six weeks before you intend to start your business.

MAIL TO: Michigan Department of Treasury
P.O. Box 30778
Lansing, MI 48909-8278

FAX TO: 517-636-4520

Registration for Michigan Taxes

It is important that you complete all items on the Registration form. Incomplete or inaccurate information will delay processing and in some cases may subject you to a penalty. Read all instructions carefully before you begin.

This form is provided under PA 122 of 1941 and the Michigan Employment Security Act of 1936. Filing is mandatory if you are required to pay business taxes in Michigan.

Complete this Registration Form if you:

- Start a new business or reinstate an old business.
- Purchase or acquire an existing business.
- Need to register for any of the Michigan taxes listed below.
- Change the type of ownership of your business (e.g., from sole proprietorship to partnership, or incorporate a sole proprietorship or partnership).

Do not complete this Registration Form if you:

- Make sales at fewer than three events in Michigan during a calendar year. Instead, file Form 2271, *Concessionaire's Sales Tax Return and Payment.*
- Wish to apply for an ID number for your bank account. Use your Social Security number for this purpose.

Register for Sales Tax if you:

- Sell tangible personal property to the end user from a Michigan location (wholesalers do not need to register).

For more information regarding Sales Tax, visit Treasury's Web site at **www.michigan.gov/businesstaxes** or call 517-636-4730, and select option 3.

Register for Use Tax if you:

- Lease tangible personal property in Michigan
- Sell telecommunication services
- Provide transient hotel or motel room rentals
- Buy goods for your own use from out-of-state unlicensed vendors
- Launder or clean textiles under a sole rental or service agreement with a term of at least five days.

For more information regarding Use Tax, visit Treasury's Web site at **www.michigan.gov/businesstaxes** or call 517-636-4730 and select option 3.

Register for Withholding Tax if you:

- Are an employer withholding federal income tax from employee compensation (see *Federal Employer's Tax Guide Circular E*).
- Are a partnership, LLC or S Corporation with nonresident partners, members or shareholders (flow-through entity Withholding Tax).

For more information regarding Withholding Tax, visit Treasury's Web site at **www.michigan.gov/businesstaxes** or call 517-636-4730, and select option 3.

Individual owners and partners may not remit withholding on their wages through their business account numbers. They must file quarterly income tax estimates. For information about quarterly estimates, call 1-800-827-4000.

Register for Single Business Tax if you:

- Have adjusted gross receipts greater than $350,000. Special circumstances apply for controlled groups.

For more information regarding Single Business Tax, visit Treasury's Web site at www.michigan.gov/treasury or call 517-636-4700.

Register for Motor Fuel Tax if you:

- Operate a terminal or refinery for gasoline, diesel or aviation fuel or import from a foreign country.
- Transport fuel across a Michigan border for hire.
- Are a position holder in a fuel terminal.
- Sell diesel fuel for use in watercraft.
- Sell LPG for highway use.
- Sell aviation fuel for resale.
- Operate a diesel-powered vehicle for transport across Michigan's borders, having three or more axles, or having two axles and a gross vehicle weight over 26,000 pounds.

For more information regarding Motor Fuel Tax, visit Treasury's Web site at **www.michigan.gov/treasury** or call 517-636-4600.

Register for Tobacco Products Tax if you:

- Sell cigarettes or other tobacco products for resale.
- Purchase any tobacco products from unlicensed out-of-state sources.
- Sell cigarettes or other tobacco products in a vending machine.

For more information regarding Tobacco Tax, visit Treasury's Web site at **www.michigan.gov/tobacco taxes** or call 517-636-4630.

If, after reviewing your registration, Treasury determines that you need to file Motor Fuel or Tobacco products returns, we will send you the necessary applications.

Register for State Unemployment Tax if you:

- Have employees performing services in Michigan.
- Plan to have employees working in Michigan.
- Have acquired all/part of the payroll, accounts, services or assets of a business having employees in Michigan.

All employers must complete UIA Schedule A, *Liability Questionnaire* and UIA Schedule B, *Successorship Questionnaire*.

For more information, visit Treasury's Web site at **www.michigan.gov/businesstaxes** or UIA's Web site at **www.michigan.gov/uia**.

For specific information regarding missing UIA payments, reports, penalties, and/or interest, in Michigan call 1-800-638-3994. Be sure to note the last three digits of your UIA Account Number, or if you do not have a UIA Account Number, then by the last three digits of your Federal Employer Identification Number (FEIN) as you will be transferred to the appropriate tax team based on the last three digits of your number.

Mailing Instructions

Mail your completed registration and UIA schedules to:

Michigan Department of Treasury
P.O. Box 30778
Lansing, MI 48909-8278

Mail your application at least six weeks, but not more than six months, before you intend to start your business to allow your registration to be processed. Treasury will forward your application to UIA. You may also fax your forms to 517-636-4520.

Treasury will mail your personalized Sales, Use and Withholding Tax returns. UIA will issue your unemployment account number.

Instructions for Completing Form 518, Registration for Michigan Taxes

Lines not listed are explained on the form.

Reason for This Application. Check the box that best describes the reason why you are completing this application.

Line 1, Federal Employer Identification Number (FEIN). The Internal Revenue Service (IRS) issues the FEIN. If you need an FEIN, contact the IRS at 1-800-829-3676 and ask for Form SS-4, or visit the IRS Web site at **www.irs.ustreas.gov/formspubs/index.html** to download the form.

Line 2, Company Name. If your company is a partnership or corporation, enter the appropriate indicator in this box: LLP, LLC, Corp, Inc, PC or LC. If your business is a sole proprietorship, enter the owner's name here and the business name on line 3.

Line 4, Legal Address. Enter the street address where your books and records are kept for audit purposes. You must also receive mail there.

Line 5, Mailing Address. This may be a Post Office box or any other address where you want business tax forms mailed.

Line 6, Physical Address. Enter the physical address if the actual location of your business is different from the legal address, line 4.

Line 7, Business Ownership Type Code. Using the list below, enter the business type code for which you are registering.

Sole Proprietorship	10
Husband/Wife Proprietorship	20
Flow-Through Entity Withholding	25
Limited Partnership	33
- Submit a list of all general partners – Lines 27-30.	
Any Other Type of Partnership	30
Limited Liability Company (LLC, LC, LLP)	34
Michigan S Corporation	41
Michigan Professional Corporation	42
Any Other Michigan Corporation	40
Any Non-Michigan S Corporation	51
Any Other Non-Michigan Corporation	50
Trust or Estate (Fiduciary)	60
Joint Stock Club or Investment Company	70
Social Club or Fraternal Organization	80
Any Other Type of Business	90

Line 8, Michigan Department of Labor and Economic Growth (DLEG) Corporate ID Number. This item is only applicable if you have a Michigan business entity. A non-Michigan entity will not be issued a DLEG Corporate ID number.

Line 9, Business Code. Locate the three-digit code that best describes your business on the list of Standard Industry Codes (SIC) on pages 7 and 8 in this booklet and enter that code on line 9. **You must supply an SIC code.**

Line 10, Business Activity. Briefly describe the specific business activity or affairs the business will be transacting or conducting in Michigan.

Line 11, Products You Sell. Briefly describe what products you will sell to the final consumer.

Lines 12 to 15, Taxes. Check the box for each tax type you expect to pay. Indicate in the space next to each tax type the date your liability for that tax begins. For Sales Tax, Use Tax and Income Tax, check the box that indicates how much each month you expect to

pay of that tax. Please note that you are required to pay the Single Business Tax if your business' gross receipts exceed $350,000 in a year.

Line 16, Unemployment Insurance Tax. If you will be paying this tax, you should already have received an FEIN from the IRS. Be sure to enter this number on Line 1 and complete the attached Unemployment Insurance Agency (UIA) Schedule A and Schedule B. If this is the only tax you will be paying, send these forms and other requested documents to Unemployment Insurance Agency Tax Office at:

UIA	Or Fax to:
P.O. Box 8068	313-456-2130
Royal Oak, MI 48068-8068	

Line 17. Check this box if your business will be selling motor fuel or if your business will include operation of a commercial transport vehicle.

Line 19, Number of Locations. Enter the number of Michigan locations that will need a Sales Tax License.

Line 20, Fiscal Year. Enter the two-digit number that corresponds to the month in which you close your tax books. For instance, if your tax year is from July to June, enter "06" for June.

Line 21, Seasonal Business. Complete this only if your business is not open the entire year. Enter two two-digit numbers corresponding to the months your business opens and closes, respectively. For example, if your business is open from October to May, enter "10" on the first line and "05" on the second line.

Do not submit this form solely for the purpose of making sales at only one or two events in Michigan per year. Instead, submit Form 2271, *Concessionaire's Sales Tax Return and Payment.* This form can be found on Treasury's Web site at **www.michigan.gov/treasurynewbusiness**, or you can call 517-636-4660 to have this form mailed to you.

Line 22, Payroll Service. This refers to you only if you contract with a company that prints payroll checks for your business (or processes EFT payments to your employees) and makes payments on your company's behalf for income tax withholding. If you contract with such a company, you must file Form 3683, *Payroll Service Provider Combined Power of Attorney Authorization and Corporate Officer Liability (COL) Certificate for Business.* This form can be found on Treasury's Web site at **www.michigan.gov/treasurynewbusiness**, or call 517-636-4660 to have this form mailed to you.

Do not check this box if you or your company produce your own paychecks for your employees and you hire an accounting firm that manages your payroll. If you do have a payroll service, provide its name so that Registration staff can assist you with this.

Line 23. If your business succeeds or replaces an existing business or businesses because of incorporation, purchase or merger, provide the names and account numbers of those previous business(es).

Lines 27 to 30. You must supply at least one name. If there are more than four owners or partners (other than non-officer shareholders), attach a separate sheet of paper.

Note: You must provide a signature certifying that the information provided on the form is true, correct and complete to the best of your knowledge and belief.

BUSINESS CODES

1. AGRICULTURE, FORESTRY & FISHERIES

Farms

011 Field Crop
012 Fruit, Tree, Nut, Vegetable
013 Livestock
014 General
019 Miscellaneous Commercial
021 Non-Commercial

Agricultural Services, Animal Husbandry, Horticultural

071 Agricultural Services Fertilizing, Harvesting
072 Animal Husbandry Services, Grooming Kennels, Stables, Veterinary, etc.
073 Horticulture Services, Landscaping. Tree Trimming, Mowing, Snow Plowing, etc.

Forestry

082 Forest Nurseries, Tree Seed Gathering, Extracting
085 Forestry Services

Fisheries

091 Fisheries

2. MINING

Metal Mining

101 Iron Ores
109 Miscellaneous Metal Ores

Crude Petroleum & Natural Gas

131 Crude Petroleum & Natural Gas
138 Oil & Gas Exploration & Field Services

Quarrying

144 Sand & Gravel

3. CONTRACT CONSTRUCTION

151 General Building, Dwellings, Farm, Industrial, etc.
161 Highway & Street Construction, Except Elevated Highways
162 Heavy Construction, Elevated Highways, Tunnels, Sidewalks, Refineries, Sewage & Water Treatment Plants, etc.

Special Trade Contractors

171 Plumbing, Heating, Air Conditioning, Refrigeration
172 Painting, Paper Hanging, Decorating, Interior, Exterior
173 Electrical Work, At the Site
174 Masonry, Stonework, Tile Setting, Plastering, Bricklaying
175 Carpentry, Wood Flooring, Tile Flooring
176 Roofing, Sheet Metal Work
177 Concrete Work, Asphalt & Blacktop Driveways, etc.
178 Water Well Drilling & Services
179 Miscellaneous Special Trade Contractor

4. MANUFACTURING

Food & Kindred Products

201 Meat Products, Slaughter, Dressing, Packing, Freezing, etc.
202 Milk Processing & Dairy Products
203 Canning & Preserving Fruits, Vegetables, Sea Foods
204 Milling & Grain Mill Products
205 Bakery Products
206 Sugar, Except Refining Only
207 Confectionery & Related Products, Candy, Gum
208 Beverage Industries, Flavoring Extracts, Syrups
209 Miscellaneous Food Preparations & Kindred Products

Textile Mill Products

229 Miscellaneous Textile Goods, Felt, Lace, Padding, Twine, etc.

Apparel, Curtains, etc.

238 Misc. Apparel & Accessories
239 Miscellaneous Fabricated Textile Products, Curtains, Draperies, etc.

Lumber & Wood Products - Except Furniture

241 Logging Camps & Logging Contractors
242 Sawmills & Planing Mills
243 Millwork, Veneer, Plywood, Prefabricated Structural Wood Products
244 Wooden Containers
249 Misc. Wood Products, Shaping, Treating, Preserving, etc.

Furniture & Fixtures

251 Household Furniture
252 Office Furniture
254 Partitions, Shelving, Lockers, Office & Store Fixtures
259 Miscellaneous Furniture Fixtures

Paper & Allied Products

262 Paper Mills, Except Building Paper Mills
263 Paperboard Mills
264 Converted Paper & Paperboard Products, Except Containers & Boxes
265 Paperboard Containers & Boxes

Printing, Publishing & Allied Industries

271 Newspapers, Publishing, Publishing & Printing
272 Periodicals, Publishing, Publishing & Printing
273 Books
274 Miscellaneous Publishing
275 Commercial Printing, Unspecified
278 Bookbinding, Blank Books, Loose Leaf Binders, Related Industries
279 Printing Services Industries, Typesetting

Chemical & Allied Products

281 Industrial Inorganic & Organic Chemicals
282 Plastics Materials & Synthetic Resins, Synthetic Rubber, Synthetic & Other Human-Made Fibers, Except Glass
283 Drugs for Human or Veterinary Use
284 Soap, Detergents & Cleaning Preparations, Perfumes, Cosmetics, etc.
285 Paints, Varnishes, Lacquers, Enamels, Allied Products
286 Gum & Wood Chemicals
287 Agricultural Chemicals
289 Miscellaneous Chemical Products

Petroleum Refining

291 Petroleum Refining
299 Misc. Petroleum Products

Rubber & Misc. Plastic Products

301 Tires & Inner Tubes
306 Fabricated Rubber Products
307 Miscellaneous Plastics Products

Leather & Leather Products

314 Footwear, Except Rubber
319 Leather Goods, Other

Stone, Clay, Glass Products

323 Glass Products Made of Purchased Glass
326 Pottery, Related Products
327 Concrete, Gypsum, Plaster Products
328 Cut Stone, Stone Products
329 Abrasive, Asbestos, Misc. NonmetallicMineral

Primary Metal Industries

331 Blast Furnaces, Steel Works, Rolling & Finishing Mills
332 Iron & Steel Foundries
335 Rolling, Drawing & Extruding of Nonferrous Metals
336 Nonferrous Foundries
339 Misc. Primary Metal Industries

Fabricated Metal Products, Except Machinery & Transportation

343 Heating Apparatus, Except Electric & Plumbing Fixtures
344 Fabricated Structural Metal Products
345 Screw Machine Products, Bolts, Nuts, Screws, Rivets & Washers
346 Metal Stampings
347 Coating, Engraving, Allied Services
348 Misc. Fabricated Wire Products
349 Misc. Fabricated Metal Products

Machinery, Except Electrical

351 Engines & Turbines
352 Farm Machinery & Equipment
353 Construction, Mining, Materials Handling Machinery
354 Metalworking Machinery
355 Special Industry Machinery, Except Metalworking Machinery
356 Industrial Machinery & Equipment
357 Office, Computing, Accounting Machines
358 Service Industry Machines
359 Miscellaneous Machinery (Except Electrical), Machine Shops

Electrical Machinery, Equipment, etc.

361 Electric Transmission & Distribution Equipment
362 Electrical Industrial Apparatus
363 Household Appliances
364 Electric Lighting & Wiring Equipment
365 Radio & TV Receiving Sets, Satellite Dishes, Except Communication Types
366 Communication Equipment
367 Electronic Components & Accessories
369 Misc. Electrical Machinery, Equipment, Supplies

Transportation Equipment

371 Motor Vehicles & Motor Vehicle Equipment
372 Aircraft & Parts
373 Ship & Boat Building & Repairing
375 Motorcycles, Bicycles & Parts
379 Misc. Transportation Equipment

Professional, Scientific, Controlling Instruments, Photographic & Optical Goods, Watches & Clocks

381 Engineering, Laboratory, Scientific & Research Instruments & Associated Equipment
382 Instruments for Measuring, Controlling, Physical Characteristics
383 Optical Instruments & Lenses
384 Surgical, Medical, Dental Instruments & Supplies
385 Ophthalmic Goods
386 Photographic Equip. & Supplies
387 Watches, Clocks, Clockwork Operated Devices & Parts

Misc. Manufacturing Industries

391 Jewelry, Silverware, Plated Ware
393 Musical Instruments & Parts
394 Toys, Amusement, Sporting & Athletic Goods
395 Pens, Pencils, Other Office & Artist Materials
396 Costume Jewelry, Buttons, Misc. Notions, Except Precious Metal
398 Misc. Manufacturing Industries

5. TRANSPORTATION, COMMUNICATION, ELECTRIC, GAS, SANITARY SEWERS

Railroad Transportation

401 Railroads, Steam, Diesel, Electric, etc.

Local, Suburban & Interurban Passenger Transportation

411 Local & Suburban Passenger & Ambulance
412 Taxicabs & Limousines
413 Intercity & Rural Highway Passenger Transportation
417 Terminal & Service Facilities for Motor Vehicle Passengers

Motor Freight Transportation & Warehousing

421 Trucking, Local & Long Distance
422 Public Warehousing
423 Terminal & Terminal Maintenance Facilities for Motor Freight

Water Transportation

433 Great Lakes, St. Lawrence Seaway Transportation
446 Services Incidental to Water Transportation - Charter Boats, Marinas Without Retail Sales

Air Transportation

451 Air Transportation, Scheduled Carriers
452 Air Transportation Nonscheduled Carriers
458 Fixed Facilities & Services

Pipe Line Transportation

461 Pipe Lines

Transportation Services

471 Freight Forwarding
472 Arrangement of Transportation, Travel Agents, Shipping Agents & Brokers
478 Miscellaneous Services Incidental to Transportation

Communication

481 Telephone Communication, Wire or Radio
483 Radio Broadcasting & Television
489 Communication Services, Cable TV, etc.

Electric, Gas & Sanitary Services

491 Electric Companies & Systems
492 Gas Companies & Systems
493 Combination Companies
494 Water Supply
495 Sanitary Services, Landfill, Garbage Pickup, etc.

6. WHOLESALE TRADE

501 Motor Vehicle & Automotive Equipment
502 Drugs, Chemicals, Allied Products
503 Piece Goods & Apparel
504 Groceries, Related Products
505 Farm Products, Raw Materials, Grain Elevators
506 Electrical Goods
507 Hardware, Plumbing, Heating, Cooling Equipment & Supplies
508 Machinery, Equipment, Supplies, Chain Saws, Vending Machines, etc.
509 Miscellaneous Wholesalers - Import/Export, Jewelry, Unspecified Distributors
511 Metals & Minerals
512 Petroleum Bulk Stations & Related Products
513 Scrap & Waste Materials
514 Tobacco & Tobacco Products
515 Beer, Wine, Distilled Alcoholic Beverages

BUSINESS CODES, Continued

516 Paper & Related Products
517 Furniture & Home Furnishings
518 Lumber & Construction Materials

7. RETAIL TRADE

Retail Building Materials, Hardware & Farm Equipment

521 Lumber & Other Building Materials Dealers
522 Heating, Plumbing, Air Conditioning Equipment, Hot Tubs, Water Conditioners & Purifiers
523 Paint, Glass, Wallpaper Stores
524 Electrical Supply Stores
525 Hardware & Farm Equipment, Chain Saws, Fire Alarms, Security Systems, Drilling Equipment, etc.

Retail General Merchandise

531 Major Department Stores
532 Other Department Stores & Mail Order Houses - Catalog Sales
533 Variety Stores
534 General Stores
535 Direct Sellers, Peddlers, Party Plan Merchandisers
536 Vending Machines, (Excluding Food, Beverages, Music Amuse- ment
539 Fabric & General Merchandise

Retail Food

541 Grocery Stores, Delicatessens
542 Meat, Fish, Sea Food Markets
543 Fruit Stores & Vegetable Markets
544 Candy, Nuts & Confectionery
545 Dairy Products
546 Retail Bakeries
547 Retail Milk Route
549 Health Food, Soda Pop, Miscellaneous Food

Retail Automotive Dealers & Gasoline Service Stations

551 New & Used Car Dealers
552 Used Car Dealers Only
553 Tire, Battery, Automotive Acces- sory, Car Radio & Phone Dealers
554 Gasoline Service Stations
555 Mobile Homes, Motor Homes, Camping Vehicles, New & Used
556 Aircraft Sales & Service
557 Watercraft Sales & Service, Marinas with Retail Sales
558 Motorcycle, Snowmobile, ATV, New & Used
559 Vehicle Dealers Not Elsewhere Classified

Retail Apparel & Accessories

561 Men's & Boy's Clothing
562 Women's Clothing, Bridal, Lingerie, etc.
563 Women's Accessories & Specialty Stores
564 Children's & Infants Wear Stores
565 Family Clothing Stores
566 Shoe Stores
567 Custom Tailors
568 Furrier & Fur Shops
569 Miscellaneous Apparel & Accessory Stores, Screen Printing on Cloth

Retail Furniture, Home Furnishing Stores, etc.

571 Furniture Stores & Custom Cabinet Work
572 Household Appliance Stores
573 Radio, TV & Satellite, Antenna Stores
574 Floor Covering Stores
575 Drapery, Curtain, Upholstery, Interior Decorators with Stock
576 China, Glassware, Metalware Stores
577 Records, Tapes & Musical Instruments

579 Miscellaneous Home Furnishing - Pictures, Mirrors

Retail Eating & Drinking Places

581 Class C Tavern, with Liquor, Food Incidental
582 Tavern, Beer & Wine Only, Food incidental
583 Night Clubs, Cabarets, Discotheques
584 Hotel Dining Rooms
585 Family Restaurants & Cafeterias
586 Lunch Counters, Dairy Bars, Fast Food, Pizzerias
587 Caterers, Concessions, Food Vending Machines

Miscellaneous Retail Stores

591 Prescription Drugs, etc.
592 Party & Liquor Stores
593 Antique & Secondhand, Flea Markets
594 Book & Stationary Stores, Cards, Book Clubs, Office Supplies
595 Sporting Goods, Bicycles, Small Arms, Ammunition, Tack Supplies, Bait & Tackle, Tennis & Golf Shoes, etc.
596 Farm & Garden Supply Stores
597 Jewelry Stores
598 Fuel, Ice & Firewood
599 Retail Stores Not Elsewhere Classified, Florists, Cigars, Cameras, Arts & Crafts, Hobbies, Opticians & Optical, Picture Frames

8. FINANCE, INSURANCE, REAL ESTATE BANKING

601 Federal Reserve Banks
602 Commercial & Stock Savings Banks
603 Mutual Savings Banks
604 Trust Companies Not Engaged In Deposit Banking
605 Establishments Closely Related to Banking - Foreign Banks, Exchanges, Travelers Checks, Check Clearing Houses

Credit Agencies Other Than Banks

611 Rediscount & Financing Institutions for Credit Agencies Other Than Banks - Mortgage Companies Than Originate Loans
612 Savings & Loans Associations
613 Agricultural Credit Unions
614 Personal Credit Institutions
615 Business Credit Institutions
616 Mortgage & Brokers

Security & Commodity Brokers, Dealers, Exchanges, Services

621 Security Brokers, Dealers, Flotation Companies
622 Commodity Contracts Brokers & Dealers
628 Services Allied with the Exchange of Securities or Commodities

Insurance Carriers

631 Life Insurance
632 Accident & Health Insurance
633 Fire, Marine, Casualty Insurance
635 Surety Insurance
636 Title Insurance
639 Other Insurance Carriers

Insurance Brokers, Brokers, Services

641 Insurance Agents, Brokers, Unspecified Services & Claims Adjustors
651 Real Estate Investments, Real Estate Operators & Lessors, Except Developers
653 Real Estate Agents, Brokers, Managers & Unspecified
654 Title Abstract Companies

655 Subdividers, Developers Cemetery Assoc.
656 Operative Builders

Combinations of Real Estate, Insurance, Loan & Law Offices

661 Combinations of Real Estate, Insurance, Loans & Law Offices

Holding & Other Investment Companies

671 Holding Companies
672 Investment Companies
673 Trusts
679 Miscellaneous Investing Institutions, Franchisors, Selling or Licensing, Gas & Oil Leases

9. SERVICES

Hotels, Rooming Houses, Camps & Other Lodging Places

701 Hotels, Motels, Tourist Courts
702 Rooming & Boarding Houses, Bed & Breakfasts
703 Trailer Parks, Camps
704 Organization Hotels & Lodging Houses, on Membership Basis

Personal Services

721 Dry Cleaning & Dyeing Plants, Diaper Service, Laundries, etc.
722 Photographic Studios, Aerial Maps
723 Beauty, Cosmetology, Nail Shops & Schools
724 Barber Shops & Schools
725 Shoe Repair & Shine
726 Funeral Service & Crematories
727 Pressing, Alteration, Garment Repair
729 Misc. Personal Services - Debt Counseling, Invalid Supply Rental, Massages, Reducing & Sun Tan Salons, Valet Parking, etc.

Miscellaneous Business Services

731 Advertising, Sign Painting
732 Consumer Credit Reporting, Mercantile Reporting, Adjustment & Collection Agencies
733 Duplicating, Addressing, Blueprinting, Photocopying, Mailing, Mailing List Compilers, Stenographic Services
734 Services to Dwellings Including Mobile Homes, Window Cleaning, Janitorial, Maintenance, Extermi- nating, etc.
735 News Syndicates
736 Private Employment Agencies
737 Computer Rental, Consultants, Software
739 Business Services, Management, Training, Consulting, Rentals, Sales & Manufacturing Representatives, Coin-Operated Amusement Devices

Automobile Repair, Services, Garages

751 Car & Truck Rentals, without Drivers
752 Automobile Parking
753 Automobile Repair Shops, Van Conversions
754 Automobile Services, Car Wash, Driver Education

Miscellaneous Repair Services

762 Electrical Repair Shops
763 Watch, Clock, Jewelry Repair
764 Reupholstery & Furniture Repair
769 Miscellaneous Repair Shops & Related Services - Locksmiths, Taxidermists, Welding, Specialized Repairs

Motion Pictures

781 Motion Picture Production & Distribution

783 Motion Picture Theaters & Drive-In Theaters
784 Video Film Rentals

Amusement & Recreation Services, Except Motion Pictures

791 Dance Halls, Studios, Schools
792 Theatrical Producers, Bands, Orchestras & Entertainers
793 Bowling Alleys, Billiard & Pool Parlors
794 Sports Promoters & Commercial Operators, Miscellaneous Amusement & Recreation Services, Health Spas & Gyms

Medical & Other Health Services

801 Physicians & Surgeons
802 Dentists & Dental Surgeons
803 Osteopathic Physicians
804 Chiropractors
806 Hospitals
807 Medical & Dental Laboratories
809 Miscellaneous Health & Allied Services, Nursing Homes, Optometrists

Legal Services

811 Legal Services

Educational Services

821 Elementary & Secondary Schools, Day Care Nurseries & Schools
822 Colleges, Universities, Profes- sional Schools, Junior Colleges, Normal Schools
823 Libraries, Information Centers, Mobile Libraries
824 Correspondence Schools, Vocational Schools, Business Colleges
829 Miscellaneous Schools & Educational Services

Museums, Art Galleries, Botanical & Zoological Gardens

841 Museums, Art Galleries, Planetaria
842 Arboreta, Botanical & Zoological Gardens

Nonprofit Membership Organizations

861 Business Associations
862 Professional Membership Organizations
863 Labor Unions & Organizations
864 Civic, Social, Fraternal Associations
865 Political Organizations
866 Religious Organizations
867 Charitable Organizations
869 Miscellaneous Nonprofit Membership Organizations

Private Households

881 Private Households - Domestic Employees, Cleaning, Baby-sitting, Private Nursing

Miscellaneous Services

891 Engineering & Architectural
892 Nonprofit Educational & Scientific Research Agencies
893 Accounting, Auditing, Bookkeeping, Data Processing Services
899 Misc. Services, Family & Marriage Counseling, Social Work, etc.

10. GOVERNMENT

919 Federal Government
929 State Government
939 County Government
949 City Government
959 Township Government
969 School District

Michigan Unemployment Insurance Agency
518 Schedule A (Rev. 8/05)

UIA Schedule A - Liability Questionnaire

Issued under authority of the Michigan Employment Security Act of 1936, as amended, MCL 421.1 et seq. Filing is mandatory for all employers. **You must complete all items on this form accurately and completely. Failure to do so may subject you to the penalties provided under the MES Act.**

UIA Account Number, if already assigned

Federal Employer Identification No. (required)

An employing unit becomes liable to pay Michigan unemployment taxes when the employing unit meets any of the following criteria:

- Pays $1,000 or more in gross wages for covered employment in a calendar year.
- Employs one or more employees in 20 different weeks within a calendar year.
- Acquires all or part of an existing Michigan business.
- Pays at least $1,000 in cash, not including room and board, for domestic service within a calendar quarter.
- Pays at least $20,000 in cash, not including room and board, for agricultural service within a calendar quarter, **OR** employs at least 10 agricultural workers in each of 20 different weeks in the current or preceding calendar year.
- Elects coverage under the terms of the Michigan Employment Security (MES) Act.
- Is subject to federal unemployment tax.

When any one of the above criteria is met, you must submit Form 518, *Registration for Michigan Taxes,* and UIA Schedule A - *Liability Questionnaire* and UIA Schedule B - *Successorship Questionnaire.* You must also begin quarterly filing of Form UIA 1020, *Employer's Quarterly Tax Report,* Form UIA 1020-R, *Reimbursing Employer's Quarterly Payroll Report* and Form UIA 1017, *Wage Detail Report.* Unemployment taxes are due and payable beginning with the first calendar quarter in which you had payroll. Due dates for tax and wage reports are April 25, July 25, October 25 and January 25.

Providing inaccurate or incomplete information in this Registration, or UIA Schedules A or B, will be evidence of intentional misrepresentation and may subject you to the civil and/or criminal penalties provided in Sections 54 and 54b of the *Michigan Employment Security (MES) Act.*

On what date did/will you first employ anyone in Michigan? ....

Month	Day	Year

Complete only **one** of the seven items below that best describes your business.

1. EMPLOYERS OTHER THAN DOMESTIC OR AGRICULTURAL

A. If you have had a gross payroll of $1,000 or more within a calendar year, enter the date it was reached or will be reached. ....

Month	Day	Year

B. If you have had 20 or more calendar weeks in which one or more persons performed services for you within a calendar year, enter the date the 20th week was reached or will be reached. The weeks do not have to be consecutive nor the persons the same. ....

Month	Day	Year

2. AGRICULTURAL EMPLOYERS

A. If you have had a total cash payroll of $20,000 or more for agricultural services performed within a calendar quarter in either the current or preceding calendar year, not including room and board, enter the date the $20,000 was reached or will be reached. ....

Month	Day	Year

B. If you have had at least 10 agricultural workers in each of 20 different weeks in the current or preceding calendar year, enter the date the 20th week was reached or will be reached. The weeks do not have to be consecutive nor the persons the same. ....

Month	Day	Year

3. DOMESTIC/HOUSEHOLD EMPLOYERS

A. If you have had a cash payroll of $1,000 or more for domestic services within a calendar quarter in either the current or preceding calendar year, not including room and board, enter the date the $1,000 was reached or will be reached. ....

Month	Day	Year

4. NONPROFIT EMPLOYERS

Nonprofit organizations finance their unemployment liability by either (1) paying unemployment taxes on the taxable wages of their employees (contributing) or (2) making a specific prior election to reimburse the UIA for any unemployment benefits paid to their former employees (reimbursing). A nonprofit organization that does not elect to be reimbursing will be, by default, contributing. To elect reimbursing status, see paragraphs 4A-4D.

A. Nonprofit employers electing reimbursing status must provide the UIA with a copy of the documentation from the Internal Revenue Service (IRS) granting 501(c)(3) status.

☐ Check this box if you elect to be a reimbursing employer. Attach a copy of your IRS 501(c)(3) documentation. Failure to check this box will result in the establishment of your liability as a contributing employer.

Continued on page 2

518 Schedule A, Page 2

4. NONPROFIT EMPLOYERS (continued)

B.   If you are a nonprofit employer electing reimbursing status, enter the amount (or estimate) of your gross annual payroll ....

$ [   ]

C.   **Bonding Requirements.** Section 13a of the *Michigan Employment Security (MES) Act* requires that **nonprofit** employers electing reimbursing status on or after December 21, 1989, and that have, or expect to have, a gross payroll of more than $100,000 during any calendar year must notify the UIA of that fact immediately and must provide a surety bond, irrevocable letter of credit, or other banking device approved by the UIA, in an amount to be determined by the UIA to secure the employer's obligations under the MES Act. If you exceed $100,000 in gross payroll in a later year, you are obligated to notify the UIA, and provide the bond at that time.

D.   If your organization is funded more than 50 percent by a grant, list the source and duration of the grant.

Source	Start Date	End Date

5. GOVERNMENTAL AGENCIES, INDIAN TRIBES AND TRIBAL UNITS

Governmental entities generally reimburse unemployment insurance benefits paid to former employees on a dollar-for-dollar basis unless they elect to make quarterly "contribution" payments.

A.   If you are a governmental agency, or Indian tribe or tribal unit, identify the type (i.e., city, township, commission, authority, tribe, etc.) ....

Month   Day

B.   Enter your fiscal year beginning date ....

Under the MES Act, a governmental agency or Indian tribe finances its unemployment liability by (1) reimbursing the UIA for any unemployment benefits paid to their former employees (reimbursing) or (2) electing to pay unemployment taxes on the taxable wages of its employees (contributing).

C.   ☐ Check this box if you elect to be a contributing employer. Failure to check this box will result in the establishment of your liability as a reimbursing employer. Indian tribes and tribal units are subject to the same bonding requirements as nonprofit employers (see Line 4C, above).

6. FEDERAL UNEMPLOYMENT TAX ACT (FUTA) SUBJECTIVITY. Select this option ONLY if you are NOT liable for UIA taxes under any of the other employer types (1-5 above).

State

If you are already subject to FUTA, enter the state, other than Michigan, where you became liable ....

Note: "Subject to FUTA" refers to filing Form 940 with the IRS. If you are required to file Form 940 (FUTA) with the IRS in other states, you are required to file and pay state unemployment taxes in Michigan.

7. ELECTIVE COVERAGE. For employers who would not otherwise be liable for unemployment taxes, such as churches.

☐ Check this box if you wish to elect coverage under the MES Act. Approval is subject to UIA review; some qualifiers apply. Your election, if granted, will apply to all your employees.

Give your reason for electing coverage in the space provided below. If you are an individual owner or partnership electing to cover family members, specify their relationship to the owner or partners. You may not elect coverage for your parents or spouse, nor for your child under the age of 18. Individual owners and partners cannot elect coverage for themselves. You may not elect coverage for domestic employment below the statutory requirements stated above. Election of coverage remains in effect for a minimum of two calendar years.

Print Name of Owner/Officer			Signature of Owner/Officer
Title	Telephone Number	Date	
Print Name of Owner/Officer			Signature of Owner/Officer
Title	Telephone Number	Date	

Attach this schedule to Form 518, *Registration for Michigan Taxes* and mail it to the Michigan Department of Treasury.

BCS/CD-600 (Rev. 12/03)

MICHIGAN DEPARTMENT OF LABOR & ECONOMIC GROWTH BUREAU OF COMMERCIAL SERVICES	
Date Received	(FOR BUREAU USE ONLY)
This registration will expire 10 years from the stamped registration date.	
MARK IDENTIFICATION NUMBER	**M** ☐ ☐ **-** ☐ ☐ ☐

APPLICATION FOR REGISTRATION OF TRADEMARK/SERVICE MARK
(Please read information and instructions on last page)

Pursuant to the provisions of Act 242, Public Acts of 1969, as amended, the undersigned executes the following Application:

1. This Application is for the purpose of registering a: (check one)

   ☐ Trademark   ☐ Service mark

2. The mark: (Complete only one of the following)

   a) **WORDS ONLY:**
   If the mark is only words, the words in the mark are: (Include type style if it is an inherent part of the mark)

   b) **DESIGN ONLY:**
   If the mark is a design only, describe the design: (Include colors if they are an inherent part of the mark)

   c) **WORDS AND DESIGN:**
   Describe the design and list the words in the mark: (Include color and type style if they are an inherent part of the mark)

Please note: Complete either Item 3 **or** Item 4. Designate only one mark and one classification code per application.

Trademarks only

3. a) List the goods in connection with which the mark is used.

   b) The mode or manner in which the trademark is used in connection with the goods.

   c) Numerical classification of goods:_____

220

Service marks only

4. a) List the services in connection with which the mark is used.

   b) The mode or manner in which the mark is used in connection with the services.

   c) Numerical classification of services:_____

5. a) The mark was first used in Michigan by the applicant, or a predecessor, in_____
      on_____ .   (city)
          (month / day / year)
   b) The mark was first used in the United States by the applicant, or a predecessor, in_____
                                                                              (city)
      _____ on _____ .
              (state)   (month / day / year)

6. a) The name of the individual or other entity applying for the registration is:

   b) The business name of the applicant, if different than 6(a):

   c) The business address of the applicant is:

7. a) The applicant is a: (check one)
      ☐ Corporation   ☐ Partnership   ☐ Individual   ☐ Limited Liability Company   ☐ Other

   b) If a corporation, the state where incorporated: _____

8. Two copies, photographs, facsimiles or specimens of the mark, as actually in use must accompany this Application. The sample should be 8.5 x 11 inches or smaller so it may be scanned to optical disk media.

State of _____

County of _____ } SS

I, being first sworn, hereby depose and say that I have read the above application, including any attached papers, and the facts set out therein are true; the applicant is the owner of the mark and none other has the right to use the mark in Michigan either in the identical form or in a form which so nearly resembles the mark as to be likely to deceive or to be mistaken for the mark; the specimens of the mark as filed herewith are true and correct. FURTHER, the Bureau of Commercial Services, Michigan Department of Labor & Economic Growth is hereby appointed as the applicant's agent for service of process only in actions relating to the registration or the application for registration of this mark.

Signature	Type or Print Name	Type or Print Title

Subscribed and sworn to before me this _____ day of_____ , _____ .

_____
(Signature of Notary)

_____
(Type or Print Name of Notary)

Notary Public for_____County,

State of _____

(Notary Seal)   My Commission expires_____

Preparer's name_____

Business telephone number _____

INFORMATION AND INSTRUCTIONS

1. This application must be used to register a Trademark/Service Mark. A document required or permitted to be filed under this act cannot be filed unless it contains the minimum information required by the act. This is a legal document and agency staff cannot provide legal advice.

2. Submit one original of this document. Upon filing, a Certificate of Registration will be mailed to the applicant or his/her representative to the address provided on this Application.

   Since this application will be maintained on electronic format, it is important that the filing be legible. Documents with poor black and white contrast, or otherwise illegible, will be rejected.

3. This Application is to be used pursuant to Section 3(1) of Act 242, P.A. of 1969 for the purpose of registering a trademark or service mark. A trademark is any word, name, symbol, or device, or any combination thereof, other than a trade name in its entirety, adopted and used by a person to identify goods made or sold by him or her and to distinguish them from similar goods made or sold by others. Similarly, a service mark is a mark used by a person in the sale or advertising of services to identify his or her services and distinguish them from the similar services of others. The term person, as used above, means an individual, firm, partnership, corporation, association, union, or other organization. A mark is not registrable until it has actually been adopted and used in Michigan. The registration is effective for ten years and is renewable for successive terms of 10 years upon the filing of an application for renewal, on a form provided by the Bureau, within six months prior to the expiration date.

4. The Department of Labor and Economic Growth, Bureau of Commercial Services is appointed as the applicant's agent for service of process in actions relating to the registration or application for registration if: (1) the applicant is or becomes a nonresident individual, partnership or association, (2) the applicant is or becomes a foreign corporation or limited liability company without a certificate of authority to transact business in Michigan, or (3) the applicant cannot be found in Michigan.

5. Item 2 - Complete section (a), (b) or (c) depending on the type of mark that is being registered.

6. **Trademarks only:**
   Item 3(a) - List the good(s) on which the mark is used.
   Item 3(b) - List how the mark is used on the good(s) i.e. tag, label, etc.
   Item 3(c) - List the classification of the good, but be aware that only one classification can be designated per application.
      A list of the classification codes can be found on the back of this Application.

7. **Service marks only:**
   Item 4(a) - List the service(s) in connection with which the mark is used.
   Item 4(b) - List how the mark is used i.e. in advertising, signs, letterhead, etc.
   Item 4(c) - List the classification of the good, but be aware that only one classification can be designated per application.
      A list of the classification codes can be found on the back of this Application.

8. Item 5 - A trademark is considered "used in Michigan" when affixed to the product, container, tags or labels and sold in Michigan. For services, the mark must be used or displayed in this state in the sale or advertising of services rendered in Michigan.

9. Item 8 - **Two copies, photographs, facsimiles or specimens of the mark, as actually in use must accompany this Application. The sample should be 8.5 x 11 inches or smaller so it may be maintained on electronic format.**

10. This Application must be signed by:
    Individual - by the applicant
    Corporation - by an authorized officer or agent.
    Limited Liability Company - by a manager if management is vested in one or more managers or by a member if management is reserved for members.
    Partnership - by a partner.

11. **NONREFUNDABLE FEE:** Make remittance payable to the State of Michigan **$50.00**

To submit by mail:	To submit in person:
Michigan Department of Labor & Economic Growth	2501 Woodlake Circle
Bureau of Commercial Services	Okemos, MI
Corporation Division	Telephone: (517) 241-6470
7150 Harris Drive	
P.O. Box 30054	Fees may be paid by VISA or Mastercard when
Lansing, MI 48909	delivered in person to our office.

TRADEMARK UNIFORM CLASSIFICATION OF GOODS

1. Raw or partly prepared materials
2. Receptacles
3. Baggage, animal equipments, portfolios and pocketbooks
4. Abrasives and polishing materials
5. Adhesives
6. Chemicals and chemical compositions
7. Cordage
8. Smokers' articles, not including tobacco products
9. Explosives, firearms, equipments and projectiles
10. Fertilizers
11. Inks and inking materials
12. Construction materials
13. Hardware and plumbing and steam fitting supplies
14. Metals and metal castings and forgings
15. Oils and greases
16. Paints and painters' materials
17. Tobacco products
18. Medicines and pharmaceutical preparations
19. Vehicles
20. Linoleum and oiled cloth
21. Electrical apparatus, machines and supplies
22. Games, toys and sporting goods
23. Cutlery, machinery and tools, and parts thereof
24. Laundry appliances and machines
25. Locks and safes
26. Measuring and scientific appliances
27. Horological instruments
28. Jewelry and precious-metal ware
29. Brooms, brushes and dusters
30. Crockery, earthenware and porcelain
31. Filters and refrigerators
32. Furniture and upholstery
33. Glassware
34. Heating, lighting and ventilating apparatus
35. Belting, hose, machinery packing, and non-metallic tires
36. Musical instruments and supplies
37. Paper and stationery
38. Prints and publications
39. Clothing
40. Fancy goods, furnishings and notions
41. Canes, parasols and umbrellas
42. Knitted, netted and textile
43. Thread and yarn
44. Dental, medical and surgical appliances
45. Soft drinks and carbonated waters
46. Foods and ingredients of foods
47. Wines
48. Malt beverages and liquors
49. Distilled alcoholic liquors
50. Merchandise not otherwise classified
51. Cosmetics and toilet preparations
52. Detergents and soaps

SERVICE MARK UNIFORM CLASSIFICATION OF SERVICES

100. Miscellaneous
101. Advertising and business
102. Insurance and financial
103. Construction and repair
104. Communication
105. Transportation and storage
106. Material treatment
107. Education and entertainment

Form **SS-8** (Rev. November 2006) Department of the Treasury Internal Revenue Service	**Determination of Worker Status for Purposes of Federal Employment Taxes and Income Tax Withholding**	OMB No. 1545-0004

Name of firm (or person) for whom the worker performed services	Worker's name
Firm's address (include street address, apt. or suite no., city, state, and ZIP code)	Worker's address (include street address, apt. or suite no., city, state, and ZIP code)

Trade name	Daytime telephone number ( )	Worker's social security number
Telephone number (include area code) ( )	Firm's employer identification number	Worker's employer identification number (if any)

Note. If the worker is paid by a firm other than the one listed on this form for these services, enter the name, address, and employer identification number of the payer.

Disclosure of Information

The information provided on Form SS-8 may be disclosed to the firm, worker, or payer named above to assist the IRS in the determination process. For example, if you are a worker, we may disclose the information you provide on Form SS-8 to the firm or payer named above. The information can only be disclosed to assist with the determination process. If you provide incomplete information, we may not be able to process your request. See *Privacy Act and Paperwork Reduction Act Notice* on page 5 for more information. **If you do not want this information disclosed to other parties, do not file Form SS-8.**

Parts I–V. All filers of Form SS-8 must complete all questions in Parts I–IV. Part V must be completed if the worker provides a service directly to customers or is a salesperson. If you cannot answer a question, enter "Unknown" or "Does not apply." If you need more space for a question, attach another sheet with the part and question number clearly identified.

Part I	**General Information**

1 This form is being completed by: ☐ Firm ☐ Worker; for services performed _____ to _____ .
    (beginning date)   (ending date)

2 Explain your reason(s) for filing this form (for example, you received a bill from the IRS, you believe you erroneously received a Form 1099 or Form W-2, you are unable to get worker's compensation benefits, or you were audited or are being audited by the IRS). ....
    ----

3 Total number of workers who performed or are performing the same or similar services _____ .

4 How did the worker obtain the job? ☐ Application   ☐ Bid   ☐ Employment Agency   ☐ Other (specify) _____

5 Attach copies of all supporting documentation (contracts, invoices, memos, Forms W-2 or Forms 1099-MISC issued or received, IRS closing agreements, IRS rulings, etc.). In addition, please inform us of any current or past litigation concerning the worker's status. If no income reporting forms (Form 1099-MISC or W-2) were furnished to the worker, enter the amount of income earned for the year(s) at issue $ _____ .

    If both Form W-2 and Form 1099-MISC were issued or received, explain why. ....
    ----

6 Describe the firm's business. ....
    ----

7 Describe the work done by the worker and provide the worker's job title. ....
    ----

8 Explain why you believe the worker is an employee or an independent contractor. ....
    ----

9 Did the worker perform services for the firm in any capacity before providing the services that are the subject of this determination request?
    ☐ Yes   ☐ No   ☐ N/A
    If "Yes," what were the dates of the prior service? ....
    If "Yes," explain the differences, if any, between the current and prior service. ....
    ----

10 If the work is done under a written agreement between the firm and the worker, attach a copy (preferably signed by both parties). Describe the terms and conditions of the work arrangement. ....

For Privacy Act and Paperwork Reduction Act Notice, see page 5.   Cat. No. 16106T   Form **SS-8** (Rev. 11-2006)

Part II   Behavioral Control

1   What specific training and/or instruction is the worker given by the firm? ....

2   How does the worker receive work assignments? ....

3   Who determines the methods by which the assignments are performed? ....

4   Who is the worker required to contact if problems or complaints arise and who is responsible for their resolution? ....

5   What types of reports are required from the worker? Attach examples. ....

6   Describe the worker's daily routine such as, schedule, hours, etc. ....

7   At what location(s) does the worker perform services (e.g., firm's premises, own shop or office, home, customer's location, etc.)? Indicate the appropriate percentage of time the worker spends in each location, if more than one. ....

8   Describe any meetings the worker is required to attend and any penalties for not attending (e.g., sales meetings, monthly meetings, staff meetings, etc.). ....

9   Is the worker required to provide the services personally? . . . . ☐ **Yes**   ☐ **No**

10   If substitutes or helpers are needed, who hires them? ....

11   If the worker hires the substitutes or helpers, is approval required? . . . . ☐ **Yes**   ☐ **No**
     If "Yes," by whom? ....

12   Who pays the substitutes or helpers? ....

13   Is the worker reimbursed if the worker pays the substitutes or helpers? . . . . ☐ **Yes**   ☐ **No**
     If "Yes," by whom?

Part III   Financial Control

1   List the supplies, equipment, materials, and property provided by each party:
     The firm ....
     The worker ....
     Other party ....

2   Does the worker lease equipment? . . . . ☐ **Yes**   ☐ **No**
     If "Yes," what are the terms of the lease? (Attach a copy or explanatory statement.) ....

3   What expenses are incurred by the worker in the performance of services for the firm? ....

4   Specify which, if any, expenses are reimbursed by:
     The firm ....
     Other party ....

5   Type of pay the worker receives: ☐ Salary   ☐ Commission   ☐ Hourly Wage   ☐ Piece Work
     ☐ Lump Sum   ☐ Other (specify) ....
     If type of pay is commission, and the firm guarantees a minimum amount of pay, specify amount $ _____ .

6   Is the worker allowed a drawing account for advances? . . . . ☐ **Yes**   ☐ **No**
     If "Yes," how often? ....
     Specify any restrictions. ....

7   Whom does the customer pay? . . . . ☐ Firm   ☐ Worker
     If worker, does the worker pay the total amount to the firm?   ☐ **Yes**   ☐ **No**   If "No," explain. ....

8   Does the firm carry worker's compensation insurance on the worker? . . . . ☐ **Yes**   ☐ **No**

9   What economic loss or financial risk, if any, can the worker incur beyond the normal loss of salary (e.g., loss or damage of equipment, material, etc.)? ....

Part IV   Relationship of the Worker and Firm

1   List the benefits available to the worker (e.g., paid vacations, sick pay, pensions, bonuses, paid holidays, personal days, insurance benefits). ....

2   Can the relationship be terminated by either party without incurring liability or penalty? . . . . ☐ **Yes**   ☐ **No**
If "No," explain your answer. ....

3   Did the worker perform similar services for others during the same time period? . . . . ☐ **Yes**   ☐ **No**
If "Yes," is the worker required to get approval from the firm? . . . . ☐ **Yes**   ☐ **No**

4   Describe any agreements prohibiting competition between the worker and the firm while the worker is performing services or during any later period. Attach any available documentation. ....

5   Is the worker a member of a union? . . . . ☐ **Yes**   ☐ **No**

6   What type of advertising, if any, does the worker do (e.g., a business listing in a directory, business cards, etc.)? Provide copies, if applicable.
....

7   If the worker assembles or processes a product at home, who provides the materials and instructions or pattern? ....

8   What does the worker do with the finished product (e.g., return it to the firm, provide it to another party, or sell it)? ....

9   How does the firm represent the worker to its customers (e.g., employee, partner, representative, or contractor)? ....

10   If the worker no longer performs services for the firm, how did the relationship end (e.g., worker quit or was fired, job completed, contract ended, firm or worker went out of business)? ....

Part V   For Service Providers or Salespersons. Complete this part if the worker provided a service directly to customers or is a salesperson.

1   What are the worker's responsibilities in soliciting new customers? ....
....

2   Who provides the worker with leads to prospective customers? ....

3   Describe any reporting requirements pertaining to the leads. ....

4   What terms and conditions of sale, if any, are required by the firm? ....

5   Are orders submitted to and subject to approval by the firm? . . . . ☐ **Yes**   ☐ **No**

6   Who determines the worker's territory? ....

7   Did the worker pay for the privilege of serving customers on the route or in the territory? . . . . ☐ **Yes**   ☐ **No**
If "Yes," whom did the worker pay? ....
If "Yes," how much did the worker pay? $ _____

8   Where does the worker sell the product (e.g., in a home, retail establishment, etc.)? ....
....

9   List the product and/or services distributed by the worker (e.g., meat, vegetables, fruit, bakery products, beverages, or laundry or dry cleaning services). If more than one type of product and/or service is distributed, specify the principal one. ....

10   Does the worker sell life insurance full time? . . . . ☐ **Yes**   ☐ **No**

11   Does the worker sell other types of insurance for the firm? . . . . ☐ **Yes**   ☐ **No**
If "Yes," enter the percentage of the worker's total working time spent in selling other types of insurance . . . . _____ %

12   If the worker solicits orders from wholesalers, retailers, contractors, or operators of hotels, restaurants, or other similar establishments, enter the percentage of the worker's time spent in the solicitation . . . . _____ %

13   Is the merchandise purchased by the customers for resale or use in their business operations? . . . . ☐ **Yes**   ☐ **No**
Describe the merchandise and state whether it is equipment installed on the customers' premises. ....
....

Sign Here

Under penalties of perjury, I declare that I have examined this request, including accompanying documents, and to the best of my knowledge and belief, the facts presented are true, correct, and complete.

_____ Title _____ Date _____
Type or print name below signature.

General Instructions

Section references are to the Internal Revenue Code unless otherwise noted.

Purpose

Firms and workers file Form SS-8 to request a determination of the status of a worker for purposes of federal employment taxes and income tax withholding.

A Form SS-8 determination may be requested only in order to resolve federal tax matters. If Form SS-8 is submitted for a tax year for which the statute of limitations on the tax return has expired, a determination letter will not be issued. The statute of limitations expires 3 years from the due date of the tax return or the date filed, whichever is later.

The IRS does not issue a determination letter for proposed transactions or on hypothetical situations. We may, however, issue an information letter when it is considered appropriate.

Definition

Firm. For the purposes of this form, the term "firm" means any individual, business enterprise, organization, state, or other entity for which a worker has performed services. The firm may or may not have paid the worker directly for these services.

If the firm was not responsible for payment for services, be sure to enter the name, address, and employer identification number of the payer on the first page of Form SS-8, below the identifying information for the firm and the worker.

The SS-8 Determination Process

The IRS will acknowledge the receipt of your Form SS-8. Because there are usually two (or more) parties who could be affected by a determination of employment status, the IRS attempts to get information from all parties involved by sending those parties blank Forms SS-8 for completion. Some or all of the information provided on this Form SS-8 may be shared with the other parties listed on page 1. The case will be assigned to a technician who will review the facts, apply the law, and render a decision. The technician may ask for additional information from the requestor, from other involved parties, or from third parties that could help clarify the work relationship before rendering a decision. The IRS will generally issue a formal determination to the firm or payer (if that is a different entity), and will send a copy to the worker. A determination letter applies only to a worker (or a class of workers) requesting it, and the decision is binding on the IRS. In certain cases, a formal determination will not be issued. Instead, an information letter may be issued. Although an information letter is advisory only and is not binding on the IRS, it may be used to assist the worker to fulfill his or her federal tax obligations.

Neither the SS-8 determination process nor the review of any records in connection with the determination constitutes an examination (audit) of any federal tax return. If the periods under consideration have previously been examined, the SS-8 determination process will not constitute a reexamination under IRS reopening procedures. Because this is not an examination of any federal tax return, the appeal rights available in connection with an examination do not apply to an SS-8 determination. However, if you disagree with a determination and you have additional information concerning the work relationship that you believe was not previously considered, you may request that the determining office reconsider the determination.

Completing Form SS-8

Answer all questions as completely as possible. Attach additional sheets if you need more space. Provide information for all years the worker provided services for the firm. Determinations are based on the entire relationship between the firm and the worker. Also indicate if there were any significant changes in the work relationship over the service term.

Additional copies of this form may be obtained by calling 1-800-829-4933 or from the IRS website at *www.irs.gov.*

Fee

There is no fee for requesting an SS-8 determination letter.

Signature

Form SS-8 must be signed and dated by the taxpayer. A stamped signature will not be accepted.

The person who signs for a corporation must be an officer of the corporation who has personal knowledge of the facts. If the corporation is a member of an affiliated group filing a consolidated return, it must be signed by an officer of the common parent of the group.

The person signing for a trust, partnership, or limited liability company must be, respectively, a trustee, general partner, or member-manager who has personal knowledge of the facts.

Where To File

Send the completed Form SS-8 to the address listed below for the firm's location. However, only for cases involving federal agencies, send Form SS-8 to the Internal Revenue Service, Attn: CC:CORP:T:C, Ben Franklin Station, P.O. Box 7604, Washington, DC 20044.

Firm's location:	Send to:
Alaska, Arizona, Arkansas, California, Colorado, Hawaii, Idaho, Illinois, Iowa, Kansas, Minnesota, Missouri, Montana, Nebraska, Nevada, New Mexico, North Dakota, Oklahoma, Oregon, South Dakota, Texas, Utah, Washington, Wisconsin, Wyoming, American Samoa, Guam, Puerto Rico, U.S. Virgin Islands	Internal Revenue Service SS-8 Determinations P.O. Box 630 Stop 631 Holtsville, NY 11742-0630
Alabama, Connecticut, Delaware, District of Columbia, Florida, Georgia, Indiana, Kentucky, Louisiana, Maine, Maryland, Massachusetts, Michigan, Mississippi, New Hampshire, New Jersey, New York, North Carolina, Ohio, Pennsylvania, Rhode Island, South Carolina, Tennessee, Vermont, Virginia, West Virginia, all other locations not listed	Internal Revenue Service SS-8 Determinations 40 Lakemont Road Newport, VT 05855-1555

Instructions for Workers

If you are requesting a determination for more than one firm, complete a separate Form SS-8 for each firm.

Form SS-8 is not a claim for refund of social security and Medicare taxes or federal income tax withholding.

If the IRS determines that you are an employee, you are responsible for filing an amended return for any corrections related to this decision. A determination that a worker is an employee does not necessarily reduce any current or prior tax liability. For more information, call 1-800-829-1040.

Time for filing a claim for refund. Generally, you must file your claim for a credit or refund within 3 years from the date your original return was filed or within 2 years from the date the tax was paid, whichever is later.

Filing Form SS-8 does not prevent the expiration of the time in which a claim for a refund must be filed. If you are concerned about a refund, and the statute of limitations for filing a claim for refund for the year(s) at issue has not yet expired, you should file Form 1040X, Amended U.S. Individual Income Tax Return, to protect your statute of limitations. File a separate Form 1040X for each year.

On the Form 1040X you file, do not complete lines 1 through 24 on the form. Write "Protective Claim" at the top of the form, sign and date it. In addition, you should enter the following statement in Part II, Explanation of Changes: "Filed Form SS-8 with the Internal Revenue Service Office in (Holtsville, NY; Newport, VT; or Washington, DC; as appropriate). By filing this protective claim, I reserve the right to file a claim for any refund that may be due after a determination of my employment tax status has been completed."

Filing Form SS-8 does not alter the requirement to timely file an income tax return. Do not delay filing your tax return in anticipation of an answer to your SS-8 request. In addition, if applicable, do not delay in responding to a request for payment while waiting for a determination of your worker status.

Instructions for Firms

If a **worker** has requested a determination of his or her status while working for you, you will receive a request from the IRS to complete a Form SS-8. In cases of this type, the IRS usually gives each party an opportunity to present a statement of the facts because any decision will affect the employment tax status of the parties. Failure to respond to this request will not prevent the IRS from issuing a determination letter based on the information he or she has made available so that the worker may fulfill his or her federal tax obligations. However, the information that you provide is extremely valuable in determining the status of the worker.

If you are requesting a determination for a particular class of worker, complete the form for one individual who is representative of the class of workers whose status is in question. If you want a written determination for more than one class of workers, complete a separate Form SS-8 for one worker from each class whose status is typical of that class. A written determination for any worker will apply to other workers of the same class if the facts are not materially different for these workers. Please provide a list of names and addresses of all workers potentially affected by this determination.

If you have a reasonable basis for not treating a worker as an employee, you may be relieved from having to pay employment taxes for that worker under section 530 of the 1978 Revenue Act. However, this relief provision cannot be considered in conjunction with a Form SS-8 determination because the determination does not constitute an examination of any tax return. For more information regarding section 530 of the 1978 Revenue Act and to determine if you qualify for relief under this section, you may visit the IRS website at *www.irs.gov*.

Privacy Act and Paperwork Reduction Act Notice. We ask for the information on this form to carry out the Internal Revenue laws of the United States. This information will be used to determine the employment status of the worker(s) described on the form. Subtitle C, Employment Taxes, of the Internal Revenue Code imposes employment taxes on wages. Sections 3121(d), 3306(a), and 3401(c) and (d) and the related regulations define employee and employer for purposes of employment taxes imposed under Subtitle C. Section 6001 authorizes the IRS to request information needed to determine if a worker(s) or firm is subject to these taxes. Section 6109 requires you to provide your taxpayer identification number. Neither workers nor firms are required to request a status determination, but if you choose to do so, you must provide the information requested on this form. Failure to provide the requested information may prevent us from making a status determination. If any worker or the firm has requested a status determination and you are being asked to provide information for use in that determination, you are not required to provide the requested information. However, failure to provide such information will prevent the IRS from considering it in making the status determination. Providing false or fraudulent information may subject you to penalties. Routine uses of this information include providing it to the Department of Justice for use in civil and criminal litigation, to the Social Security Administration for the administration of social security programs, and to cities, states, and the District of Columbia for the administration of their tax laws. We may also disclose this information to other countries under a tax treaty, to federal and state agencies to enforce federal nontax criminal laws, or to federal law enforcement and intelligence agencies to combat terrorism. We may provide this information to the affected worker(s), the firm, or payer as part of the status determination process.

You are not required to provide the information requested on a form that is subject to the Paperwork Reduction Act unless the form displays a valid OMB control number. Books or records relating to a form or its instructions must be retained as long as their contents may become material in the administration of any Internal Revenue law. Generally, tax returns and return information are confidential, as required by section 6103.

The time needed to complete and file this form will vary depending on individual circumstances. The estimated average time is: Recordkeeping, 22 hrs.; Learning about the law or the form, 47 min.; and Preparing and sending the form to the IRS, 1 hr., 11 min. If you have comments concerning the accuracy of these time estimates or suggestions for making this form simpler, we would be happy to hear from you. You can write to the Internal Revenue Service, Tax Products Coordinating Committee, SE:W:CAR:MP:T:T:SP, 1111 Constitution Ave. NW, IR-6406, Washington, DC 20224. Do not send the tax form to this address. Instead, see *Where To File* on page 4.

This page intentionally blank.

Form **8850**
(Rev. June 2007)
Department of the Treasury
Internal Revenue Service

Pre-Screening Notice and Certification Request for the Work Opportunity Credit

See separate instructions.

OMB No. 1545-1500

Job applicant: Fill in the lines below and check any boxes that apply. Complete only this side.

Your name _____   Social security number _____

Street address where you live _____

City or town, state, and ZIP code _____

Telephone number (___) ___ - _____

If you are under age 40, enter your date of birth (month, day, year) ___ / ___ / ___

---

1 ☐ Check here if you are completing this form **before** August 28, 2007, and you lived in the area impacted by Hurricane Katrina on August 28, 2005. If so, please enter the address, including county or parish and state where you lived at that time.

_____

2 ☐ Check here if you received a conditional certification from the state workforce agency (SWA) or a participating local agency for the work opportunity credit.

3 ☐ Check here if **any** of the following statements apply to you.

I am a member of a family that has received assistance from Temporary Assistance for Needy Families (TANF) for any 9 months during the past 18 months.

I am a veteran and a member of a family that received food stamps for at least a 3-month period during the past 15 months.

I was referred here by a rehabilitation agency approved by the state, an employment network under the Ticket to Work program, or the Department of Veterans Affairs.

I am at least age 18 but **not** age 40 or older and I am a member of a family that:
  a Received food stamps for the past 6 months, **or**
  b Received food stamps for at least 3 of the past 5 months, **but** is no longer eligible to receive them.

During the past year, I was convicted of a felony or released from prison for a felony.

I received supplemental security income (SSI) benefits for any month ending during the past 60 days.

4 ☐ Check here if you are a veteran entitled to compensation for a service-connected disability **and,** during the past year, you were:

Discharged or released from active duty in the U.S. Armed Forces, **or**

Unemployed for a period or periods totaling at least 6 months.

5 ☐ Check here if you are a member of a family that:

Received TANF payments for at least the past 18 months, **or**

Received TANF payments for any 18 months beginning after August 5, 1997, **and** the earliest 18-month period beginning after August 5, 1997, ended during the past 2 years, **or**

Stopped being eligible for TANF payments during the past 2 years because federal or state law limited the maximum time those payments could be made.

Signature—All Applicants Must Sign

Under penalties of perjury, I declare that I gave the above information to the employer on or before the day I was offered a job, and it is, to the best of my knowledge, true, correct, and complete.

Job applicant's signature _____   **Date** ___ / ___ / ___

For Privacy Act and Paperwork Reduction Act Notice, see page 2.   Cat. No. 22851L   Form **8850** (Rev. 6-07)

For Employer's Use Only

Employer's name _____ Telephone no. (___) - _____ EIN _____

Street address _____

City or town, state, and ZIP code _____

Person to contact, if different from above _____ Telephone no. (___) - _____

Street address _____

City or town, state, and ZIP code _____

If, based on the individual's age and home address, he or she is a member of group 4 or 6 (as described under Members of Targeted Groups in the separate instructions), enter that group number (4 or 6) . . . . _____

Date applicant: Gave information   __/__/__   Was offered job   __/__/__   Was hired   __/__/__   Started job   __/__/__

Complete Only If Box 1 on Page 1 is Checked

State and county or parish of job   _____

☐ Check if the individual was not your employee on August 28, 2005, and this is the first time the employee has been hired by you since August 28, 2005.

Under penalties of perjury, I declare that the applicant completed this form on or before the day a job was offered to the applicant and that the information I have furnished is, to the best of my knowledge, true, correct, and complete. Based on the information the job applicant furnished on page 1, I believe the individual is a member of a targeted group. I hereby request a certification that the individual is a member of a targeted group.

Employer's signature _____ **Title** _____ **Date** __/__/__

Privacy Act and Paperwork Reduction Act Notice

Section references are to the Internal Revenue Code.

Section 51(d)(13) permits a prospective employer to request the applicant to complete this form and give it to the prospective employer. The information will be used by the employer to complete the employer's federal tax return. Completion of this form is voluntary and may assist members of targeted groups in securing employment. Routine uses of this form include giving it to the state workforce agency (SWA), which will contact appropriate sources to confirm that the applicant is a member of a targeted group. This form may also be given to the Internal Revenue Service for administration of the Internal Revenue laws, to the Department of Justice for civil and criminal litigation, to the Department of Labor for oversight of the certifications performed by the SWA, and to cities, states, and the District of Columbia for use in administering their tax laws. We may also disclose this information to other countries under a tax treaty, to federal and state agencies to enforce federal nontax criminal laws, or to federal law enforcement and intelligence agencies to combat terrorism.

You are not required to provide the information requested on a form that is subject to the Paperwork Reduction Act unless the form displays a valid OMB control number. Books or records relating to a form or its instructions must be retained as long as their contents may become material in the administration of any Internal Revenue law. Generally, tax returns and return information are confidential, as required by section 6103.

The time needed to complete and file this form will vary depending on individual circumstances. The estimated average time is:

Recordkeeping . . . .5 hrs., 30 min.

Learning about the law or the form . . . . .24 min.

Preparing and sending this form to the SWA . . . . .30 min.

If you have comments concerning the accuracy of these time estimates or suggestions for making this form simpler, we would be happy to hear from you. You can write to the Internal Revenue Service, Tax Products Coordinating Committee, SE:W:CAR:MP:T:T:SP, 1111 Constitution Ave. NW, IR-6406, Washington, DC 20224.

Do not send this form to this address. Instead, see *When and Where To File* in the separate instructions.

Instructions for Form 8850

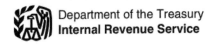 **Department of the Treasury
Internal Revenue Service**

(Rev. June 2007)

Pre-Screening Notice and Certification Request for the Work Opportunity Credit

General Instructions

Section references are to the Internal Revenue Code unless otherwise noted.

What's New

The Small Business and Work Opportunity Act of 2007 made the following changes.
• The work opportunity credit has been extended to cover individuals who begin work for you before September 1, 2011.
• For individuals who begin work for you after May 25, 2007, the qualified veterans group is expanded to include veterans entitled to compensation for a service-connected disability and who, during the one-year period ending on the hiring date, were (a) discharged or released from active duty in the U.S. Armed Forces or (b) unemployed for a period or periods totaling at least 6 months. The first-year wages taken into account for these disabled veterans is $12,000.
• For individuals who begin work for you after May 25, 2007, the high-risk youth group has been renamed "designated community residents" and expanded to include individuals who are at least age 18 but not yet age 40. In addition, residents of rural renewal counties (see page 4) have been added to this group.

 You should use this version of Form 8850 for individuals who begin work for you after May 25, 2007. Use the February 2007 revision for individuals who began work for you before May 26, 2007.

Purpose of Form

Employers use Form 8850 to pre-screen and to make a written request to their state workforce agency (SWA) (unless the employee checks only the Hurricane Katrina employee box) to certify an individual as a member of a targeted group for purposes of qualifying for the work opportunity credit.

Submitting Form 8850 to the SWA (unless the employee checks only the Hurricane Katrina employee box) is but one step in the process of qualifying for the work opportunity credit. The state work opportunity tax credit (WOTC) coordinator for the SWA must certify the job applicant is a member of a targeted group. After starting work, the employee must meet the minimum number-of-hours-worked requirement for the work opportunity credit. The employer elects to take the credit by filing Form 5884, Work Opportunity Credit.

 The certification requirements described above do not apply to Hurricane Katrina employees. For an employer of a Hurricane Katrina employee, this form is used to accept reasonable evidence that the worker is a Hurricane Katrina employee. It is the employer's responsibility to ascertain that the place where the employee lived on August 28, 2005, (the address on line 1 of the form) is in fact in the Gulf Opportunity Zone (core disaster area) (see pages 2 and

3 for a list of these areas). The employer is not required to ask employees to furnish any documentary evidence.

Who Should Complete and Sign the Form

The job applicant gives information to the employer on or before the day a job offer is made. This information is entered on Form 8850. Based on the applicant's information, the employer determines whether or not he or she believes the applicant is a member of a targeted group (as defined under Members of Targeted Groups). If the employer believes the applicant is a member of a targeted group, the employer completes the rest of the form no later than the day the job offer is made. Both the job applicant and the employer must sign Form 8850 no later than the date for submitting the form to the SWA.

Instructions for Employer

When and Where To File

Do not file Form 8850 with the Internal Revenue Service. Instead, if required, file it with your SWA no later than the 28th day after the job applicant begins work for you. Although electronic filing of Form 8850 is permitted, at the time these instructions were published, Colorado was the only state equipped to receive Form 8850 electronically. See Announcement 2002-44 for details. You can find Announcement 2002-44 on page 809 of Internal Revenue Bulletin 2002-17 at *www.irs.gov/pub/irs-irbs/irb02-17.pdf*.

To get the name, address, phone and fax numbers, and email address of the WOTC coordinator for your state, visit the Department of Labor Employment and Training Administration (ETA) website at *www.doleta.gov/business/Incentives/opptax*.

 Never attach Form 8850 to a tax return or otherwise send it to the IRS, regardless of the employee's targeted group. Form 8850 should be filed with the SWA unless the employee checks only the Hurricane Katrina employee box, in which case the employer should keep the Form 8850 for its records.

Additional Requirements for Certification

In addition to filing Form 8850, you must complete and send to your state WOTC coordinator either:
• ETA Form 9062, Conditional Certification Form, if the job applicant received this form from a participating agency (e.g., the Jobs Corps) or
• ETA Form 9061, Individual Characteristics Form, if the job applicant did not receive a conditional certification.

You can get ETA Form 9061 from your local public employment service office or you can download it from the ETA website at *www.doleta.gov/business/Incentives/opptax.*

Recordkeeping

Keep copies of Forms 8850, any transmittal letters that you submit to your state WOTC coordinator, and certification letters you receive from your WOTC coordinator as long as they may be needed for the administration of the provisions relating to the work opportunity credit. Records that support the credit usually must be kept for 3 years from the date any income tax return claiming the credit is due or filed, whichever is later.

Members of Targeted Groups

A job applicant may be certified as a member of a targeted group if he or she is described in one of the following groups.

1. **Qualified IV-A recipient.** An individual who is a member of a family receiving assistance under a state plan approved under part A of title IV of the Social Security Act relating to Temporary Assistance for Needy Families (TANF). The assistance must be received for any 9 months during the 18-month period that ends on the hiring date.

2. **Qualified veteran.** A veteran who is any of the following.

• A member of a family receiving assistance under the Food Stamp program for at least a 3-month period during the 15-month period ending on the hiring date.

• Entitled to compensation for a service-connected disability and is hired not more than 1 year after being discharged or released from active duty in the U.S. Armed Forces.

• Entitled to compensation for a service-connected disability and was unemployed for a period or periods totaling at least 6 months (whether or not consecutive) in the 1-year period ending on the hiring date.

To be considered a veteran, the applicant must:

• Have served on active duty (not including training) in the Armed Forces of the United States for more than 180 days or have been discharged or released from active duty for a service-connected disability, and

• Not have a period of active duty (not including training) of more than 90 days that ended during the 60-day period ending on the hiring date.

3. **Qualified ex-felon.** An ex-felon who has been convicted of a felony under any federal or state law, and is hired not more than 1 year after the conviction or release from prison for that felony.

4. **Designated community resident.** An individual who is at least age 18 but not yet age 40 on the hiring date and lives within an empowerment zone, renewal community, or rural renewal county (defined later).

5. **Vocational rehabilitation referral.** An individual who has a physical or mental disability resulting in a substantial handicap to employment and who was referred to the employer upon completion of (or while receiving) rehabilitation services by a rehabilitation agency approved by the state, an employment network under the Ticket to Work program, or the Department of Veterans Affairs.

6. **Summer youth employee.** An individual who:

• Performs services for the employer between May 1 and September 15,

• Is age 16 but not yet age 18 on the hiring date (or later, on May 1),

• Has never worked for the employer before, and

• Lives within an empowerment zone or renewal community.

7. **Food stamp recipient.** An individual who:

• Is at least age 18 but not yet age 40 on the hiring date, and

• Is a member of a family that—

a. Has received food stamps for the 6-month period ending on the hiring date or

b. Is no longer eligible for such assistance under section 6(o) of the Food Stamp Act of 1977, but the family received food stamps for at least 3 months of the 5-month period ending on the hiring date.

8. **SSI recipient.** An individual who is receiving supplemental security income benefits under title XVI the Social Security Act (including benefits of the type described in section 1616 of the Social Security Act or section 212 of Public Law 93-66) for any month ending during the 60-day period ending on the hiring date.

9. **Long-term family assistance recipient.** An individual who is a member of a family that:

• Has received TANF payments for at least 18 consecutive months ending on the hiring date, or

• Receives TANF payments for any 18 months (whether or not consecutive) beginning after August 5, 1997, and the earliest 18-month period beginning after August 5, 1997, ended during the past 2 years, or

• Stopped being eligible for TANF payments because federal or state law limits the maximum period such assistance is payable and the individual is hired not more than 2 years after such eligibility ended.

10. **Hurricane Katrina employee.** A Hurricane Katrina employee is a person who, on August 28, 2005, had a main home in the Gulf Opportunity (GO) Zone (core disaster area) and, during a two-year period beginning this date, is hired to perform services principally in the GO Zone. Certification does not apply to this group.

Member of a Family

With respect to the qualified IV-A recipient, qualified veteran, food stamp recipient, and long-term family assistance recipient, an individual whose family receiv assistance for the requisite period meets the family assistance requirement of the applicable group if the individual is included on the grant (and thus receives assistance) for some portion of the specified period.

Gulf Opportunity (GO) Zone (Core Disaster Area)

The GO Zone (also called the core disaster area) cove the portion of the Hurricane Katrina disaster area determined by the Federal Emergency Management Agency (FEMA) to be eligible for either individual only both individual and public assistance from the Federal Government. The GO Zone covers the following areas three states.

Alabama. The counties of Baldwin, Choctaw, Clarke, Greene, Hale, Marengo, Mobile, Pickens, Sumter, Tuscaloosa, and Washington.

Louisiana. The parishes of Acadia, Ascension, Assumption, Calcasieu, Cameron, East Baton Rouge, East Feliciana, Iberia, Iberville, Jefferson, Jefferson Davis, Lafayette, Lafourche, Livingston, Orleans,

Plaquemines, Pointe Coupee, St. Bernard, St. Charles, St. Helena, St. James, St. John the Baptist, St. Martin, St. Mary, St. Tammany, Tangipahoa, Terrebonne, Vermilion, Washington, West Baton Rouge, and West Feliciana.

Mississippi. The counties of Adams, Amite, Attala, Choctow, Claiborne, Clarke, Copiah, Covington, Forrest, Franklin, George, Greene, Hancock, Harrison, Hinds, Holmes, Humphreys, Jackson, Jasper, Jefferson, Jefferson Davis, Jones, Kemper, Lamar, Lauderdale, Lawrence, Leake, Lincoln, Lowndes, Madison, Marion, Neshoba, Newton, Noxubee, Oktibbeha, Pearl River, Perry, Pike, Rankin, Scott, Simpson, Smith, Stone, Walthall, Warren, Wayne, Wilkinson, Winston, and Yazoo.

Empowerment Zones

The following paragraphs describe current designations of empowerment zones. The designations will generally remain in effect until the end of 2009.

Urban areas. Parts of the following urban areas are empowerment zones. You can find out if your business or an employee's residence is located within an urban empowerment zone by using the RC/EZ/EC Address Locator at *www.hud.gov/crlocator* or by calling 1-800-998-9999.
- Pulaski County, AR
- Tucson, AZ
- Fresno, CA
- Los Angeles, CA (city and county)
- Santa Ana, CA
- New Haven, CT
- Jacksonville, FL
- Miami/Dade County, FL
- Chicago, IL
- Gary/Hammond/East Chicago, IN
- Boston, MA
- Baltimore, MD
- Detroit, MI
- Minneapolis, MN
- St. Louis, MO/East St. Louis, IL
- Cumberland County, NJ
- New York, NY
- Syracuse, NY
- Yonkers, NY
- Cincinnati, OH
- Cleveland, OH
- Columbus, OH
- Oklahoma City, OK
- Philadelphia, PA/Camden, NJ
- Columbia/Sumter, SC
- Knoxville, TN
- El Paso, TX
- San Antonio, TX
- Norfolk/Portsmouth, VA
- Huntington, WV/Ironton, OH

Washington, DC. Under section 1400, parts of Washington, DC, are treated as an empowerment zone. This treatment will generally remain in effect until the end of 2007. For details, use the RC/EZ/EC Address Locator at *www.hud.gov/crlocator* or see Notice 98-57 on page 9 of Internal Revenue Bulletin 1998-47 at *www.irs.gov/pub/irs-irbs/irb98-47.pdf.*

Rural areas. Parts of the following rural areas are empowerment zones. You can find out if your business or an employee's residence is located within a rural empowerment zone by using the RC/EZ/EC Address Locator at *www.hud.gov/crlocator* or by calling 1-800-998-9999.
- Desert Communities, CA (part of Riverside County)
- Southwest Georgia United, GA (part of Crisp County and all of Dooly County)
- Southernmost Illinois Delta, IL (parts of Alexander and Johnson Counties and all of Pulaski County)
- Kentucky Highlands, KY (part of Wayne County and all of Clinton and Jackson Counties)
- Aroostook County, ME (part of Aroostook County)
- Mid-Delta, MS (parts of Bolivar, Holmes, Humphreys, Leflore, Sunflower, and Washington Counties)
- Griggs-Steele, ND (part of Griggs County and all of Steele County)
- Oglala Sioux Tribe, SD (parts of Jackson and Bennett Counties and all of Shannon County)
- Middle Rio Grande FUTURO Communities, TX (parts of Dimmit, Maverick, Uvalde, and Zavala Counties)
- Rio Grande Valley, TX (parts of Cameron, Hidalgo, Starr, and Willacy Counties)

Renewal Communities

Parts of the following areas are designated as renewal communities. The designations will generally remain in effect until the end of 2009. You can find out if your business or an employee's residence is located within a renewal community by using the RC/EZ/EC Address Locator at *www.hud.gov/crlocator* or by calling 1-800-998-9999.
- Greene-Sumter County, AL
- Mobile County, AL
- Southern Alabama
- Los Angeles, CA
- Orange Grove, CA
- Parlier, CA
- San Diego, CA
- San Francisco, CA
- Atlanta, GA
- Chicago, IL
- Eastern KY
- Central Louisiana
- New Orleans, LA
- Northern Louisiana
- Ouachita Parish, LA
- Lawrence, MA
- Lowell, MA
- Detroit, MI
- Flint, MI
- West Central Mississippi
- Turtle Mountain Band of Chippewa, ND
- Camden, NJ
- Newark, NJ
- Buffalo-Lackawanna, NY
- Jamestown, NY
- Niagara Falls, NY
- Rochester, NY
- Schenectady, NY
- Hamilton, OH
- Youngstown, OH
- Philadelphia, PA
- Charleston, SC
- Chattanooga, TN
- Memphis, TN
- Corpus Christi, TX
- El Paso County, TX
- Burlington, VT

- Tacoma, WA
- Yakima, WA
- Milwaukee, WI

Rural Renewal Counties

A rural renewal county is a county in a rural area that lost population during the 5-year periods 1990 through 1994 and 1995 through 1999. Rural renewal counties are listed below.

Alabama. The counties of Butler, Dallas, Macon, Perry, Sumter, and Wilcox.

Alaska. The census areas of Aleutians West, Wrangell-Petersburg, and Yukon-Koyukuk.

Arkansas. The counties of Arkansas, Chicot, Clay, Desha, Jackson, Lafayette, Lee, Little River, Monroe, Nevada, Ouachita, Phillips, Union, and Woodruff.

Colorado. The counties of Cheyenne, Kiowa, and San Juan.

Georgia. The counties of Randolph and Stewart.

Illinois. The counties of Alexander, Edwards, Franklin, Gallatin, Greene, Hancock, Hardin, Jasper, Knox, McDonough, Montgomery, Pulaski, Randolph, Richland, Scott, Warren, Wayne, and White.

Indiana. Perry County.

Iowa. The counties of Adair, Adams, Appanoose, Audubon, Butler, Calhoun, Cass, Cherokee, Clay, Clayton, Emmet, Floyd, Franklin, Fremont, Hancock, Humboldt, Ida, Keokuk, Kossuth, Montgomery, Osceola, Palo Alto, Pocahontas, Poweshiek, Sac, Taylor, Union, Wayne, Winnebago, and Worth.

Kansas. The counties of Atchison, Barber, Barton, Brown, Clay, Cloud, Comanche, Decatur, Edwards, Elk, Ellsworth, Gove, Graham, Greeley, Greenwood, Harper, Hodgeman, Jewell, Kiowa, Labette, Lane, Lincoln, Marshall, Mitchell, Montgomery, Ness, Osborne, Phillips, Rawlins, Republic, Rooks, Rush, Russell, Scott, Sheridan, Sherman, Smith, Stafford, Trego, Wallace, Washington, Wichita, and Woodson.

Kentucky. The counties of Bell, Caldwell, Floyd, Harlan, Hickman, Leslie, Letcher, Pike, and Union.

Louisiana. The parishes of Bienville, Claiborne, Franklin, Jackson, Morehouse, St. Mary, Tensas, Vernon, and Webster.

Maine. The counties of Aroostook and Piscataquis.

Michigan. The counties of Gogebic, Marquette, and Ontonagon.

Minnesota. The counties of Big Stone, Chippewa, Cottonwood, Faribault, Jackson, Kittson, Koochiching, Lac Qui Parle, Lincoln, Marshall, Martin, Murray, Norman, Pipestone, Red Lake, Redwood, Renville, Stevens, Traverse, Wilkin, and Yellow Medicine.

Mississippi. The counties of Adams, Coahoma, Humphreys, Montgomery, Quitman, Sharkey, Tallahatchie, and Washington.

Missouri. The counties of Atchison, Carroll, Chariton, Clark, Holt, Knox, Mississippi, New Madrid, Pemiscot, and Worth.

Montana. The counties of Carter, Daniels, Dawson, Deer Lodge, Fallon, Garfield, Hill, Liberty, McCone, Petroleum, Phillips, Powder River, Prairie, Richland, Roosevelt, Rosebud, Sheridan, Valley, and Wibaux.

Nebraska. The counties of Antelope, Banner, Boone, Box Butte, Boyd, Burt, Cedar, Chase, Deuel, Dundy, Fillmore, Franklin, Garden, Garfield, Greeley, Hayes, Hitchcock, Holt, Jefferson, Johnson, Logan, Nance, Nemaha, Nuckolls, Pawnee, Perkins, Red Willow, Richardson, Rock, Sheridan, Sherman, Thayer, Thomas, Valley, Webster, and Wheeler.

Nevada. The counties of Esmeralda, Lander, and Mineral.

New Hampshire. Coos County.

New Mexico. The counties of Harding and Quay.

New York. The counties of Clinton and Montgomery.

North Dakota. The counties of Adams, Barnes, Benson, Billings, Bottineau, Burke, Cavalier, Dickey, Divide, Dunn, Eddy, Emmons, Foster, Golden Valley, Grant, Griggs, Hettinger, Kidder, LaMoure, Logan, McHenry, McIntosh, McKenzie, McLean, Mercer, Mountrail, Nelson, Oliver, Pembina, Pierce, Ramsey, Ransom, Renville, Sargent, Sheridan, Slope, Stark, Steele, Stutsman, Towner, Traill, Walsh, Wells, and Williams.

Ohio. The counties of Crawford, Monroe, Paulding, Seneca, and Van Wert.

Oklahoma. The counties of Alfalfa, Beaver, Cimarron, Custer, Dewey, Ellis, Grant, Greer, Harmon, Harper, Kiowa, Major, Roger Mills, Seminole, Tillman, and Woodward.

Pennsylvania. The counties of Venango and Warren.

South Carolina. Marlboro County.

South Dakota. The counties of Aurora, Campbell, Clark, Day, Deuel, Douglas, Faulk, Grant, Gregory, Haakon, Hand, Harding, Hutchinson, Jones, Kingsbury, Marshall, McPherson, Miner, Perkins, Potter, Sanborn, Spink, Tripp, and Walworth.

Texas. The counties of Andrews, Bailey, Baylor, Borden, Briscoe, Brooks, Castro, Cochran, Coleman, Collingsworth, Cottle, Crane, Culberson, Deaf Smith, Dimmit, Eastland, Fisher, Floyd, Foard, Gray, Hall, Hardeman, Haskell, Hemphill, Hockley, Hutchinson, Kenedy, Kent, Knox, Lamb, Martin, McCulloch, Morris, Nolan, Oldham, Reagan, Reeves, Refugio, Roberts, Scurry, Stonewall, Terrell, Terry, Upton, Ward, Wheeler, Wilbarger, Winkler, Yoakum, and Zavala.

Virginia. The counties of Buchanan, Dickenson, Highland, and Lee and the independent cities of Clifton Forge, Covington, Norton, and Staunton.

West Virginia. The counties of Calhoun, Gilmer, Logan, McDowell, Mercer, Mingo, Summers, Tucker, Webster, Wetzel, and Wyoming.

Wyoming. The counties of Carbon and Niobrara.

IRS Form 8300 (Rev. December 2004)

OMB No. 1545-0892
Department of the Treasury
Internal Revenue Service

Report of Cash Payments Over $10,000 Received in a Trade or Business

▶ See instructions for definition of cash.

▶ Use this form for transactions occurring after December 31, 2004. Do not use prior versions after this date.
For Privacy Act and Paperwork Reduction Act Notice, see page 5.

FinCEN Form 8300 (Rev. December 2004)

OMB No. 1506-0018
Department of the Treasury
Financial Crimes
Enforcement Network

---

1 Check appropriate box(es) if: **a** ☐ Amends prior report; **b** ☐ Suspicious transaction.

Part I   Identity of Individual From Whom the Cash Was Received

2 If more than one individual is involved, check here and see instructions . . . . ▶ ☐

3 Last name | **4** First name | **5** M.I. | **6** Taxpayer identification number

7 Address (number, street, and apt. or suite no.) | **8** Date of birth . ▶ M M D D Y Y Y Y (see instructions)

9 City | **10** State | **11** ZIP code | **12** Country (if not U.S.) | **13** Occupation, profession, or business

14 Identifying document (ID) | **a Describe ID** ▶ .... | **b Issued by** ▶ ....
c Number ▶

Part II   Person on Whose Behalf This Transaction Was Conducted

15 If this transaction was conducted on behalf of more than one person, check here and see instructions . . . . . ▶ ☐

16 Individual's last name or Organization's name | **17** First name | **18** M.I. | **19** Taxpayer identification number

20 Doing business as (DBA) name (see instructions) | Employer identification number

21 Address (number, street, and apt. or suite no.) | **22** Occupation, profession, or business

23 City | **24** State | **25** ZIP code | **26** Country (if not U.S.)

27 Alien identification (ID) | **a Describe ID** ▶ .... | **b Issued by** ▶ ....
c Number ▶

Part III   Description of Transaction and Method of Payment

28 Date cash received M M D D Y Y Y Y | **29** Total cash received $ .00 | **30** If cash was received in more than one payment, check here . . . ▶ ☐ | **31** Total price if different from item 29 $ .00

32 Amount of cash received (in U.S. dollar equivalent) (must equal item 29) (see instructions):

a U.S. currency $ _____ .00 (Amount in $100 bills or higher $ _____ .00)
b Foreign currency $ _____ .00 (Country ▶ _____)
c Cashier's check(s) $ _____ .00 ⎫ Issuer's name(s) and serial number(s) of the monetary instrument(s) ▶
d Money order(s) $ _____ .00 ⎬ ....
e Bank draft(s) $ _____ .00 ⎪ ....
f Traveler's check(s) $ _____ .00 ⎭

33 Type of transaction

a ☐ Personal property purchased
b ☐ Real property purchased
c ☐ Personal services provided
d ☐ Business services provided
e ☐ Intangible property purchased
f ☐ Debt obligations paid
g ☐ Exchange of cash
h ☐ Escrow or trust funds
i ☐ Bail received by court clerks
j ☐ Other (specify in item 34) ▶

34 Specific description of property or service shown in 33. Give serial or registration number, address, docket number, etc. ▶ ....

Part IV   Business That Received Cash

35 Name of business that received cash | **36** Employer identification number

37 Address (number, street, and apt. or suite no.) | Social security number

38 City | **39** State | **40** ZIP code | **41** Nature of your business

42 Under penalties of perjury, I declare that to the best of my knowledge the information I have furnished above is true, correct, and complete.

Signature ▶ _____ Authorized official   Title ▶ _____

43 Date of signature M M D D Y Y Y Y | **44** Type or print name of contact person | **45** Contact telephone number ( )

IRS Form 8300 (Rev. 12-2004)   Cat. No. 62133S   **FinCEN Form 8300** (Rev. 12-2004)

IRS Form **8300** (Rev. 12-2004)   Page **2**   FinCEN Form **8300** (Rev. 12-2004)

Multiple Parties

(Complete applicable parts below if box 2 or 15 on page 1 is checked)

Part I   Continued—Complete if box 2 on page 1 is checked

3 Last name	4 First name	5 M.I.	6 Taxpayer identification number

7 Address (number, street, and apt. or suite no.)	8 Date of birth . . ▶ (see instructions) M M D D Y Y Y Y

9 City	10 State	11 ZIP code	12 Country (if not U.S.)	13 Occupation, profession, or business

14 Identifying document (ID)	a **Describe ID** ▶ .... c **Number** ▶	b **Issued by** ▶ ....

3 Last name	4 First name	5 M.I.	6 Taxpayer identification number

7 Address (number, street, and apt. or suite no.)	8 Date of birth . . ▶ (see instructions) M M D D Y Y Y Y

9 City	10 State	11 ZIP code	12 Country (if not U.S.)	13 Occupation, profession, or business

14 Identifying document (ID)	a **Describe ID** ▶ .... c **Number** ▶	b **Issued by** ▶ ....

Part II   Continued—Complete if box 15 on page 1 is checked

16 Individual's last name or Organization's name	17 First name	18 M.I.	19 Taxpayer identification number

20 Doing business as (DBA) name (see instructions)	Employer identification number

21 Address (number, street, and apt. or suite no.)	22 Occupation, profession, or business

23 City	24 State	25 ZIP code	26 Country (if not U.S.)

27 Alien identification (ID)	a **Describe ID** ▶ .... c **Number** ▶	b **Issued by** ▶ ....

16 Individual's last name or Organization's name	17 First name	18 M.I.	19 Taxpayer identification number

20 Doing business as (DBA) name (see instructions)	Employer identification number

21 Address (number, street, and apt. or suite no.)	22 Occupation, profession, or business

23 City	24 State	25 ZIP code	26 Country (if not U.S.)

27 Alien identification (ID)	a **Describe ID** ▶ .... c **Number** ▶	b **Issued by** ▶ ....

Comments – Please use the lines provided below to comment on or clarify any information you entered on any line in Parts I, II, III, and IV

_____

_____

_____

_____

IRS Form **8300** (Rev. 12-2004)   FinCEN Form **8300** (Rev. 12-2004)

Section references are to the Internal Revenue Code unless otherwise noted.

Important Reminders

- Section 6050I (26 United States Code (U.S.C.) 6050I) and 31 U.S.C. 5331 require that certain information be reported to the IRS and the Financial Crimes Enforcement Network (FinCEN). This information must be reported on IRS/FinCEN Form 8300.
- Item 33 box i is to be checked only by clerks of the court; box d is to be checked by bail bondsmen. See the instructions on page 5.
- For purposes of section 6050I and 31 U.S.C. 5331, the word "cash" and "currency" have the same meaning. See *Cash* under *Definitions* on page 4.

General Instructions

Who must file. Each person engaged in a trade or business who, in the course of that trade or business, receives more than $10,000 in cash in one transaction or in two or more related transactions, must file Form 8300. Any transactions conducted between a payer (or its agent) and the recipient in a 24-hour period are related transactions. Transactions are considered related even if they occur over a period of more than 24 hours if the recipient knows, or has reason to know, that each transaction is one of a series of connected transactions.

Keep a copy of each Form 8300 for 5 years from the date you file it.

Clerks of Federal or State courts must file Form 8300 if more than $10,000 in cash is received as bail for an individual(s) charged with certain criminal offenses. For these purposes, a clerk includes the clerk's office or any other office, department, division, branch, or unit of the court that is authorized to receive bail. If a person receives bail on behalf of a clerk, the clerk is treated as receiving the bail. See the instructions for Item 33 on page 5.

If multiple payments are made in cash to satisfy bail and the initial payment does not exceed $10,000, the initial payment and subsequent payments must be aggregated and the information return must be filed by the 15th day after receipt of the payment that causes the aggregate amount to exceed $10,000 in cash. In such cases, the reporting requirement can be satisfied either by sending a single written statement with an aggregate amount listed or by furnishing a copy of each Form 8300 relating to that payer. Payments made to satisfy separate bail requirements are not required to be aggregated. See Treasury Regulations section 1.6050I-2.

Casinos must file Form 8300 for nongaming activities (restaurants, shops, etc.).

Voluntary use of Form 8300. Form 8300 may be filed voluntarily for any suspicious transaction (see *Definitions*) for use by the IRS, even if the total amount does not exceed $10,000.

Exceptions. Cash is not required to be reported if it is received:
- By a financial institution required to file Form 104, Currency Transaction Report.
- By a casino required to file (or exempt from filing) Form 103, Currency Transaction Report by Casinos, if the cash is received as part of its gaming business.
- By an agent who receives the cash from a principal, if the agent uses all of the cash within 15 days in a second transaction that is reportable on Form 8300 or on Form 104, and discloses all the information necessary to complete Part II of Form 8300 or Form 104 to the recipient of the cash in the second transaction.
- In a transaction occurring entirely outside the United States. See Publication 1544, Reporting Cash Payments Over $10,000 (Received in a Trade or Business), regarding transactions occurring in Puerto Rico, the Virgin Islands, and territories and possessions of the United States.
- In a transaction that is not in the course of a person's trade or business.

When to file. File Form 8300 by the 15th day after the date the cash was received. If that date falls on a Saturday, Sunday, or legal holiday, file the form on the next business day.

Where to file. File the form with the Internal Revenue Service, Detroit Computing Center, P.O. Box 32621, Detroit, MI 48232.

Statement to be provided. You must give a written or electronic statement to each person named on a required Form 8300 on or before January 31 of the year following the calendar year in which the cash is received. The statement must show the name, telephone number, and address of the information contact for the business, the aggregate amount of reportable cash received, and that the information was furnished to the IRS. Keep a copy of the statement for your records.

Multiple payments. If you receive more than one cash payment for a single transaction or for related transactions, you must report the multiple payments any time you receive a total amount that exceeds $10,000 within any 12-month period. Submit the report within 15 days of the date you receive the payment that

causes the total amount to exceed $10,000. If more than one report is required within 15 days, you may file a combined report. File the combined report no later than the date the earliest report, if filed separately, would have to be filed.

Taxpayer identification number (TIN). You must furnish the correct TIN of the person or persons from whom you receive the cash and, if applicable, the person or persons on whose behalf the transaction is being conducted. You may be subject to penalties for an incorrect or missing TIN.

The TIN for an individual (including a sole proprietorship) is the individual's social security number (SSN). For certain resident aliens who are not eligible to get an SSN and nonresident aliens who are required to file tax returns, it is an IRS Individual Taxpayer Identification Number (ITIN). For other persons, including corporations, partnerships, and estates, it is the employer identification number (EIN).

If you have requested but are not able to get a TIN for one or more of the parties to a transaction within 15 days following the transaction, file the report and attach a statement explaining why the TIN is not included.

Exception: *You are not required to provide the TIN of a person who is a nonresident alien individual or a foreign organization if that person does not have income effectively connected with the conduct of a U.S. trade or business and does not have an office or place of business, or fiscal or paying agent, in the United States. See Publication 1544 for more information.*

Penalties. You may be subject to penalties if you fail to file a correct and complete Form 8300 on time and you cannot show that the failure was due to reasonable cause. You may also be subject to penalties if you fail to furnish timely a correct and complete statement to each person named in a required report. A minimum penalty of $25,000 may be imposed if the failure is due to an intentional or willful disregard of the cash reporting requirements.

Penalties may also be imposed for causing, or attempting to cause, a trade or business to fail to file a required report; for causing, or attempting to cause, a trade or business to file a required report containing a material omission or misstatement of fact; or for structuring, or attempting to structure, transactions to avoid the reporting requirements. These violations may also be subject to criminal prosecution which, upon conviction, may result in imprisonment of up to 5 years or fines of up to $250,000 for individuals and $500,000 for corporations or both.

Definitions

Cash. The term "cash" means the following:

- U.S. and foreign coin and currency received in any transaction.
- A cashier's check, money order, bank draft, or traveler's check having a face amount of $10,000 or less that is received in a designated reporting transaction (defined below), or that is received in any transaction in which the recipient knows that the instrument is being used in an attempt to avoid the reporting of the transaction under either section 6050I or 31 U.S.C. 5331.

Note. Cash does not include a check drawn on the payer's own account, such as a personal check, regardless of the amount.

Designated reporting transaction. A retail sale (or the receipt of funds by a broker or other intermediary in connection with a retail sale) of a consumer durable, a collectible, or a travel or entertainment activity.

Retail sale. Any sale (whether or not the sale is for resale or for any other purpose) made in the course of a trade or business if that trade or business principally consists of making sales to ultimate consumers.

Consumer durable. An item of tangible personal property of a type that, under ordinary usage, can reasonably be expected to remain useful for at least 1 year, and that has a sales price of more than $10,000.

Collectible. Any work of art, rug, antique, metal, gem, stamp, coin, etc.

Travel or entertainment activity. An item of travel or entertainment that pertains to a single trip or event if the combined sales price of the item and all other items relating to the same trip or event that are sold in the same transaction (or related transactions) exceeds $10,000.

Exceptions. A cashier's check, money order, bank draft, or traveler's check is not considered received in a designated reporting transaction if it constitutes the proceeds of a bank loan or if it is received as a payment on certain promissory notes, installment sales contracts, or down payment plans. See Publication 1544 for more information.

Person. An individual, corporation, partnership, trust, estate, association, or company.

Recipient. The person receiving the cash. Each branch or other unit of a person's trade or business is considered a separate recipient unless the branch receiving the cash (or a central office linking the branches), knows or has reason to know the identity of payers making cash payments to other branches.

Transaction. Includes the purchase of property or services, the payment of debt, the exchange of a negotiable instrument for cash, and the receipt of cash to be held in escrow or trust. A single transaction may not be broken into multiple transactions to avoid reporting.

Suspicious transaction. A transaction in which it appears that a person is attempting to cause Form 8300 not to be filed, or to file a false or incomplete form. The term also includes any transaction in which there is an indication of possible illegal activity.

Specific Instructions

You must complete all parts. However, you may skip Part II if the individual named in Part I is conducting the transaction on his or her behalf only. For voluntary reporting of suspicious transactions, see Item 1 below.

Item 1. If you are amending a prior report, check box 1a. Complete the appropriate items with the correct or amended information only. Complete all of Part IV. Staple a copy of the original report to the amended report.

To voluntarily report a suspicious transaction (see *Definitions*), check box 1b. You may also telephone your local IRS Criminal Investigation Division or call 1-800-800-2877.

Part I

Item 2. If two or more individuals conducted the transaction you are reporting, check the box and complete Part I for any one of the individuals. Provide the same information for the other individual(s) on the back of the form. If more than three individuals are involved, provide the same information on additional sheets of paper and attach them to this form.

Item 6. Enter the taxpayer identification number (TIN) of the individual named. See *Taxpayer identification number (TIN)* on page 3 for more information.

Item 8. Enter eight numerals for the date of birth of the individual named. For example, if the individual's birth date is July 6, 1960, enter 07 06 1960.

Item 13. Fully describe the nature of the occupation, profession, or business (for example, "plumber," "attorney," or "automobile dealer"). Do not use general or nondescriptive terms such as "businessman" or "self-employed."

Item 14. You must verify the name and address of the named individual(s). Verification must be made by examination of a document normally accepted as a means of identification when cashing checks (for example, a driver's license, passport, alien registration card, or other official

document). In item 14a, enter the type of document examined. In item 14b, identify the issuer of the document. In item 14c, enter the document's number. For example, if the individual has a Utah driver's license, enter "driver's license" in item 14a, "Utah" in item 14b, and the number appearing on the license in item 14c.

Note. You must complete all three items (a, b, and c) in this line to make sure that Form 8300 will be processed correctly.

Part II

Item 15. If the transaction is being conducted on behalf of more than one person (including husband and wife or parent and child), check the box and complete Part II for any one of the persons. Provide the same information for the other person(s) on the back of the form. If more than three persons are involved, provide the same information on additional sheets of paper and attach them to this form.

Items 16 through 19. If the person on whose behalf the transaction is being conducted is an individual, complete items 16, 17, and 18. Enter his or her TIN in item 19. If the individual is a sole proprietor and has an employer identification number (EIN), you must enter both the SSN and EIN in item 19. If the person is an organization, put its name as shown on required tax filings in item 16 and its EIN in item 19.

Item 20. If a sole proprietor or organization named in items 16 through 18 is doing business under a name other than that entered in item 16 (e.g., a "trade" or "doing business as (DBA)" name), enter it here.

Item 27. If the person is not required to furnish a TIN, complete this item. See *Taxpayer Identification Number (TIN)* on page 3. Enter a description of the type of official document issued to that person in item 27a (for example, "passport"), the country that issued the document in item 27b, and the document's number in item 27c.

Note. You must complete all three items (a, b, and c) in this line to make sure that Form 8300 will be processed correctly.

Part III

Item 28. Enter the date you received the cash. If you received the cash in more than one payment, enter the date you received the payment that caused the combined amount to exceed $10,000. See *Multiple payments* under *General Instructions* for more information.

Item 30. Check this box if the amount shown in item 29 was received in more than one payment (for example, as installment payments or payments on related transactions).

Item 31. Enter the total price of the property, services, amount of cash exchanged, etc. (for example, the total cost of a vehicle purchased, cost of catering service, exchange of currency) if different from the amount shown in item 29.

Item 32. Enter the dollar amount of each form of cash received. Show foreign currency amounts in U.S. dollar equivalent at a fair market rate of exchange available to the public. The sum of the amounts must equal item 29. For cashier's check, money order, bank draft, or traveler's check, provide the name of the issuer and the serial number of each instrument. Names of all issuers and all serial numbers involved must be provided. If necessary, provide this information on additional sheets of paper and attach them to this form.

Item 33. Check the appropriate box(es) that describe the transaction. If the transaction is not specified in boxes a–i, check box j and briefly describe the transaction (for example, "car lease," "boat lease," "house lease," or "aircraft rental"). If the transaction relates to the receipt of bail by a court clerk, check box i, "Bail received by court clerks." This box is only for use by court clerks. If the transaction relates to cash received by a bail bondsman, check box d, "Business services provided."

Part IV

Item 36. If you are a sole proprietorship, you must enter your SSN. If your business also has an EIN, you must provide the EIN as well. All other business entities must enter an EIN.

Item 41. Fully describe the nature of your business, for example, "attorney" or "jewelry dealer." Do not use general or nondescriptive terms such as "business" or "store."

Item 42. This form must be signed by an individual who has been authorized to do so for the business that received the cash.

Comments

Use this section to comment on or clarify anything you may have entered on any line in Parts I, II, III, and IV. For example, if you checked box b (Suspicious transaction) in line 1 above Part I, you may want to explain why you think that the cash transaction you are reporting on Form 8300 may be suspicious.

Privacy Act and Paperwork Reduction Act Notice. Except as otherwise noted, the information solicited on this form is required by the Internal Revenue Service (IRS) and the Financial Crimes Enforcement Network (FinCEN) in order to carry out the laws and regulations of the United States Department of the Treasury. Trades or businesses, except for clerks of criminal courts, are required to provide the information to the IRS and FinCEN under both section 6050I and 31 U.S.C. 5331. Clerks of criminal courts are required to provide the information to the IRS under section 6050I. Section 6109 and 31 U.S.C. 5331 require that you provide your social security number in order to adequately identify you and process your return and other papers. The principal purpose for collecting the information on this form is to maintain reports or records which have a high degree of usefulness in criminal, tax, or regulatory investigations or proceedings, or in the conduct of intelligence or counterintelligence activities, by directing the Federal Government's attention to unusual or questionable transactions.

You are not required to provide information as to whether the reported transaction is deemed suspicious. Failure to provide all other requested information, or providing fraudulent information, may result in criminal prosecution and other penalties under Title 26 and Title 31 of the United States Code.

Generally, tax returns and return information are confidential, as stated in section 6103. However, section 6103 allows or requires the IRS to disclose or give the information requested on this form to others as described in the Code. For example, we may disclose your tax information to the Department of Justice, to enforce the tax laws, both civil and criminal, and to cities, states, the District of Columbia, to carry out their tax laws. We may disclose this information to other persons as necessary to obtain information which we cannot get in any other way. We may disclose this information to Federal, state, and local child support agencies; and to other Federal agencies for the purposes of determining entitlement for benefits or the eligibility for and the repayment of loans. We may also provide the records to appropriate state, local, and foreign criminal law enforcement and regulatory personnel in the performance of their official duties. We may also disclose this information to other countries under a tax treaty, or to Federal and state agencies to enforce Federal nontax criminal laws and to combat terrorism.

The IRS authority to disclose information to combat terrorism expired on December 31, 2003. Legislation is pending that would reinstate this authority. "In addition, FinCEN may provide the information to those officials if they are conducting intelligence or counter-intelligence activities to protect against international terrorism."

You are not required to provide the information requested on a form that is subject to the Paperwork Reduction Act unless the form displays a valid OMB control number. Books or records relating to a form or its instructions must be retained as long as their contents may become material in the administration of any law under Title 26 or Title 31.

The time needed to complete this form will vary depending on individual circumstances. The estimated average time is 21 minutes. If you have comments concerning the accuracy of this time estimate or suggestions for making this form simpler, you can write to the Tax Products Coordinating Committee, Western Area Distribution Center, Rancho Cordova, CA 95743-0001. Do not send this form to this office. Instead, see *Where To File* on page 3.

Index

proprietorship, 11, 14, 15, 60, 147, 148, 151
publicity, 3, 19, 39, 63, 65, 67, 69

R

registering, 15, 20–27, 42, 64, 65, 67, 72, 137-
138, 158–160, 164
Registration for Michigan Taxes, 157
Regulation Z, 130, 131
renting, 4, 5, 35, 37–39, 42, 60, 148
Report of Cash Payments Over $10,000 (IRS
Form 8300), 127
retail, 4, 36, 41, 46, 112, 114, 129, 131, 143,
158
retirement, 30, 100, 150

S

S corporation, 12–14, 17, 147, 149, 152
sale, 5, 16, 27, 40, 45, 46, 54, 55, 70, 97, 103,
112–114, 117–121, 126, 129, 130–132,
135, 142, 150, 157, 158, 163, 164
service mark, 25–27, 138
sexual harassment, 93–96
shareholder, 12, 13, 152
smoking, 82–84
Social Security, 88, 89, 149, 151, 154, 155, 160
solicitation, 117, 119
stock, 13, 15, 16, 33, 38, 150

T

telephone, 35, 36, 47, 96, 117, 119, 120, 133-
134, 142, 156
theft, 3, 61
trade association, 5, 80
trade name, 20, 25, 26

trade secret, 87, 138, 139
trademark, 19, 20, 25–28, 64, 68, 137, 138

U

unemployment, 49, 85, 89, 109, 151, 156, 157,
160
union, 62, 87, 107, 161
usury, 131

W

wage, 88, 93, 96–99, 106–109, 152, 154–156,
158
wage, minimum, 96–98, 107
worker, migrant, 109
workers' compensation, 49, 57–59, 89, 92

Z

zoning, 37, 39, 41, 42